D1222666

The Colleges and the Courts
1962-1966

OTHER INTERSTATE BOOKS BY DR. CHAMBERS:

The Campus and the People

Organization, support, and control of higher education in the United States in the 1960's. (82 pp., card covered)

Chance and Choice in Higher Education

A discussion of what should be done to meet the problem of the mushrooming population of college-age young people and how we can go about it. (119 pp., card covered)

The Colleges and the Courts Since 1950

An examination of the principal court decisions during the period 1951 through 1961 affecting higher education in the United States. (viii+415 pp., cloth bound)

The Colleges and the Courts
1962-1966

by

M. M. CHAMBERS

School of Education

Indiana University

THE INTERSTATE

Printers & Publishers. Inc.

Danville, Illinois

CARRIE RICH MEMORIAL LIBRARY.
CAMPBELL COLLEGE
BUIES CREEK, N. C.

Copyright © 1967 by

M. M. CHAMBERS

All Rights Reserved

Library of Congress

Catalog Card Number: 67-20928

Printed and Published by

THE INTERSTATE PRINTERS & PUBLISHERS, INC.

Danville, Illinois

Printed in U.S.A.

PREFACE

A thin horizontal slice of history—encompassing roughly the four years immediately prior to 1967—is here traversed.

Sixth in a series which began in 1936, this present volume continues the spade-work by examining some 300 recent decisions of state and federal courts affecting higher education in the United States.

The effort has been made to tell the essential facts and the law as applied in each case as tersely as possible, purged of technical jargon as far as practicable without sacrifice of accuracy, and in such form and sequence as to enlist the interest of all who are concerned in any way with universities and colleges, or with education beyond the high school.

The task is not easy, and not in every instance entirely successfully executed; but my addiction to it makes it pleasant. It is a labor compatible with, and reinforcive of, my performance of duties as a professor of higher education at Indiana University and as an occasional consultant to individuals, institutions, cities and states regarding administrative, financial, and legal aspects of higher education.

"Legal aspects of higher education" connote a branch of social science dealing with the places of individuals, institutions, and agencies of education beyond the high school among the civic functions and structures of the fifty states and of the federal jurisdiction, as spelled out in the opinions of the higher courts in litigated cases. A fascinating panorama comes into view when one observes the slowly changing concepts of the rights, privileges, obligations and responsibilities of students, teachers,

57912

trustees, alumni, parents and the general public in this increasingly important area of social concern.

This book and its predecessors are in no sense intended ever to be substitutes for the professional services of attorneys at law. Any semblance of either a "how to" manual or a comprehensive technical treatise is hereby expressly disclaimed. Instead, the aim is to encourage reflection and discourse on the many unsettled philosophical issues involved, and thus to promote study and diminish ignorance by disseminating information.

For any and all errors of fact or opinion in this volume I am solely responsible. Having made that clear, I am free to make some acknowledgments:

To the people of Indiana for supporting an excellent and adaptable statewide system of public higher education, and to the trustees, administration, faculty and students of Indiana University for its progress as a university of the first rank and as a growing and flexible center of learning, my admiration goes.

To the students at the doctoral level who fill my classes, and to my congenial colleagues among the faculty members and administrative officers, goes my gratitude for pleasant associations and rewarding stimulation.

M. M. CHAMBERS

Bloomington, Indiana
May, 1967

CONTENTS

Part Three
GOVERNMENT AND CHARITY

Part Four
SUPPORT FROM PRIVATE SOURCES;
PROPERTY; OTHER MATTERS

INTRODUCTION

TOWARD A HUMANE LAW OF HIGHER EDUCATION

Even over the short period of four years, trends in the evolution of the law become visible. If there is any one which embraces most of the others and sets the tone of the times it is the tendency toward a more humane recognition of the individual worth and dignity of students, faculty members, and all persons involved in the total enterprise.

This movement is easily observable in several of the twenty-five chapters of the discourse which follows. From the decrees regarding the provision of college education for the children of divorced parents to the decisions defining due process in disciplinary proceedings against students or teachers; from the judgments advancing the implementation of racial desegregation to the opinions invalidating state statutes prescribing vague oaths of loyalty which invade the constitutional rights of teachers;——there is everywhere perceptible the approach of a social climate hospitable to the diffusion of opportunity, to the encouragement of honest intellectual curiosity, to the integrity of the search for truth, and to freedom of the individual in educational and vocational choices.

The solicitude for justice to the individual in an increasingly complex society also manifests itself strongly in the decisions on the tort responsibility of universities and colleges, public and private, to innocent parties injured through the negligence of their officers or employees. This particular trend had a great impetus as long as a quarter of a century ago, and its gradual extension continues.

The conventional doctrine that the relationship between the student and his college is almost wholly contractual—a transaction involving purchase and sale of educational services between two parties essentially "standing on an equal footing and dealing at arm's length"—comes to be largely eroded. The more modern view is that the beginning of the relationship is no longer simply the inception of a contract, because it has become less a voluntary agreement than "an act of submission" (in the words of one judge) because the projected service is so indispensable to the student that he is largely at the mercy of the other party. This means that the traditional rules of the law of contracts play a decreasing role, and are in great part supplanted by new notions which take into account the mutual obligations of the individual and of society—and of citizen and state—while the harsh rules of private treaty move from center stage toward a shady corner of the scene.

Beyond the foregoing few generalizations it is probably better not to expatiate at this point. Others are easily discernible from a scanning of the successive chapters, and it is preferable that the reader discover them and verify and appraise them for himself, without having them premasticated. Let it be added that in several sectors of the law of higher education, the winds of change moved farther and faster during the past four years than during the twelve years between 1950 and 1962.

PART ONE

STUDENTS

College Education as a "Necessary"

The Rights and Obligations of Students

The Progress of Racial Desegregation

Various Incidents of Student Life

Charitable Trusts for Student Aid; Other Types and
    Incidents of Student Aids

CHAPTER 1

COLLEGE EDUCATION AS
A "NECESSARY"

DECISIONS continue to appear concerning the question of whether divorced parents will be ordered to pay college expenses of their children. The trend in that direction is unmistakable, but continues to encounter occasional setbacks and delays.

Illinois and Indiana Cases

Three recent opinions of intermediate appellate courts in Illinois illustrate. In the first of these, the divorce was decreed in 1943, and the wife was given custody of the 2-year-old daughter, and the husband ordered to pay $8 a week for the support of the child. This was raised to $50 a week in 1954 and again modified to require $150 a month in 1958, when the girl was 17.

The father had an annual income of about $28,000 after taxes derived from a trust. He had remarried and had two younger children. The daughter of his earlier marriage had high scholastic ability, having stood third in her high school graduating class of 130. Faced with the issue of whether the father should be relieved of her support when she reached the age of 18, or be required to support her through the normal period of an undergraduate college course, the trial court

3

continued the order that the father should pay $150 a month for a period of four years.

This was affirmed by the three-judge appellate court. Justice Schwartz, commenting on the Illinois divorce act, took note of some facts of social history:[1]

> In the days when this act was passed children went to work long before they reached their majority. But even then, education beyond the high school level for children of average or better scholarship was the common aspiration of American parents. Today, it is regarded as a necessity.

And on the question of support beyond the age of majority, he added:

> When we turn to divorced parents—a disrupted family—society cannot count on normal protection for the child, and it is here that equity takes control to mitigate the hardships that may befall children of divorced parents. Shall we presume, then, that all obligation ends with minority? The statute does not say so . . . We should rather assume that the legislature of that day, more than one hundred years ago, contemplated that it had better be left unsaid, so that the mores and necessities of the times could determine what a wise discretion should do . . . It left that to be decided as the circumstances of a particular case should warrant.

Two years later another Illinois court of appeals decided a rather similar case in almost identical manner. Here the parents had been married in 1942 and divorced in 1955 when their daughter was aged 11. The husband was ordered to pay $16.50 a week for the support of the child, plus "any extraordinary medical expenses."

In 1961 the mother came into court and recited that the girl, aged 17, had graduated from Lindbloom Technical High School in Chicago and had been accepted for admission to the Ohio State University. Her yearly expenses would be $1,640, which the mother was unable to pay; but she averred that her former husband was employed, "had substantial income," and was "well able to maintain Evelyn and pay her college expenses." She asked that he be ordered to pay these expenses, plus some dental and optical fees already incurred. The trial court ordered the father to pay "for the next four years the sum of $100 per month, while the child is pursuing an education" and also $400 out of the $631 in medical expenses previously incurred.

---

[1] *Maitzen* v. *Maitzen,* 24 Ill. App. 2d 32, 163 N.E. 2d 840 (1960).

The father soon filed a petition to vacate the order, his principal contentions being that the divorce act does not require a parent to support his child after the age of majority (18 if female), and there was no evidence that the child would be unable to support herself after reaching age 18. This was denied, and both orders were affirmed by the three-judge court of appeals in an opinion by Justice Burke, in which he adopted and followed the decision in the *Maitzen* case.[2]

A third Illinois case, decided in 1964, dropped a monkey wrench into the machinery. The same court of appeals which had decided the *Maitzen* case four years earlier (but with wholly different judges) now took, by a divided vote, a literal black-letter view of the statute, and held that a trial court did not have jurisdiction to order a divorced father to pay expenses incident to the college education of his daughter after she attained age 18, where the daughter was healthy and the father had not made any formal agreement to pay her college expenses. This was the opinion of Justice Burman, with Justice Murphy concurring.

Presiding Justice English dissented, tracing the recent development of the law in this area, and saying:[3]

> It is a truism that in this country the luxuries of yesterday are the necessities of today, and it would seem that the matter of higher education, more than almost any other subject, equates itself completely and appropriately with Justice Holmes' "felt necessities of the time."

Further, said he:

> In mentioning such a trend and development of the law I do not, myself, mean to be confusing the issue of jurisdiction with the proper discretion in the ordering of payments for college education. It should be obvious that the trend referred to could not be taking place in the absence of the requisite jurisdiction.

This division of the court exemplifies the contrast between the literal legalistic view on the one hand, and the belief that the law must fit itself to changing economic and social developments, on the other. Presiding Justice English, in addition to citing the recent

---

[2] *O'Berry* v. *O'Berry*, 36 Ill. App. 2d 163, 183 N.E. 2d 539 (1962).
[3] *Crane* v. *Crane*, 45 Ill. App. 2d 316, 196 N.E. 2d 27 (1964).

Illinois decisions and other cases, also referred to a 1961 article in the *New York University Law Review* to the effect that "There is a decided trend to order the father to provide for college education, although Indiana persisted in refusing to view such as a parental obligation."[4]

This brings us to the Indiana record, which is indeed consistently reactionary. In 1959 when a trial court ordered a divorced father to continue paying $10 a week so his 18-year-old son, then in his first year at Purdue University, could continue in college, the Indiana supreme court reversed the order. Said Judge Bobbitt: "This court will not hold that it is the duty of a parent to provide such education, under the guise that it is a necessary."[5]

Progressive View in Mississippi

Probably the most widely publicized case of the period was that of a prosperous Mississippi farmer who was divorced in 1958 and ordered to pay $50 a month for the support of his daughter who was then 16 and in high school. In 1959 when she was a senior with high scholastic standing and hoping to attend the University of Mississippi at Oxford, her father was ordered to raise his monthly payments to $90 to make this possible.

In petitioning for this latter order, her mother had shown that the father owned a 283-acre farm with 100 acres under cultivation, well-equipped with necessary buildings, machinery, and livestock, including 40 cows and 24 brood sows, and that his estimated farm income was about $12,000 a year. She added that he kept for his own amusement a rack of firearms and a brace of hunting dogs.

The supreme court of Mississippi affirmed the order. Said Justice Holmes:[6]

---

[4] Henry H. Foster, Jr., "Family Law" at pp. 634-635 in *New York University Law Review* 36: 634-641 (1961).

[5] *Haag* v. *Haag*, 240 Ind. 291, 163 N.E. 2d 243 (1959). Earlier cases to the same effect: *Morris* v. *Morris*, 92 Ind. App. 65, 171 N.E. 386 (1930); *Hachat* v. *Hachat*, 117 Ind. App. 294, 71 N.E. 2d 927 (1947). The latter is discussed at pp. 13-14 in *The Colleges and the Courts 1946-50*. New York: Columbia University Press, 1952. 202 pp.

[6] *Pass* v. *Pass*, 238 Miss. 449, 118 So. 2d 769 (1960). Commented upon in *University of Pennsylvania Law Review* 109: 130-134 (November 1960).

> We hold that where the minor child is worthy of and quali-
> fied for a college education and shows an aptitude therefor it is
> the primary duty of the father, if in reason financially able to
> do so, to provide funds for the college education of his minor
> child in the custody of the mother, where the mother and
> father are divorced and living apart . . .
> A contrary view may have been justified in former times
> when the needs of the family, and of society, and of government
> were less exacting than they are today . . .

Wishing to leave no doubt as to the position of the court, he said
further:

> It is a duty which the parent not only owes to his child, but
> to the state as well, since the stability of our government must
> depend upon a well-equipped, a well-trained, and well-educated
> citizenship. We can see no good reason why this duty should not
> extend to a college education. Our statutes do not prohibit it,
> but they are rather susceptible of an interpretation to allow it.
> The fact is that the importance of a college education is being
> more and more recognized in matters of commerce, society,
> government, and all human relations, and the college graduate
> is being more and more preferred over those who are not so for-
> tunate. No parent should subject his worthy child to this dis-
> advantage if he has the financial capacity to avoid it.

Court May Decree Formation of Private
Trust for Education of Children

Two parties were divorced in Ohio in 1948, having two daughters
then aged 5 and 4. The husband was ordered to pay $100 a month
for the children, of which $75 was for ordinary general support
and $25 was to be held by the clerk of the court to build up a college
fund for the two girls. More than a decade later both girls entered
college, but both soon left to get married. These events left about
$3,500 in the college fund, which was in fact a private trust (not a
charitable trust) for the sole purpose of paying college expenses
of the two girls.

The trial court awarded this sum to the former husband, on the
ground that the standard disposition of the unexpended *res* of a private
express trust "is by resulting trust to the settlor (founder)." Not
being a charitable trust, the private trust was not appropriate for the
application of the doctrine of *cy pres* to allow the daughters to take

for other than college purposes, or to allow other college students to take in their stead.[7]

The case affords an inkling of the contrasts between private trusts and charitable trusts, which are treated in a later chapter (Chapter 19); but it is of interest at this point chiefly because the court conceived the support of young children as including the building up of a fund for their college education.

Court Should Not Act Too Precipitately

In the District of Columbia a husband and wife obtained a judgment of separate maintenance in 1960, when their daughter was aged 15 and their son aged 10. The decree ordered the father to pay "all costs incident to the necessary and reasonable education of said minor children," but did not specifically mention college expenses or any other particulars. In 1962 the daughter entered Temple University School of Oral Hygiene, and the son at age 13 was given the religious instruction and synagogue ceremonial known as *bar mitzvah*, at considerable expense.

The wife then came into the court of general sessions and showed that the husband had not paid any of the expense of college or of *bar mitzvah*, whereupon the court summarily held him in contempt, and ordered him to pay the wife $6,000 plus $350 attorneys' fees within 60 days or go to prison for 6 months. (The cost of two years in college was $3,856.49, and the cost of *bar mitzvah* was $1,562.70, including $1,045.88 for a reception in a Washington hotel.)

The District of Columbia court of appeals reversed the order and remanded the case for trial on the facts. "Questions of fact should not have been litigated by means of a motion for contempt. Contempt can only be founded on some clear and express direction of the court." To be sure, said the court:[8]

> Insofar as college expenses are concerned, most jurisdictions require a father to educate his children in a manner befitting his condition and circumstances in life. The most important factors are . . . (1) the father's ability to pay, and (2) the ability and capacity of the child for further education.

---

[7] *Schenerlein* v. *Schenerlein*, 29 Ohio App. 2d 65, 197 N.E. 2d 231 (1963).
[8] *Pincus* v. *Pincus*, (App. D.C.), 197 A. 2d 854 (1964).

Facts relevant to these matters must be heard and determined in the lower court.

Three Pennsylvania Cases

Thrice during 1963 and 1964 a Pennsylvania superior court decided in favor of divorced fathers of college students and against the petitions of the mothers, each time basing its determination on the facts of the case and not on any sweeping negative rule. In two of these cases the opinion for the seven-judge court was written by Judge Woodside, who is generally oriented toward conservative views.

A divorced father of two daughters, Joyce and Molly, was under order to pay $20 a week for the support of each. Their mother's uncle had set up trust funds of approximately $8,000 to provide both girls with a college education. When Joyce reached age 18 and enrolled in a Bachelor of Science in Nursing course at the University of Bridgeport, her mother asked the court to increase Joyce's $20 a week support-money with the result that her petition was denied and the original order for $20 a week for Joyce was vacated.

The court pointed out that Joyce would have $40 a week from the trust, an assumed $10 a week from her own earnings, and $20 a week from her father, aggregating $70 a week; whereas her father would have less than $60 a week for his own support. "This is not a case where a father should be required by law to support a child attending college," said Judge Woodside. He was careful to add: "A majority of this Court thinks an order may be entered against a father for the support of a child attending college," and even if there was no agreement to do so (as there was not in this case) the court "must examine the evidence further to determine whether under all the circumstances the father should be required, without any agreement, to support his daughter while she is attending college."[9]

Another divorced father was under order to pay $70 a week for the support of four children. On petition of the mother, the Quarter Sessions ordered this raised to $600 a month. The eldest son, aged

---

[9] *Commonwealth ex rel. Ulmer v. Somerville*, 200 Pa. Super. 640, 190 A. 2d 182 (1963).

18, had been taken by his father and enrolled in a two-year business
course at the Goldey Beacom School in Wilmington, Delaware. The
father had paid the registration fee and arranged for the boy to
live at the YMCA, but did not pay for tuition, books, or room and
board, and the mother defrayed these expenses from her own funds.

Judge Wright, for the superior court, ordered reduction of the
monthly support payments to $425, in view of the fact that the fa-
ther's annual income did not exceed $10,905 (from his own real estate
and insurance corporation). Said the judge:[10]

> We are all of the opinion that the amount of the order should
> be reduced. The asserted needs of the children must be equated
> with the father's ability to pay. Even if we assume an income
> of $10,905, as found by the court below, an order of $7,200 per
> year appears to us to impose an unreasonable burden. The pur-
> pose of a support order is the welfare of the child and not punish-
> ment of the father. It must be fair and not confiscatory in amount,
> being intended to provide such allowance for support as is
> reasonable, considering the property, income, and earning ca-
> pacity of the father, and the condition and station in life of
> the family.

In a third case the divorced parents had one son of college age.
He had entered the University of Pennsylvania in 1961 and presumably would be graduated in June 1965. He had good marks, had been
awarded a scholarship, and had been materially helped by his mother.
The father had a take-home pay of $135 a week from a family-owned
business, in which he had an equity of $30,000, but which was cur-
rently operating at an annual loss. In these circumstances the superior
court modified a support order to set it at "$150 per month for April
and May of 1964, and for each month from September 1964 to June
1965, inclusive, during which the son continues his college education."[11]

Judge Woodside, citing the two preceding cases, again stated the
rule:

> An order may be made against a father to help a child re-
> ceive an education beyond high school when the child is able
> and willing to pursue successfully his course of studies, and his

---

[10] *Commonwealth of Pennsylvania* v. *Camp*, 201 Pa. Super. 484, 193 A. 2d
685 (1963).

[11] *Commonwealth ex rel. Decker* v. *Decker*, 204 Pa. Super. 156, 203 A. 2d
343 (1964).

father has sufficient estate, earning capacity or income to enable him to pay the order without undue hardship.

New York and Minnesota Cases

An 18-year-old son of separated parents in New York was a freshman at Fairleigh Dickinson University in New Jersey. He had a $400 "work grant" because of his good marks. The father had an annual income of $12,000 to $15,000, and had been paying $50 per week for the support of the wife and $25 per week for the son. Judge Elizabeth Bass Golding of the Nassau County Family Court estimated the college costs at $2,000 a year, including $978 for tuition and $900 for room and board. She ordered that the father pay $40 a week September through May of each year for the boy in college, and $25 a week for the other weeks, *plus* the boy's clothing, medical and dental expenses.[12]

In Minnesota the parents of a girl aged 14 and twin boys aged 17 were divorced in 1964. In an order, said by the court to be "largely the result of agreements reached by the parties themselves," the father was directed to pay "$125 monthly alimony and $65 monthly support for each of the children, and, in addition, to deposit securities of $15,000 to insure payment of prospective expenses for the children's college education." It was shown that the father owned securities worth $71,000. He appealed the order to the state supreme court, where it was affirmed, in an opinion saying:[13]

> The arrangement for insuring to the children an opportunity to receive a college education is, we believe, properly the primary responsibility of the defendant (father), and the evidence clearly demonstrates that he has sufficient remaining assets and the earning capacity to meet that responsibility.

The Minnesota court, however, added that "Under the circumstances disclosed, this obligation will terminate upon each child's majority," citing as precedent a very recent decision of its own involving the divorced parents of five children, wherein one amendment to the decree required the father to pay the cost of books and tuition for the college education of a son of college age, but not beyond his

---

[12] *Weingast* v. *Weingast*, (Nassau County Family Court), 44 Misc. 2d 952, 255 N.Y.S. 2d 341 (1964).

[13] *Posselt* v. *Posselt*, (Minn.), 136 N.W. 2d 659 (1965).

majority.[14] We have noticed that in some states the courts consider a "college education" as normally extending over four years, and couch their support orders in words covering that period though this may carry the child beyond the age of majority.

A review of the foregoing cases will show a preponderance of judicial opinion moving toward the concept of college education as a "necessary."

---

[14] *Kiesow* v. *Kiesow*, 270 Minn. 374, 133 N.W. 2d 652 (1965).

CHAPTER 2

THE RIGHTS AND OBLIGATIONS
OF STUDENTS

FIVE DECISIONS of 1963 and 1964 touch (1) admission to a state university, (2) the imposition of differential fees upon nonresidents of the state, (3) due process in expulsion cases, and (4) an action for damages against a private university and its officers for allegedly maliciously depriving a student of his doctoral degree by flunking him in his general examinations.

Admission Without Vaccination When Refusal
Is Based on Religious Scruples

A New Jersey statute authorizes vaccination to be a condition of admission to public schools and colleges, but allows exceptions to be made for individuals whose refusal to be vaccinated is on religious grounds. Rutgers, the State University of New Jersey, accordingly permitted *bona fide* members of the Christian Science faith to be admitted without vaccination (eight were in attendance during a recent year).

One new applicant, upon saying his religious belief would not allow him to be vaccinated, was, as usual in such cases, handed two certificates: (1) a statement of his own religious scruples against vaccination, to be signed by him, and (2) a statement attesting his membership in some Christian Science church, to be signed by some officer of such church. This latter certificate he rejected, saying he was not a member of any Christian Science church; whereupon Rutgers excluded him. He then sued for a proper remedy, and the superior court entered judgment in his favor and directed the university to admit him.[1]

The university's procedure was, apparently, indeed rather blunderingly disregardful of individual liberty of conscience. The opinion of Judge Martino speaks of it with some scorn:[2]

> The policy of recommending or suggesting a religion to a person who professes a different religion is contrary to the law of this land. The suggestion that plaintiff does not have a *bona fide* religion to qualify for this exemption, in view of the facts and the law on this question, indicates an arbitrary and capricious policy for a state university . . . Membership in a recognized religious group cannot be required as a condition of exemption from vaccination under our statute and constitutional law.

The school history of the young man in question showed that he had, with the concurrence of his mother, refused vaccination twice before—once in elementary school and again in high school—and had been allowed to continue in school.

Obligation to Pay Nonresident Fees in State University

Colorado has a statute (CRS 1953, sec. 124-18-1 *et seq.*, as amended by SL 1961, Ch. 229):

> It is the intent of the General Assembly that the state institutions of higher education shall apply uniform rules, as herein prescribed and not otherwise, in determining whether students shall be classified as in-state students or out-of-state students for tuition purposes. . . .
> An emancipated minor or adult student who has registered for more than five hours per term shall not qualify for a change

---

[1] The university appealed, and this decision was modified by the state supreme court, apparently only because the plaintiff had meantime become a student elsewhere. In order to determine if the case were moot, the supreme court obtained from him an affidavit that he would be interested in the future in graduate work at the university, and accordingly held the case not moot and essentially affirmed the judgment for its declaratory value to this plaintiff.

[2] *Kolbeck* v. *Kramer*, 84 N.J. Super. 569, 202 A. 2d 889 (1964); modified and declaratory value affirmed in 46 N.J. 46, 214 A. 2d 408 (1965).

in his classification for tuition purposes unless he shall have completed twelve continuous months of residence while not attending an institution of higher learning in the state or while serving in the armed forces.

In 1964 the Colorado supreme court held that the classification prescribed in this statute is not unreasonable, and that the statute is not in violation of any clause of the state constitution or of the United States Constitution.[3] The missing element in both the statute and the decision seems to be that neither takes an account of individual *intent*. Many courts in many states have held that a minor who leaves his parental roof and goes to another state for the purposes of attending college there, presumptively intends to leave that state as soon as he has completed his college course; but this presumption is not as strong in the case of an adult student, or one who is wholly self-supporting, or one who is married and has his family with him; and justice would require that it be susceptible of being completely overthrown in cases where the student declares (and demonstrates with suitable evidence) that he fully *intends* to continue as a permanent resident of the state after his college course has been completed.

It seems difficult to find any significant difference between the Colorado statute and the Idaho rule of the state board of education which the supreme court of Idaho unanimously declared to be unjustly discriminatory and invalid, in a 1960 decision.[4]

Differences in the forms of action in the two cases may have affected the different outcomes. The aggrieved student in Idaho was merely seeking to be heard on the question of his rights as a resident. The Colorado student, in contrast, had completed four years at the university as a nonresident, during which time he had paid the university some $2,331 in fees in excess of what he would have paid if he had been classified as a resident. He then sued for compensatory and punitive *damages* in the sum of $5,500. In affirming the trial court judgment against him, the Colorado supreme court swept aside all his pleas regarding equal protection and due process under

---

[3] *Landwehr* v. *Regents* of the University of Colorado, (Colo.), 396 p. 2d 451 (1964).

[4] *Newman* v. *Graham et al., State Board of Education*, 82 Ida. 90, 349 p. 2d 716, 83 A.L.R. 2d 492 (1960); discussed at pages 16-17 in *The Colleges and the Courts Since 1950*. Danville, Illinois: The Interstate Printers & Publishers, Inc., 1964. 415 pp.

the Fourteenth Amendment, the power of Congress to regulate commerce among the states, the privileges and immunities of citizens of the several states, and the civil rights clauses of the Colorado constitution, merely by saying all these are inapplicable if the classification prescribed in the statute is reasonable; and by holding that it is reasonable, citing the fact that the state similarly distinguishes among residents and nonresidents who receive legacies from Colorado decedents, for purposes of the state inheritance tax. (Legacies going to nonresidents are taxed at higher rates than those going to resident legatees.) The Idaho reasoning seems somehow more convincing and more solicitous of the rights of individuals.

A more recent decision by a special three-judge federal court in Iowa clarifies this a bit. George Clarke, a resident of Illinois, went to Iowa City and entered the State University of Iowa there in 1961, and attended the university continuously thereafter. In 1966, at the age of 22, he had completed his first year in the College of Law. Throughout the period he had been classified as a nonresident of the state, and charged the out-of-state tuition fees. This was believed to be in accord with a section of the university rules which states the usual principle as follows:

> A student from another state who has enrolled for a full program, or substantially a full program, in any type of educational institution will be presumed to be in Iowa primarily for educational purposes, and will be considered not to have established residence in Iowa. Continued residence in Iowa during vacation periods or occasional periods of interruption to the course of study does not of itself overcome the presumption.

Decisions are made by the university registrar but may be appealed to a review committee, whose findings are final. It appeared to be the practice of the registrar never to reclassify a continuous full-time nonresident student, except in cases where such student is able to show that he is under the age of 21 and his parents have moved into Iowa from another state.

Noting that the quoted rule is not absolute, but is based on a presumption susceptible of being overcome by suitable evidence, the court held that "The regulation classifying students as residents or nonresidents for tuition payment purposes is not arbitrary or unreasonable and bears a rational relation to Iowa's object and purpose of financing, operating and maintaining its educational institutions."

Although it thought the registrar's interpretation too rigid, the court observed that the interpretations of the review committee seemed to be somewhat more flexible, but nevertheless concluded that "While the Review Committee's interpretation of the regulations is correct, its application of them in this instance appears to be unduly rigid. It is the view of this Court that the plaintiff herein has established a substantial basis for being classified as a resident for tuition payment purposes." Consequently the case was remanded to the review committee for reconsideration, with the court retaining jurisdiction for such further relief as either party might request.[5]

Clarke had based his plea for classification as a resident of Iowa upon (1) his declared intent to reside in Iowa and practice law immediately after his graduation, and (2) the fact that he had married a girl who was an Iowa resident.

The review committee, after reconsidering his case as directed by the federal court, decided by a vote of 3 to 1 to reclassify him a resident student *only if* he would make a contract with the university to the effect that if he did not remain in Iowa and practice law following his graduation (or following service in the armed forces if that intervened) then he would pay the difference between the nonresident and resident tuition fees at the Law School.

The court, faced with this determination, promptly declared it arbitrary and unreasonable, ordered it set aside, and found that "George Clarke has established that he was a resident of the State of Iowa for tuition payment purposes effective with the commencement of his second year of law school in September, 1966"; and an order that he be so classified was issued.[6]

This decision, let it be understood, did not invalidate any part of the rules of the University of Iowa; it merely held that the interpretation of the rules by the university authorities in this particular instance was in violation of the plaintiff student's rights under 42 United States Code, Section 1983:

---

[5] *Clarke* v. *Iowa State Board of Regents,* (U.S.D.C., Ia.), So. Dist., Central Div., Civil No. 6-1773-C-1, September 15, 1966. Before Circuit Judge Matthes and District Judges Stephenson and Hanson.

[6] *Clarke* v. *Redeker et al., Iowa State Board of Regents,* (U.S.D.C., Ia.), So. Dist., Central Div., Civil No. 6-1773-C-1, January 9, 1967.

Every person who, under color of any statute, ordinance, regulation, custom, or usage, of any State or Territory, subjects, or causes to be subjected, any citizen of the United States or other person within the jurisdiction thereof to the deprivation of any rights, privileges, or immunities secured by the Constitution and laws, shall be liable to the party injured in an action at law, suit in equity, or other proper proceeding for redress.

It was under that section that George Clarke brought his action to enjoin the university from continuing to classify him as a nonresident. It is also noteworthy that in addition to his plea regarding his own resident status, he also sought in vain to prove (1) charging higher rates of tuition fees to a nonresident student than to a resident student by a state university is a violation of the equal protection and privileges and immunities clauses of the Fourteenth Amendment, and (2) the tuition regulations of the University of Iowa unreasonably discriminate between a nonresident male whose wife is a resident of Iowa and a nonresident female whose husband is a resident of Iowa, because they follow the traditional rule that the residence of a wife is that of her husband. This latter, said the court, does not prevent the appropriate university officials from considering his marriage when he is attempting to overcome the rebuttable presumption of nonresidency. Thus the decision changes no law, but merely rectifies an administrative determination in a single case.

A very different type of suit reached a decision in an Idaho county court January 16, 1967. A disgruntled taxpayer sought to restrain and prohibit the Board of Regents of the University of Idaho from establishing any policy regarding the fees of out-of-state students other than one which would require them to pay fees substantially equal to the entire cost to the state of Idaho of providing their education. To make a long story short, District Judge Merlin S. Young concluded a lengthy opinion by saying: "The non-resident tuition policy (of the Regents) is within their discretion and cannot be said to be a spending of public money for the private benefit of nonresidents of Idaho, as a matter of law," and entered judgment against the plaintiff.[7]

He noted that the "very minimum" average cost per student per

---

[7] *Cobbs* v. *State Board of Education* (*acting as Regents of the University of Idaho*), (Dist. Ct. of Third Judicial Dist. of State of Idaho, in and for County of Ada), Civil No. 36600 (January 16, 1967).

year at the University of Idaho was $1,200 to $1,400, and that on January 1, 1966 the nonresident tuition fee was raised to $500. This could be interpreted in a very general way as meaning the average subsidy to an out-of-state student would be at least $700, also that about 20 per cent of the students at the University of Idaho were nonresidents, mostly from 10 western states, and somewhat more than half from the neighboring state of Washington. In the graduate programs the percentages were higher, running as high as 50 per cent in some instances; and instructional costs per student were markedly higher in the graduate programs than in the undergraduate schools. The nonresident fees charged by the 10 western states ranged from $585 to $825—all higher than Idaho's nonresident fee. "No state university sets its non-resident tuition fees upon the basis of the actual cost of education of the student in that university," the court observed, and continued:

> The Board of Regents does not attempt to set non-resident tuition upon a basis of costs per student or any other cost basis. It does use its best collective judgment to arrive at a figure for non-resident tuition which it believes will attract high quality non-resident students to the University of Idaho . . . (It) believes that a substantial percentage of a college student body should come from outside of the state and that this is essential to prevent a university from becoming provincial in outlook and that non-resident students are necessary to attract a good faculty.

Remarking that the benefits derived from the admission of Idaho students to other state universities on a somewhat informal nonresident reciprocal basis and the benefits to Idaho universities received from the attendance of nonresident students are "public benefits," the court conceded that "the public benefit derived from paying a substantial part of the cost of educating non-resident students is an intangible thing which cannot be established in dollars and cents," and decided that such a problem of educational policy was within the discretion of the board of regents, and the court should not undertake to substitute its judgment for that of the board.

The opinion is of great interest because it is perhaps the first instance in which there is a clear judicial pronouncement of some of the important values inherent in interstate migration of university students, and also of the fact that not all aspects of university operation can be in accord with strict cost accounting.

Quasi-Judicial Power May Be Lawfully
Delegated to a Student Court

In May 1961 an instructor in Latin accused a girl student at the University of North Carolina of having cheated in a make-up examination, and brought his charges to the Women's Honor Council, a student court authorized to hear and determine such cases under the rules of the university. After due notice to the accused, the council conducted a hearing, and found her guilty as charged, and recommended that she be suspended.

She immediately wrote to Chancellor Aycock (top executive of the Chapel Hill institution, where the foregoing events occurred) asking him to place the matter in the hands of a faculty committee for review. A week later he declined this request, but informed her of her right to appeal to President Friday (executive of three institutions, including Chapel Hill, composing the "greater" or "consolidated" University of North Carolina). This she did, and Friday affirmed Aycock's decision. Her next appeal was to the executive committee of the board of trustees, which met in July and affirmed the disposition by President Friday. She then appealed to the full board at its meeting in February 1962. The board appointed a special committee to investigate the entire matter and report at its next meeting. This committee advised that no injustice had been done, and recommended that the board take no action, and suggested that the matter be left in the hands of the chancellor and faculty at Chapel Hill. The board adopted this report in May 1962.

The accused girl then sued in the superior court of Orange County, and Judge Heman R. Clark held a *de novo* hearing in November 1962, and heard testimony of the Latin instructor, the head of the Latin department, Chancellor Aycock, the chairman and the secretary of the Women's Honor Council, and of the accused and her legal counsel. Late in December Judge Clark entered a twofold order: (1) "petitioner's contention that the decision of the Board was an unconstitutional delegation of authority is without merit in her case;" but (2) "All of the evidence offered against Miss Carter fails to rebut the presumption of innocence. . . . To deny her readmission solely on the grounds of the suspension for cheating, on the evidence in this case would, in the opinion of this Court, be arbitrary and capricious."

Already almost two years had elapsed, and another year was lost because meantime the plaintiff had instituted another action in the superior court of Wake County asking the court to order the university to show cause why she should not be restored to good standing. This case was heard by Judge Clawson L. Williams in July 1963, and he issued an order in November 1963 directing that the case be heard *de novo* by the faculty committee on discipline at Chapel Hill, and declining to entertain any further proceedings until the faculty committee could hold its hearing and make its report. This was immediately appealed to the supreme court of North Carolina, where the record of both actions came under review. Early in 1964 the supreme court published its decision, which in effect reversed the order of Judge Williams and affirmed the order of Judge Clark, which had concluded by declaring the case[8]

> remanded to the Board of Trustees of the University of North Carolina, and the Board is directed to refer the matter to the proper administrative authority for a review of the proceeding, including the additional evidence disclosed in this court and for other and further administrative action as is appropriate.

Justice Parker, in a lengthy opinion, after making clear that the board of trustees could delegate disciplinary authority to the chancellor and faculty, continued:

> and in the discharge of this duty, delegation of such authority may be made to established agencies of student government; . . . provided, that in the discharge of this duty it shall be the duty of the chancellor and faculty to secure to every student the right of due process and fair hearing, the presumption of inno-

---

[8] *In re Carter*, 262 N.C. 360, 137 S.E. 2d 150 (1964). The duration of the litigation was nearly four years. The plaintiff, Miss Carter, was first suspended from the university in May 1961. She attended summer school at a nearby institution in 1961. She studied abroad during the 1961-62 academic year. In January 1962 her suspension was cancelled, in accord with the university's usual custom of reinstating suspended students after two semesters. She attended the university's summer school in 1962, but took only one course. She was denied readmission in the Fall of 1962 on the ground that her summer school credits were not sufficient to make up her academic deficiencies. Subsequently she attended an Eastern university, and eventually transferred to a Southern college. At about the time of the conclusion of the litigation she was married; and further facts of her career are not known. Standing on the records of the North Carolina courts is the statement of Superior Court Judge Heman R. Clark that "All of the evidence offered against Miss Carter fails to rebut the presumption of innocence."

cence until found guilty, the right to know the evidence and to face witnesses testifying against him, and the right to such advice and assistance in his own defense as may be allowable under the regulations of the institution. . . .

Due Process in Disciplinary Actions

The Florida Agricultural and Mechanical University has a rule to the effect that "Students convicted by city, county, state, or federal authorities for violation of any criminal or civil law shall be disciplined by the faculty discipline committee."

In October 1963 two students, together with several others, were arrested and convicted of contempt in the local district court for alleged violation of an injunction against student disturbances (specifically, "sit-in" efforts to gain unsegregated use of theater facilities). Fourteen days after their conviction these two students were called by telephone at their homes by the assistant dean of students and asked if they had received written notice of a hearing before the faculty discipline committee. Both replied in the negative and each was thereupon advised orally that they would be expected to appear at the hearing on the afternoon of that same day. They appeared between 3 and 5 p.m. One was before the committee about 45 minutes, and the other about half that long.

Both admitted their convictions but asserted they had not been leaders in the demonstration and should not be singled out for more severe punishment than others "also charged and convicted in like circumstances." Neither claimed to misunderstand the charge against him. Neither requested the privilege of calling witnesses or of obtaining legal counsel. No record of the proceedings was kept. After each had been given opportunity to make a summarizing statement, the committee voted to suspend both indefinitely and so notified them. They were also made aware of their right to appeal to the board of control, governing all Florida's state universities.

Their subsequent petition in federal district court for reinstatement by injunction was denied.[9] Chief Judge Carswell found that the procedure as indicated in the record was sufficient to meet the

---

[9] *Due* v. *Florida Agricultural and Mechanical University*, (U.S.D.C.), 233 F. Supp. 396 (1963).

requirements of due process in such cases as outlined by Circuit Judge Rives in the landmark case of *Dixon* v. *Alabama State Board of Education.*[10]

Probably it should be noted here that the handling of the accused students at Florida Agricultural and Mechanical University as above described seems to approach perilously close to a summary dismissal, and it is possible that there might be other judges who would not share Chief Judge Carswell's view that the minimum requirements set forth in *Dixon* v. *Alabama* were actually met.

Exclusion for Academic Failure:
Two Medical School Cases

At the University of Vermont a third-year medical student was enrolled in a 12-week course in pediatrics and obstetrics, March through June, 1964. From May 11 to June 7 he was absent due to illness, and "made up" the lost time from July 1 to July 16. On July 17 he was advised that he had failed and could not advance to his fourth year because a rule of the College of Medicine forbade the advancement of any student who failed 25% or more of his major courses of the third year.

He then petitioned for permission to repeat his third year, but was denied; and subsequently he was permanently expelled.

In court he alleged that his expulsion was wrongful, arbitrary, and unjust, and asked the court to order it rescinded. His work had been "passing" prior to his absence, he said (87% and 82% in the respective parts of the course), and early in July his teacher decided that "he would not give him a passing grade regardless of his prior work and regardless of the quality of his work in the make-up period."

The university met this allegation with a motion to dismiss the case and a motion for summary judgment in its favor. The federal district judge denied these motions and ordered the case set for hearing on the limited issue of whether the university had acted arbi-

---

[10] (U.S.C.A.), 294 F. 2d 150 (1961); *certiorari* denied, 368 U.S. 930, 82 S.Ct. 368, 7 L.Ed. 2d 193 (1961). Discussed at pages 31-32 in *The Colleges and the Courts Since 1950.*

trarily, capriciously, or in bad faith in dismissing the student; and said, "Should the plaintiff (student) prevail on that issue, this court will then order the defendant University to give the plaintiff a fair and impartial hearing on his dismissal order."

The court will not undertake to appraise the quality of a medical student's work, nor to interpose its own judgment of that as a substitute for the discretion of the medical faculty; but the allegation that the student was declared an academic failure without regard to the quality of his work is one which a court is bound not to ignore. The burden of proof is on the student, but he has a right to be heard in court in an effort to prove his allegation.[11]

In support of its motions to dismiss the case and for summary judgment, the university put forward some technical matters to which the court's responses are of some interest. First, it was asserted that the court should not take jurisdiction because of the Eleventh Amendment prohibition of a state being sued by a citizen of another state. Not so, said the court. The University of Vermont is clearly a public corporation having its own entity apart from that of the state, and a suit of this kind against it is not a suit against the state within the prohibition of the Eleventh Amendment.

Second, it was asserted that the court should not take jurisdiction because the statutory minimum amount of money involved for that purpose was not present. To this the court responded: "The value of the right of a third-year medical student to complete his fourth year and obtain a degree is worth, for purposes of determining the jurisdictional amount, in excess of $10,000."

A student entered the medical school of the University of Miami (Florida) in the fall of 1959. A year later he was admitted to the second year on probation. His second year's work having been unsatisfactory, he was allowed to repeat it, after which he was promoted to the third year with a grade point average of 1.92 (slightly below the customarily required "C" average). He was promoted to the fourth year on probation, conditioned upon additional satisfactory work in (a) pediatrics, and (b) obstetrics-gynecology. During the summer of 1963 he successfully completed (a) but not

---

[11] *Connelly* v. *University of Vermont and State Agricultural College*, (U.S.D.C., Vt.), 244 F. Supp. 156 (1965).

(b), and at the close of the summer the executive committee of the school of medicine dismissed him for academic failure.

He sought a writ of *mandamus* to compel his promotion to the fourth year, alleging that his dismissal was "arbitrary, capricious, and without just cause . . . , and not in good faith." The local circuit court, seemingly accepting these averments as findings of fact, issued an interlocutory writ, which was quashed by the court of appeal.[12] The local circuit court later granted a peremptory writ,. which the court of appeal nullified by reversing the judgment, on the ground that the allegations were without basis in evidence. *Mandamus* will not be used to control an exercise of discretion.

The court did not let the fact that the University of Miami is a private institution go unmentioned, but said the applicable principle is the same for public and private institutions:

> It is generally accepted that the terms and conditions for graduation are those offered by the publications of the college at the time of enrollment. As such, they have some of the characteristics of a contract between the parties, and are sometimes subject to civil remedies in courts of law.

The fact that the University of Miami Medical School receives a large part of its annual operating income in payments of tax funds of the state of Florida has no effect on the situation.[13]

Alleged Malicious Deprivation of Doctoral Degree

A graduate student at the American University sued the university and its officers as joint defendants, for damages for unjustly and maliciously depriving him of his doctoral degree by failing him in his general examinations. The federal district court dismissed the complaint "as to the American University only" and ordered final judgment as to the university, but made no ruling as to the individual defendants. The federal court of appeals held this disposition of the case to be in error, saying the claims against defendant members of the university staff must also be decided in the first instance by the district court. Accordingly the case was remanded to the district court with instructions to retain full control of the entire case until

---

[12] *University of Miami* v. *Militana*, (Fla. App.), 168 So. 2d 88 (1964).
[13] *University of Miami* v. *Militana*, (Fla. App.), 184 So. 2d 701 (1966).

final judgment is rendered as to all defendants. At this writing no report of further proceedings is available.[14]

Cases of Student Activists Accused of Violating Criminal Statutes

A New Jersey "Disaster Control Act" provides that any person refusing to obey the lawful orders of authorized Civil Defense personnel shall be adjudged a disorderly person, and establishes a penalty of imprisonment up to one year or fine up to $175, or both.

A small group of students at Drew University formed "ARROW" (Associated Realists Resisting Organization for War) to disrupt "Operation Alert 1961," an air-raid drill ordered by the state Civil Defense authorities. They issued a leaflet requesting students to attend an open-air meeting just before the scheduled alarm and to either remain at the meeting or go about distributing leaflets to the persons who had taken cover or were doing so.

ARROW's "Statement of Intention and Purpose" stressed the following, concerning Civil Defense: (1) its "functional futility"; (2) its "creation of an atmosphere of fear and hatred"; (3) its character as "an integral part of the strategy of military action"; and (4) its alleged "promotion of public apathy toward disarmament negotiations."

The offenders were convicted in the county court and fined $50 each. On appeal the convictions were affirmed in an opinion by Judge Walter J. Freund, who said: "The motive does not appear to be primarily religious; even if it were, *actions* contrary to penal law can not be excused by religious beliefs, even though the right to religious *belief* is absolute."[15]

The only earlier case of record directly in point (a New York case) terminated in the same manner.[16]

Indiana has an Anti-Sedition Act (Acts 1951, Ch. 226) which

---

[14] *Robbin* v. *American University*, (U.S.C.A.), 117 App. D.C. 351, 330 F. 2d 225 (1964).

[15] *State of New Jersey* v. *Congdon*, 76 N.J. Super. 493, 185 A. 2d 21 (1962).

[16] *People* v. *Parilli*, 1 Misc. 2d 201, 147 N.Y.S. 2d 618 (1955); affirmed in *People* v. *Peck*, 195 N.Y.S. 2d 637, 7 N.Y. 2d 76 (1959); appeal dismissed and *certiorari* denied in 364 U.S. 662, 81 S.Ct. 389, 5 L.Ed. 2d 372 (1961).

forbids described acts and makes violation a felony. A small group of students at Indiana University were indicted by a grand jury which alleged that on May 2, 1963 they "did then and there assemble for the purpose of advocating and teaching the doctrine that the government of the United States and of the State of Indiana should be overthrown by force, violence, and any unlawful means, voluntarily participating therein by their presence, aid and instigation, contrary to the . . . peace and dignity of the State of Indiana."

In the trial court Judge Nat U. Hill of Bloomington concluded that the statute was unconstitutional and ordered the indictment quashed and the accused persons discharged. This judgment was reversed by the state supreme court in an opinion by Chief Justice Arterburn, with Judges Achor and Myers concurring, Judge Landis not participating, and with Judge Jackson entering a vigorous dissent. The majority opinion turned largely on rejection of the defense argument that the field of the statute had been pre-empted by the federal statute of 1940 (54 Stat. 670, as amended in United States Code Section 2385) known as the Smith Act, thus closing the door to state legislation.

After a study of two relevant opinions of the United States Supreme Court rendered in 1956 and 1959, both decided by closely divided votes (*Pennsylvania* v. *Nelson*, 350 U.S. 497, 76 S.Ct. 477, 100 L.Ed. 640 [1956], opinion by Chief Justice Warren, with Justices Burton, Minton, and Reed dissenting; and *Uphaus* v. *Wyman*, 360 U.S. 72, 79 S.Ct. 1040, 3 L.Ed. 2d 1090 [1959], opinion by Justice Clark, with Justices Warren, Brennan, Black, and Douglas dissenting), the view of the majority was, in the words of Justice Clark, that the prevailing federal law "rejects the notion that it stripped the states of the right to protect themselves, ..." and made clear that "a state could proceed with prosecutions for sedition against the state itself."

Chief Justice Arterburn also wrote some restrained and well-reasoned statements about freedom of speech and "freedom of organization among college and university students and their right to hear all shades of opinion expressed by outside speakers. . . . ," stressing the fact that no liberties are absolute, and that the weight of judicial opinion upholds the right of the states to protect their classrooms and campuses by legislation against seditious acts.

In his dissent, Judge Jackson set out in full the text of the Indiana Anti-Sedition Act, and concluded: [17]

> A reading of the above statute clearly and indisputably shows it to be unconstitutionally vague. A statute, invoking the police powers of the state in order to provide for internal security and public safety, and thereby impinging upon the constitutionally protected areas of free speech and assembly, must so clearly and specifically define the proscribed acts as to leave no doubts of the nature of the offense and the charge to be met by the defendant. *Herndon* v. *Lowry*, 301 U.S. 242, 57 S.Ct. 732, 81 L.Ed. 1066 (1937).

As appears in Chapter 7, *infra*, this doctrine of strict specification in statutes carrying criminal penalties has recently been used more than once by the United States Supreme Court in striking down as unconstitutional the loyalty oath statutes of some states, on the ground of vagueness.

California Sustains Action of Juvenile Court
Concerning Unlawful "Sit-in"

One aftermath of the nonviolent civil disobedience on the Berkeley campus of the University of California of December 2, 1964, consisting chiefly of hundreds of students refusing to leave Sproul Hall at closing time and being eventually removed by force by policemen, was that a group of the students who were minors were processed in the juvenile court of Alameda County, where they were charged with violating Penal Code Sections 148 (resisting an officer), 409 (unlawful assembly), and 602, subdivision "o" (failure to leave a public building after closing time), all of which are misdemeanors.

The juvenile court's order regarding each one found guilty was that the student be

> ... placed on probation without wardship upon the condition that he be of good conduct and obey all laws; obey parents; maintain good school attendance, behavior and performance; report to and follow directions of the probation officer; and spend four weekends at the probation department's Training Academy (reducible to two weekends at the discretion of the probation officer).

---

[17] *State* v. *Levitt*, (Ind.), 203 N.E. 2d 821 (1965).

It was reported that the juvenile judge had said the weekends "probably" meant manual labor from 8 to 5 on Saturday and Sunday. Some of the cases were taken to the court of appeal, chiefly on the ground that execution of the order would deprive the parents of the physical custody of their children on weekends. Justice Molinari, affirming the order for the three-judge court, noted that[18]

> As the record stands there is nothing to indicate that appellants will be required to do any manual labor at all or that the program will consist of anything more than an educational program.

Freedom of Students to Invite to the Campus
Outside Speakers and to Hear All Shades of Opinion

There has been a wave toward enacting various types of "speaker bans" by some state legislatures and some institutional governing boards. Often these proposed measures have been defeated after exposure to debate, and it can be said that they are not widely popular. In 1963 the North Carolina legislature enacted a law prohibiting the appearance on state-owned campuses of "known Communists" and persons who have pleaded the Fifth Amendment in loyalty investigations. In 1965 this was amended to vest in the institutional boards of trustees the discretion to decide whether speakers in the named categories should be allowed to speak.

Early in 1966 two such speakers were twice denied permission to speak on the Chapel Hill campus of the University of North Carolina—Herbert Aptheker and Frank Wilkinson—though recognized student groups wished to invite them, and did invite them for off-campus appearances. As a result, on March 31, 1966 the president of the student government and other student leaders, joined by the two leftist speakers, instituted a suit in the United States district court at Greensboro against the board of trustees of the University of North Carolina.

Alleging that the students and the speakers are denied the constitutional rights of freedom of speech and assembly (including the right to listen as well as to speak) and "equal protection of the laws," the plaintiffs hope for a decision "establishing clearly the right of

---

[18] *In re Bacon*, (Cal. App.), 49 Cal. Rptr. 322 (1966).

members of an academic community to listen to speakers they choose to invite." The North Carolina Conference of the American Association of University Professors is helping to finance the litigation, and the national AAUP has been reported as considering whether to file a supporting "friend of the court" brief in the case.

For years the Ohio State University has been a hotbed of controversy over a "speakers' rule." One of the hot spots in the history was in March 1962 when the organization known as Students for Liberal Action scheduled one Phillip A. Luce to speak to them, and the president of the university ordered the doors of the Law Building auditorium locked some hours before Luce's scheduled appearance there. The president again refused, in November 1962, to allow Frank Wilkinson to address the same organization; and in March 1963 Wilkinson and the president of the student liberal organization jointly filed suit in the federal district court for the southern district of Ohio, asking that the president and board of trustees of the university be ordered to permit Wilkinson to speak on the campus, and that the current "speakers' rule" be declared violative of constitutional rights and void. It was reported early in 1966 that the action had been summarily dismissed by District Judge Mel G. Underwood, granting the Ohio attorney general's motion for dismissal on the ground that the president and the board of trustees have the general authority to act as they think in the best interests of the university in controlling students inside and outside the classroom. It has been reported more recently that the board of trustees, in an effort to quiet the long-continued and more or less continual acrid argument over the matter, has voted to recede somewhat from the rigid version which gave sole and absolute authority to the president of the university to admit or exclude campus speakers; but apparently the board has not yet arrived at a recognition of the fact that here is an area in which the best rule is no rule at all.

Privilege of Student Editor Not to Identify Sources of News Stories

It seems to be a cherished ethic of journalism that editors and reporters should have the privilege of quoting or paraphrasing the words of anonymous interviewees without disclosing their names as sources of the information. The theory apparently is that without the protection of anonymity the respondents would often refuse to divulge the information (sometimes for fear of self-incrimination) and as a result news-gatherers would be handicapped and the public would be deprived of facts of which it should be informed.

Some states have statutes intended to protect a fiduciary relationship between journalists and their sources of information; but there is no such statute in Oregon. In 1966 Annette Buchanan, editor of the *Oregon Daily Emerald*, the University of Oregon student newspaper, published a story on the use of marijuana by students, purportedly based on interviews with marijuana users. Since the use of marijuana is a crime in Oregon, Judge Edward Leavy of the circuit court at Eugene ordered Miss Buchanan to reveal the names of her interviewees to the Lane County grand jury early in June, or stand in contempt of court with a possible maximum penalty of six months in jail and a $300 fine.

Miss Buchanan declined to reveal the names, saying it would be a breach of a fiduciary relationship. Her attorney sought the intervention of the state supreme court.

Prohibition of Local Chapters of National Fraternities by Trustees of State University of New York

Local chapters of national fraternities at the former University of Buffalo, which became a unit of the State University of New York in 1963, sued to have the ban prohibiting these chapters declared invalid in 1965, but it continues to be valid on all campuses of the university.[19]

The trustees banned national fraternities at SUNY campuses as early as 1953, after receiving a report on the subject from the then president of SUNY, in which the reasoning on which the ban is based was set forth substantially as follows:

1. The university must be in a position to control the discipline and tone of the campus, and the presence of student organizations answerable to, or under the dominance of, outside national headquarters is anomalous, and endangers or destroys the university's position;

---

[19] *Beta Sigma Rho, Inc.* v. *Moore*, 46 Misc. 2d 1030, 261 N.Y.S. 2d 658 (1965).

2. The university is obligated to abstain from discrimination on grounds of race, color, sex, religion, or national origin; and "The academic and extracurricular programs of a university intertwine to such a degree in educating and molding a student that they cannot be severed and each judged by contradictory standards"; and

3. The university has an obligation to make its services available to qualified students at the lowest practicable expense to the student and his parents, and the sums included in fraternity fees and dues for the purpose of supporting a national headquarters and field staff add unduly and unnecessarily to the cost of education to the student.

Buffalo local chapters of certain national fraternities asked the local trial court for a declaratory judgment to hold the 12-year-old ban invalid. This was refused. Justice Matthew J. Jasen held that the trustees did not act arbitrarily in requiring Buffalo local chapters to comply with the existing state-university-wide ban of national fraternities when the University of Buffalo became a part of the state university.

University of Colorado's 1965 Rule on Racial Discrimination in Fraternities Declared Lawful by Federal District Court

On March 19, 1956, the Board of Regents of the University of Colorado adopted a resolution stipulating that any student organization denying membership to any person because of race, color, or religion would be placed on probation. Some nine years later the University suspended the privileges of "rushing" and "pledging" for Beta Mu Chapter of Sigma Chi Fraternity on the Boulder campus, "until such time as the chapter can comply with the university policy resolution."

It appeared that the regents had determined to investigate the practices of Sigma Chi after its Stanford University chapter had been suspended by the national organization when it pledged a Negro student, Kenneth Washington, son of a Denver physician. The University of Colorado chapter sought to convince the regents that it had dissociated itself from the pledging rules and practices disseminated by the national headquarters. This was ineffective because the national headquarters had never consented.

Thereafter the chapter sued in federal district court, alleging that the regents were exceeding their powers and depriving the members of the chapter of the constitutional right of free association. The case reached a three-judge federal court composed of Circuit Judge Jean S. Breitenstein and District Judges Hatfield Chilson and William E. Doyle. Their opinion, a 28-page document, was excerpted in the press in late summer 1966. Of the regents' resolution, the judges said: "It seeks to promote the principle of racial and religious equality, but there is nothing in it that can be regarded as an excessive exercise of power." Citing cases where universities have abolished fraternities altogether, they thought the resolution of 1956 was only "a mild regulatory measure."

Other parts of the opinion, as quoted, evince a thoughtful and tolerant view. Without assuming that the chapter is demanding the right to discriminate on the basis of race or creed, the judges said:

> A more apt description of the plaintiffs' contention is in terms of their seeking recognition of a right of association which grants them freedom to select members free of state regulation.
>
> The Regents, on the other hand, are not forcing plaintiffs to take members of any particular group. The extent and degree of the attempted regulation would be more accurately described as an effort to eliminate from the charters and rituals of the organization affected a provision which compels discrimination on the basis of race, color, or creed.

Decisions touching several other aspects of college and university fraternities and sororities, such as the impact of property taxation and zoning regulations upon fraternity housing, are reserved for discussion in Chapter 25, *infra* ("Accessory Educational Corporations and Associations").

Can a Student's Academic and Disciplinary Performances Be Kept Distinct, Neither Affecting the Other?

A press dispatch of September 2, 1966, reported that Jacalyn Dieffenderfer, a 20-year-old girl student at the University of Colorado residing in Boulder, filed suit in district court to compel the president and regents of the university and an instructor in English, Miss Kaye Bache, to change her grade in an English course from "F" to "B." She is said to have alleged that the mark of failure bore no relation to the quality of her work, but was given in order to discipline and punish her for alleged wrongful conduct. It seems that she had been accused of cheating by Miss Bache, but had been cleared of the charge by the university discipline committee after investigation and hearing.

The law of such cases is well stated in the decision in *Connelly* v. *University of Vermont* (Footnote 11 in this chapter). No court will order a particular scholastic mark to be awarded in the first place, or changed thereafter, for that would be substituting the judgment of the court for that of the instructor. But if it is alleged that a mark has been given capriciously or maliciously without proper appraisal of the student's work, then a court may order a trial of the facts. The burden of proof will be on the student; but if he proves his allegations, the court may then order the school to accomplish a fair evaluation of the student's work by some means involving the exercise of sound discretion by qualified teachers, and the awarding of a mark in accord with that judgment.

Exclusion of Student from College of Architecture in University of Florida; Court of Appeal and Faculty Disagree

Another case in which there seems to have been difficulty in distinguishing between the academic and disciplinary merits of a student was decided by a Florida court of appeal in 1966. It involves interesting and important questions regarding the administration of a large state university.

Briefly, the facts seem to be these: Oscar Woody, a student in the College of Architecture and Fine Arts of the University of Florida, had been advised by his major department head that he must take the course designated Art 207. Woody did not want to take this course (his reason does not appear in the record). On registration day he approached the appropriate table to have his registration cards completed and validated. There he persuaded the professor in charge at the time (not the major department head) to remove Art 207 from his cards and initial them as changed. Upon discovering this, the department head refused to accept his registration and charged him with physically altering his Course Assignment Card, an important record of the University. This charge was filed with the Faculty Discipline Committee of the University, which duly notified Woody and held a hearing at which he was present and testified. The committee decided by a divided vote, with its chairman casting the deciding vote, that "Mr. Woody was not proven guilty of physically altering the Course Assignment Card . . . but was guilty of conduct unbecoming a University of Florida student in that he did knowingly cause a university record to be altered against the stated wishes of his Department Head," and recommended that he be placed on disciplinary probation for the remainder of his undergraduate career. The president of the University approved this recommendation.

Having awaited the foregoing result, Mr. Woody two days later filed a petition with the appropriate committee of the College of Architecture and Fine Arts, asking to be permitted to register late. This petition was summarily denied. He remained out of school until the beginning of the next trimester, when he applied to the university for registration, and was denied without notice or hearing. President Reitz affirmed the determination and informed Woody's attorney that the faculty committee of the College of Architecture and Fine Arts took the position that Woody's failure to take Art 207 constituted a defiance of the college's requirements and resulted in his disqualifying himself for further attendance in the college due to *failure to maintain a satisfactory academic record.* (Note here that Woody had maintained an average of "B" in his academic work at the university; and that Chief Judge Rawls of the court of appeal later said of his exclusion: "It was based *solely upon misconduct* and not upon failure to maintain the required academic standard." The judge said this because President Reitz had noted that the committee's action was influenced by reports that his conduct and behavior had created a disturbing influence in classes and his defiance of regulations and lack of cooperation had been demonstrated in situations prior to the incident relating to failure to register for Art 207.)

The judge was shocked by the fact that the committee of the College of Architecture and Fine Arts "went beyond the question presented and expelled him permanently from that College. It made that decision without notice and hearing and based same upon incidents which are not matters of record and upon which the student had never been given an opportunity to be heard."

When Woody was given a hearing before the board of regents, President Reitz explained that the Architecture faculty "did not wish Mr. Woody to continue as a student in that College," and that according to accepted university administration principles the faculty has the right to admit or exclude any student from its program because in awarding degrees it places its stamp of approval and recommendation upon the individual.

The president therefore recommended that Woody be denied further enrollment in Architecture, *without prejudice to his enrollment in other colleges of the university*. The regents approved this recommendation, and the state board of education affirmed the determination. The only further recourse was to the courts. The trial court, having issued an alternative writ of *mandamus*, quashed it, concluding that the hearing before the board of regents had been sufficient. Of this, Chief Judge Rawls of the court of appeal was later to say with emphasis: "Even there he was not advised of the acts of misconduct upon which was grounded his exclusion from the college of his choice."

Judges Wigginton and Donald K. Carroll, both of Judge Rawls' colleagues on the appeal bench, concurred in his opinion, reversing and remanding the case with direction to reinstate the alternative writ of *mandamus* and proceed accordingly.[20]

It would appear that the court meant to give no countenance to informal, secretive, *ex parte* treatment of students by faculties, deeming this kind of practice especially inappropriate in a modern tax-supported public institution such as a state university. It hewed to the line of the distinction between *academic* and *disciplinary* matters, and noted that the catalog of the University of Florida charges each college of the university with responsibility of enforcing its own *academic* standards, but that the enforcement of *disciplinary* standards is the responsibility of an all-university faculty committee, subject to appeal to the president and thence to the board of regents.

> The action here is invalid on its face not only because (Woody) was never confronted with the charges against him and was not given an opportunity to present his case before the committee (of the College of Architecture) that excluded him, but also because that committee, instead of bringing open charges of misconduct in the usual manner before the University Disciplinary Committee, circumvented that duly authorized Committee and arrogated unto itself the authority of imposing its own penalty for (Woody's) misconduct.

---

[20] *Woody* v. *Burns, Governor, et al.*, (Fla. App.), 188 So. 2d 56 (1966).

Referring to the *Dixon* v. *Alabama* decision of 1961,[21] the court said:

> It has been held that constitutional due process requires notice and opportunity for hearing before a student of a tax-supported college or university can be expelled for misconduct. . . .
>
> The basis is that a charge of misconduct as opposed to failure to meet the scholastic standards of the college, depends upon a collection of the facts which are easily colored by the point of view of the witness.
>
> . . . .
>
> The principles of fair play require that before a student may be denied the right to continue his studies at a state-supported university due to misconduct he shall be advised of all the charges against him and be given an opportunity to refute same. When these requirements are met, the judgment of a duly constituted disciplinary committee functioning in a normal manner by well-defined procedures will not be lightly disturbed.

The decision to exclude Woody from the College of Architecture, said Chief Judge Rawls, "was made without notice and hearing . . . , was based upon matters upon which he had never had an opportunity to be heard, and in spite of these deficiencies it was approved by the President of the University, the Board of Regents, and the State Board of Education."

Evidently the court was convinced, and not without reason, that an element of personal animus against Woody had developed among some members of the Architecture faculty; and on this point its words were sharp:

> We are not aware of any delegation by the legislature or the State Board of Education or the Board of Regents to the faculty members of any college of the higher educational system of this state to arbitrarily or capriciously decide whom they desire to teach . . .
>
> This is not to say that those charged with the responsibility of operating our universities are not responsible for establishing basic standards of conduct and enforcing same . . . On the contrary it is their duty to take affirmative action to exclude from the student body those individuals not conforming to the established standards. However, the manner of enforcement must be by a duly authorized body in accordance with pro-

---

[21] *Dixon* v. *Alabama State Board of Education*, (U.S.C.A.), 294 F. 2d 150 (1961); reversing (U.S.D.C., Ala.), 186 F. Supp. 945 (1960); *certiorari* denied, 368 U.S. 930, 82 S.Ct. 368, 7 L.Ed. 2d 193 (1961). Discussed at pages 31-33 in *The Colleges and Courts Since 1950.*

cedures which permit the student an opportunity to vindicate himself, if he can and so desires.

Earlier in the opinion the court had declared: "The University of Florida is not the private property of those employed by the citizens of this state to perform the responsibility of providing a program of higher education primarily for the students of this state."

No doubt some observers may argue that the court misunderstands the functions of a faculty, and ignores the necessary autonomy of professional colleges within a university; and that the insistence that Woody's exclusion was *disciplinary* is in error, because his evasion of "Art 207" is in itself a failure to meet the *academic* requirements of the College of Architecture, regardless of what disciplinary overtones it may carry.

Knowledgeable commentators will say, too, that the actions of the president of the University of Florida in this case were in accord with recognized academic and administrative customs and practices in large universities. But this does not necessarily mean that those procedures must be perpetuated in state universities of the present and future. The view of the court of appeal, with its emphasis on the concept of a state university as existing to serve all the people of the state, rather than only the favorites of its faculties, is persuasive.

Should the Architecture faculty have "bent the rules" a bit, at least for the time being, in deference to the strong preference of this consistent "B" student, instead of "playing it by the book" and rigidly insisting that he take a course he did not want? Which is the better employment of a faculty's high prerogative—unbending enforcement of the minute letter of its rules, or a somewhat flexible administration of them, with considerable adaptation to individual differences among students? Should a faculty be inhospitable to students who show marked independence of thought and propensity to challenge faculty views? Are academic and professional degrees to be reserved exclusively for the docile, the complacent, the apathetic, the unspirited, who take the "zombie pose" and stolidly "serve time" at the university?

Hitherto these have been thought of, if at all, as questions of policy and not of law; but they are unmistakably suggested by this Florida decision. Is a new concept of the university in the making, to change it from a bureaucratic mill for the fabrication of flannel-suited robots to a community of independent scholars in which the integrity of even the most junior members is recognized and given a humane respect? Shall we really act upon the maxim that "all education is self-education," and repudiate the notions that education is regimentation, that it is largely a hazing process, and that no learning can be good unless it is repugnant and painful to the learner?

Whether the present *Woody* decision stands or falls, it serves to raise many profound issues in the future of public higher education. At some remote time it may become a benchmark in the history of academe.

CHAPTER 3

THE PROGRESS OF RACIAL DESEGREGATION

LITIGATION OF THE ADMISSION OF STUDENTS to state universities and colleges without discrimination as to race or color, though it has been in progress for more than 30 years, is not yet concluded. This chapter reviews four such cases in the states of Alabama, Louisiana, and South Carolina. Two other cases not directly involving colleges or universities are added: the long struggle over the right of the National Association for the Advancement of Colored People to operate in Alabama, and the unsuccessful libel suit by a public officer of Montgomery against the *New York Times* for publishing an allegedly inaccurate and defamatory advertisement which he averred reflected adversely upon his reputation.

To Study Architecture in South Carolina

A 19-year-old resident of Charleston sought admission to the Clemson Agricultural College of South Carolina in January 1961. The incomplete application was first denied on the ground that it appeared he was currently doing satisfactory work at Iowa State University, where he was attending. (He was a student of architecture, and some of his college expenses were being paid by the state of

South Carolina in accord with that state's practice of denying Negro applicants admission to any of its state institutions other than South Carolina State College at Orangeburg, but of subsidizing their attendance at any reputable institution outside the state which would admit them to a course of instruction desired by them and offered in any South Carolina state university or college but not available at Orangeburg, as was the case in this instance.)

Renewed and resubmitted, his application was again cancelled August 31, 1961, for the reason that his "college board" test scores, received on the preceding day, were received too late to permit consideration of his application. (He had not taken the examination until August, though one had been given in Charleston, where he lived, in late June 1961.) About 50 other applications were cut off for similar reasons. Thus the contention that his cancellation was not discriminatory was supported by substantial evidence.

He completed another formal application and submitted it in June 1962, when his transcripts for the third quarter at Iowa State University arrived at Clemson. The dean of the school of architecture at Clemson then wrote him that, though not a formal catalog requirement, the dean routinely requested all applicants to submit samples of their design work and present themselves for a personal interview.

Meantime, the United States district court having declined to order his admission or afford other appropriate relief, he appealed to the United States court of appeals. Thereafter he wrote the registrar at Clemson, offering to submit samples as requested by the dean, and received the reply that all communications should be between his and Clemson's attorneys. As to this, the United States court of appeals said in its review of the case: "The College should not have shut off Gantt's effort to comply with the request of the Dean for samples of his design work, nor should it be allowed to justify its failure to grant the application because of Gantt's failure to submit drawings which the College refused to receive, or because of his effort to enforce his constitutional rights."

As to the state's practice of subsidizing his attendance at a university outside the state, the court had only to repeat the substance

of the unanimous decision of the United States Supreme Court of a
quarter of a century before, in the landmark *Gaines Case:* [1]

> To require a Negro in all respects eligible for admission
> to a college maintained by the state to forego attendance there
> and to attend an out-of-state college, even with a state subven-
> tion, is not a satisfaction of his constitutional right to equal treat-
> ment without regard to race.

With this background, the court of appeals reversed and remanded the district court judgment adverse to Gantt, and directed
the lower court to order the admission of Gantt to Clemson College
"commencing with the opening of the next semester, for his qualification for admission is unquestioned. The injunctive order will require
only that he be treated as any other transfer student."[2]

The opinion also declared this to be a "class action," not merely
for the benefit of the plaintiff alone, but on behalf of other Negro
citizens of South Carolina similarly situated.

Alabama: Auburn University and
University of Alabama

Harold A. Franklin, a permanent resident of Talladega and a
graduate of Alabama State College at Montgomery, wished to be
admitted to the graduate school of Auburn University (the land-grant
university of Alabama) to pursue a master's degree in history and
political science. He was faced with a graduate school rule that applicants who were not graduates of an accredited college or university would not be admitted. His *alma mater*, a state college for
Negroes, was unaccredited.

He sought in the federal district court a temporary injunction
against Auburn University's refusal to admit him. The injunction was
granted. District Judge Johnson reasoned that the state of Alabama
was fully responsible for both the operation of the Auburn Uni-

---

[1] *State of Missouri ex rel. Gaines* v. *Canada,* 59 S.Ct. 232, 83 L.Ed. 207
(1938). Discussed at pages 5-6 in *The Colleges and the Courts,* 1936-40. New
York: Carnegie Foundation for the Advancement of Teaching, 1941. 126 pp.

[2] *Gantt* v. *Clemson Agricultural College of South Carolina,* (U.S.C.A.), 320
F. 2d 611 (1963); reversing and remanding 213 F. Supp. 103 (1962). Earlier de-
cision, 208 F. Supp. 416 (1962). *Certiorari* denied, 375 U.S. 814, 84 S.Ct. 46, 11
L.Ed. 2d 49 (1963).

versity graduate school and the unaccredited condition of the state's two Negro colleges. In these circumstances the rule of the graduate school against the admission of graduates of nonaccredited colleges was in effect unlawfully discriminatory on the ground of race. The judge's injunctive order specified the term beginning January 2, 1964. The action was a "class action" and the order applied to other qualified Negroes as well as to the petitioner.[3]

Readers of *The Colleges and the Courts Since* 1950 will recall that on July 1, 1955, District Judge H. H. Grooms issued an order permanently enjoining the dean of admissions of the University of Alabama from denying qualified Negro applicants the right to enroll solely on account of their race or color.[4] On May 16, 1963, the same judge declared the original order to be in continuing effect. This latter order was prompted by a motion made in his court by the 11 members of the board of trustees of the University of Alabama, in their individual capacities, personally requesting him to delay the implementation of the order because of the prevailing climate of racial unrest, in the current cases of the qualified Negro applicants, Malone and McGlathery.

On May 21, 1963, District Judge Grooms denied this motion, whereupon Governor George C. Wallace of Alabama publicly declared he would personally "bar the door" of the University of Alabama against any Negro, and this he subsequently did in a comic-opera confrontation with United States marshals who escorted the Negro applicants through the door over his protest. The United States district court issued a temporary injunction against Governor Wallace, restraining him from obstructing the implementation of its order of July 1, 1955. In this order, Chief Judge Lynne expressed his thoughts:

> Thoughtful people, if they can free themselves from tensions produced by established principles with which they violently disagree must concede that the governor of a sovereign state has no authority to obstruct or prevent the execution of the lawful orders of a court of the United States. No legalistic for-

---

[3] *Franklin* v. *Parker*, (U.S.D.C., Ala.), 283 F. Supp. 724 (1963); affirmed, with slight modification not material here, (U.S.C.A.), 331 F. 2d 841 (1964).

[4] *Lucy* v. *Adams*, (U.S.D.C., Ala.), 134 F. Supp. 235 (1955); affirmed in 228 F. 2d 619 (1955). *Certiorari* denied, 351 U.S. 931, 76 S.Ct. 790, 100 L.Ed. 1460 (1956). Discussed at page 40 in *The Colleges and the Courts Since 1950*.

mula is required to express the craving of honest, hard-working, God-fearing citizens for a moral order logically supported, —an attitude long ago expressed when Coke informed King James that there was a law above the King.

It was clear, he thought, that the plaintiffs would suffer irreparable loss if the injunctive order were not issued. After citing many cases on the law of desegregation, he concluded: "My prayer is that all of our people, in keeping with our finest traditions, will join in the resolution that law and order will be maintained, both in Tuscaloosa and in Huntsville"[5] (seats of the main campus and branch campus of the University of Alabama). His hope was fulfilled.

When State Is Violating Federal Law, It Can Be Enjoined by Federal Court

The doctrine that a state or its agency can not be sued by a citizen in a federal court without its own consent (Eleventh Amendment, United States Constitution) is subject to exceptions. When a Negro girl resident of Louisiana brought a class action against the state board of education for admission to Northeast Louisiana State College at Monroe the federal district court dismissed that action without considering the merits, but allowed the plaintiff 60 days in which to reform her plea by joining the individual members of the board as indispensable defendants, because

> The Louisiana State Board of Education is not amenable to suit in a Federal court. If redress is sought as a result of actions of the members of the Board, those members must be sued individually. The court must not allow the merits of the case to assume such proportions as to make it blind to the constitutional prohibition of a suit against an unconsenting sovereign.

The action in its original form, said the court, would violate the Eleventh Amendment. It would also be contrary to Article XIX, section 26 of the Louisiana constitution, which had been amended in 1956 expressly to withdraw the state's consent to suits against cer-

---

[5] *United States* v. *Wallace*, Governor, (U.S.D.C., Ala.), 218 F. Supp. 290 (1963).

tain of its agencies, including the state board of education.[6] The plaintiff appealed, and also immediately asked the United States court of appeals for a temporary injunction to restrain the board from excluding her, pending the result of her appeal on the merits.

The redoubtable Circuit Judge Richard T. Rives, sitting with Circuit Judge Hutcheson and District Judge Grooms, wrote the opinion directing the district court to issue the temporary order forthwith, so that Sarah Louise McCoy and other qualified Negro applicants similarly situated could enter the college at the beginning of the summer session of 1964.

Judge Rives used words which amounted to a reversal of the district court's determination. "Five times," he said, "this court (of appeals) has held that there is no immunity for a state agency from suit to enjoin it from enforcing an unconstitutional statute which requires segregation of the races and that the individual members of the Board need not be joined. The Supreme Court (of the United States) has recently indicated agreement . . . We see no reason why this court (or the district court) should depart from our previous holdings."

Rights of National Association for the Advancement of Colored People in State of Alabama

Incensed by the activities of the National Association for the Advancement of Colored People in providing legal counsel, financial support, and other forms of aid and comfort to Negroes who were suing for enforced recognition of their constitutional rights, Alabama segregationists pursued a long course of litigation aimed at having the NAACP deprived of the right to operate or exist in that state.

In 1956 the Montgomery County circuit court ordered the Alabama headquarters of the NAACP to produce numerous records in court within five days on penalty of being in contempt and subject to a fine of $100,000. Among the records was to be a listing of the individual names of all members of the organization. Substantially all the records demanded were produced, except the listing of rank-

---

[6] *McCoy* v. *Louisiana State Board of Education*, (U.S.D.C., La.), 229 F. Supp. 735 (1964). Motion for injunction pending appeal granted (U.S.C.A.), 332 F. 2d 915 (1964).

and-file members by name, which was withheld and alleged not to be within the power of the court to require. The NAACP took an appeal to the Alabama supreme court, which denied *certiorari* and dismissed the appeal.[7]

This judgment was reversed and remanded by the United States Supreme Court, in an opinion in which Justice Harlan said. "Inviolability of privacy in group association may in many circumstances be indispensable to preservation of freedom of association, particularly where a group espouses dissident beliefs."

> Petitioner has made an uncontroverted showing that on past occasions revelation of the identity of its rank-and-file members has exposed these members to economic reprisal, loss of employment, threat of physical coercion, and other manifestations of public hostility.

Thus the order of the Montgomery County court was an unlawful and a "substantial restraint upon the exercise by petitioner's members of their right to freedom of association." Subsequently, however, the Alabama supreme court affirmed the Montgomery court order, and an appeal was again taken to the Supreme Court of the United States, which reversed and remanded in a *per curiam* opinion.[8]

In 1961 the Montgomery County court dissolved its temporary injunctive order of 1956 against the NAACP, and permanently enjoined it from intrastate operation in Alabama; and this decree was affirmed by the Alabama supreme court.[9] This met with reversal by the United States Supreme Court, in an opinion again written by Justice Harlan. Dealing in some detail with the complaints advanced by the state of Alabama against the NAACP, he noted that these were in considerable part based on the giving of legal and financial aid by the NAACP to qualified Negro students to enable them to gain admission and attend the University of Alabama, and remarked:

---

[7] *Patterson* v. *NAACP*, 265 Ala. 349, 91 So. 2d 214 (1956); reversed in 357 U.S. 449, 78 S.Ct. 1163, 2 L.Ed. 2d 1488 (1958).

[8] *Patterson* v. *NAACP*, 268 Ala. 531, 109 So. 2d 138 (1959); *certiorari* granted, judgment reversed, and *mandamus* denied in 360 U.S. 240, 79 S.Ct. 1001, 3 L.Ed. 2d 1205 (1959). Rehearing denied, 361 U.S. 856, 80 S.Ct. 43, 4 L.Ed. 2d 96 (1959).

[9] *NAACP* v. *State of Alabama*, 274 Ala. 544, 150 So. 2d 677 (1963); reversed and remanded in 377 U.S. 288, 84 S.Ct. 1302, 12 L.Ed. 2d 325 (1964).

Before these proceedings were commenced, this Court had upheld the right of Autherine Lucy and Polly Anne Myers to enroll at the University of Alabama. *Lucy* v. *Adams*, 350 U.S. 1, 76 S.Ct. 33, 100 L.Ed. 3 (1955). Neither furnishing them with financial assistance, in effect a scholarship, to attend the University, nor providing them with legal counsel to assist their efforts to gain admission was unlawful or could, consistently with the decisions of this Court, be inhibited because contrary to the University's policy against admitting Negroes.

In his long list of complaints against the NAACP, the attorney general of Alabama included:

(8) that it attempted to "pressure" the mayor of Philadelphia, the Governor of Pennsylvania, and the Penn State football team into "a boycott of the Alabama football team" when the two teams were to play each other in the Liberty Bowl.

Of this, the austere Justice Harlan said:

We pass the eighth charge without comment; by no stretch can it be considered germane to the present controversy.

Reversing and remanding the Alabama decree against the NAACP, he concluded:

Should we unhappily be mistaken in our belief that the Supreme Court of Alabama will promptly implement this disposition, leave is given the Association to apply to this Court for further appropriate relief.

Meantime, in the midst of the eight-year course of litigation just sketched, the NAACP had instituted an action in federal court which produced its own separate train of decisions. In 1960 the federal district court dismissed the NAACP's suit to enjoin Alabama officers from enforcing the 1956 order of the Montgomery County court.[10] The United States court of appeals vacated this judgment and instructed the federal district court to permit determination of the issues in the state courts. This opinion was by Circuit Judge Jones, concurred in by District Judge Mize (sitting with the court of appeals), and dissented from in part by Chief Judge Elbert P. Tuttle, whose position was much like the view subsequently taken by the United States Supreme Court in the same case.

------

[10] *NAACP* v. *Gallion*, (U.S.D.C., Ala.), 190 F. Supp. 583 (1960); judgment vacated in (U.S.C.A.), 290 F. 2d 337 (1961); which was in turn vacated and remanded in 368 U.S. 16, 82 S.Ct. 4, 7 L.Ed. 2d 85 (1961).

The Supreme Court vacated the judgment of the court of appeals and remanded it with instructions to direct the district court to "proceed with the trial of the issues in this action unless the State of Alabama shall have accorded to the petitioner an opportunity to be heard within a reasonable time, no later than January 2, 1962." Trying again for a trial on the merits in the federal district court, the NAACP was told by District Judge Johnson that the United States Supreme Court—not the federal district court—was the proper tribunal to review the decisions of the Alabama supreme court, and denied the NAACP's motion for a hearing on the merits.[11]

During the same period the NAACP was embroiled in somewhat analogous litigation in some other southern states, including Louisiana and Virginia which are not digested here.[12]

Unsuccessful Suit Against Newspaper for Alleged Libel of Public Officer

Related in part to the nonviolent but bizarre activities of Negro college students seeking civil rights is the case of the *New York Times'* accepting and publishing a paid advertisement from a civil rights organization, in which a not entirely accurate recital of events involving students and police in Montgomery, Alabama, prompted the city commissioner of safety to sue the *Times* for damages for an allegedly libelous publication unjustly derogatory to his reputation.

The basis of the claim was a part of a full-page ad in the *Times* issue of March 29, 1960, under the heading "Heed Their Rising Voices."

> In Montgomery, Alabama, after students sang "My Country, 'Tis of Thee" on the State Capitol steps, their leaders were expelled from school, and truckloads of police armed with shotguns and tear gas ringed the Alabama State College campus. When the entire student body protested to state authorities by refusing to register, their dining hall was padlocked in an attempt to starve them into submission.
>
> . . . .
>
> Again and again the Southern violators have answered Dr.

---

[11] *NAACP* v. *Flowers*, (U.S.D.C., Ala.), 217 F. Supp. 70 (1963).

[12] Two of the cases reaching the United States Supreme Court were *Louisiana ex rel. Gramillion* v. *NAACP*, 366 U.S. 293, 81 S.Ct. 1333, 6 L.Ed. 2d 301 (1961); and (Virginia) *NAACP* v. *Button*, 371 U.S. 415, 83 S.Ct. 328, 9 L.Ed. 2d 405 (1963).

King's peaceful protests with intimidation and violence. They have bombed his home, almost killing his wife and child. They have assaulted his person. They have arrested him seven times— for "speeding," "loitering," and similar "offenses." And now they have charged him with "perjury"—a *felony* under which they would imprison him for *ten years....*

The advertisement did not mention the plaintiff (Montgomery City Commissioner of Safety), either by name or by title. Nevertheless an Alabama court awarded him $1 million in damages, and the judgment was affirmed by the state supreme court.

The judgment was reversed by the United States Supreme Court. Justice Brennan expressed the views of six members of the court. Justices Black and Goldberg wrote separate opinions concurring in the result, both joined by Justice Douglas, and both expressing the view that the constitutional guaranty of free speech and press afforded the defendants an absolute, unconditional privilege to publish their criticism of official conduct.

The conclusion of Justice Brennan for the majority of the court was:[13]

> (1) The rule of law applied by the Alabama courts was constitutionally deficient for failure to provide the safeguards for freedom of speech and press that are required by constitutional guaranty in a libel action brought by a public official against critics of his official conduct, and, in particular, for failing to provide a qualified privilege for honest misstatements of fact, defeasible only on a showing of actual malice; and (2) under proper standards the evidence presented in the case was constitutionally insufficient to support the judgment for the plaintiff.

The case bids fair to become a *cause célèbre* in the perennial cold war between the media of mass communication and public officers who resent criticism of their official performance. It will also be something of a landmark in the history of civil rights and interracial justice.

---

[13] *New York Times Company* v. *Sullivan,* 376 U.S. 254, 84 S.Ct. 710, 11 L.Ed. 2d 686 (1964). Reversing 272 Ala. 656, 144 So. 2d 25 (1962). Cited elsewhere in reports of the United States Supreme Court as follows: *Certiorari* granted, 371 U.S. 946, 83 S.Ct. 570 (1963). Permitted to file as *amicus curiae*: Tribune Company, 373 U.S. 907 83 S.Ct. 1310 (1963). Am. Civ. Liberties Union, 373 U.S. 820, 83 S.Ct. 1864 (1963). Washington Post, 375 U.S. 803, 84 S.Ct. 40 (1963).

Public Library Must Be Desegregated

Negro citizens and residents of the city and county of Sumter in South Carolina came into federal district court alleging that they were denied the right to use the library supported by city and county taxes, because of their race. They asked that an injunction be issued to restrain the library officials from thus denying them equal protection of the laws under the Fourteenth Amendment.

The case was clear. District Judge Simons held that the complaint set forth a cause of action; but before the case had reached him the library had already in good faith complied with the law of the land by admitting to membership persons of all races and colors under the same regulations, and it appeared that there would be no further violation of the rights of Negroes. Therefore he dismissed the complaint as moot, but not before explicitly ordering that Sec. 42-647 of the Code of Laws of South Carolina for 1962 (a segregation statute) is void and nonenforceable.[14]

Two Ways of Accomplishing Desegregation in Private Universities

Racial discrimination in state or municipal educational institutions is unlawful under the "equal protection of the laws" clause of the Fourteenth Amendment. As yet no court has held that, in the absence of any modifying circumstances, the same restraint applies to private educational institutions; but scholarly lawyers and judges have begun to anticipate the possibility of such a decision.

Meantime there is a 1965 United States court of appeals judgment that the private University of Tampa is so closely dependent on the municipality that, although it is in fact a private nonprofit corporation, nevertheless it must be held subject to the restraints of the Fourteenth Amendment. The university was said to have owed its establishment very largely to the availability of a surplus city building usable for its purposes, and the use of other city-owned land at nominal rentals.

Action by Negro complainants against discrimination had been

---

[14] *James* v. *Carnegie Public Library*, (U.S.D.C., S.C.), 235 F. Supp. 911 (1964).

dismissed in the federal district court, but this judgment was reversed by the court of appeals in an opinion by the well-known Chief Judge Tuttle, with Circuit Judges Rives and Bell concurring. An injunction against the university was not issued, because during the appeal the university's governing board had already rescinded all racial barriers and enrolled some Negro students. The court of appeals directed the district court to "retain jurisdiction for a reasonable time to permit it to determine that appellees have commenced to, and will continue to, operate without racial discrimination."[15]

Desegregation of the private Rice University at Houston was sought by a very different process. The terms of the trust instrument by which the institution was founded (which were also made a part of its charter as a nonprofit corporation) did not contemplate the admission of Negro students nor the charging of tuition fees. Recently the university asked the state courts for a determination "whether the trustees might accept qualified applicants without regard to color, and might charge tuition fees to those able to pay."

An affirmative judgment was rendered by the local district court, and an appeal to the Texas court of civil appeals was dismissed, though the issue was contested by a group of alumni and donors to the university. Said the plain-speaking Judge Coleman: "The status of appellants as former students and alumni of Rice University does not create in them a justiciable interest. An interest in the matter at issue based on sentiment alone will not support an appeal."

He went on: "The great weight of authority supports the rule that neither the donors of a fund devoted exclusively to charitable purposes, nor contributors to such a fund, have such an interest in the fund as to entitle them to maintain suit to interfere with, or direct, the management of the fund by the trustees." And finally he quoted from the article on charities in *American Jurisprudence*, 2d: "A mere contributor, to have a foothold for questioning disposition of the fund, must have some special interest in the trust or reversionary interest in the fund different from that of fellow-contributors."[16]

This case was later reversed and remanded on other technical

---

[15] *Hammond* v. *University of Tampa*, (U.S.C.A., Fla.), 344 F. 2d 951 (1965).

[16] *Coffee* v. *William Marsh Rice University*, (Tex. Civ. App.), 387 S.W. 2d 132 (1965). Application for writ of error granted.

procedural grounds which will probably not change the ultimate outcome. That aspect is discussed in Chapter 19, *infra*, in the text appertaining to Footnote 13. See also Chapter 12, *infra*, for Girard
College and Sweet Briar College.

Thus the elimination of racial barriers proceeded between 1962
and 1966. There is no mistaking the trend, but it has not yet reached
completion.

CHAPTER 4

VARIOUS INCIDENTS OF
STUDENT LIFE

NUMEROUS AND WIDELY DIVERGENT MATTERS fall within the scope of this chapter. Among them are (1) the residence of students for (a) voting purposes, and (b) for purposes of service of summons in an automobile accident case; and (2) statutes forbidding the sale of intoxicating beverages within prescribed distances from the campus. These latter have a long history behind them.

Among the less frequently litigated issues are (3) those arising out of the conduct of interscholastic athletics, such as (a) a suit for libel against a popular magazine by a college football player alleging that his team had been falsely described as indulging in unsportsmanlike and unlawful practices, and (b) the activities of a widespread ring of big-time gamblers in bribing basketball players at numerous colleges; and (4) forgery and impersonation by a non-student in a unsuccessful attempt to gain unlawful possession of the transcript of credits of a recently graduated student. Finally (5) there is a small spate of cases involving automobile liability insurance policies when a student's vehicle is in a traffic accident while driven by a person other than the insured.

Voting Residence of Students

Max and Charlotte Livingston, husband and wife, were born, reared, and always resided in the vicinity of Farragut, Iowa, except when Max was away for two years in military service, and when both went to Tarkio, Missouri, for a year for the sole purpose of completing Max's undergraduate education in senior year at Tarkio College.

In a hotly-contested school bond election in the Farragut Community School District their votes were challenged on the ground that they were residents of another state. The supreme court of Iowa readily decided this comparatively simple case in harmony with one of its own decisions nearly a century old, holding that one who becomes a resident of a locality for the purpose of attending college and who has formed no intention of remaining after the completion of his college course is not entitled to vote in such locality. "To constitute a residence within the law as to qualification of voters the fact of residence and intent to remain must concur."[1] Hence Max and Charlotte had never lost their voting residence in Farragut, Iowa.

This is the rudimentary and conservative rule, not everywhere followed. Witness, for example, the 1947 New York decision holding that Columbia University students under the "G. I. Bill" who had their families with them and lived in quarters rented from the university on agreements stipulating that they must vacate whenever they ceased to be students, were entitled to vote in the political subdivision in which the dwellings were located, and their wives and adult relatives living with them had the same right. This was on the practical ground that the adult students and adult members of their households had no other homes. Therefore the question of "intent to remain" beyond the completion of the course of study was entirely ignored; and this may well be the more modern view regarding adult students.[2]

---

[1] *Frakes* v. *Farragut Community School District,* 225 Iowa 88, 121 N.W. 2d 636, 48 A.L.R. 2d 484 (1963); citing *Vanderpoel* v. *O'Hanlon,* 53 Iowa 246, 5 N.W. 119 (1880).

[2] *Robbins* v. *Chamberlain,* 297 N.Y. 108, 75 N.E. 2d 617 (1947). Discussed at pages 30-31 in *The Colleges and the Courts, 1946-50.* New York: Columbia University Press, 1952. 202 pp.

Residence for Service of Summons in
Automobile Accident Case

A girl student of minor age at Bowling Green State University in Ohio was sued for damages for injuries sustained by the plaintiff whose parked car was struck by a vehicle driven by her. Service of summons was made by the sheriff of Wood County (in which the university is located) upon the girl student in person, and upon the housemother in Treadway Hall, the dormitory in which both lived. Since the girl had neither parent nor guardian in that county, service was later made upon her father, a resident of Mobile, Alabama, by registered mail through the office of the secretary of state.

Some four years later her attorney moved to quash the service of summons, and the motion was sustained by the court of common pleas, only to be reversed and remanded by the court of appeals. It was decided that the service of summons upon the girl and her housemother in the dormitory was in exact conformity with the Ohio statute governing the subject (Revised Code sec. 2703.13):[3]

> When the defendant is a minor the service of summons must be upon him, and also upon his guardian or father, or, if neither can be found, upon his mother, or the person having the care of such infant, or with whom he lives. The manner of service must be the same as in the case of adults, and shall be made on such persons in the order named in this section.

Statutory Prohibition of Sales of Alcoholic Beverages
in Vicinity of Colleges or Universities

Three recent cases have joined the long train in this area. None seems to be of earth-shaking significance.

California Penal Code section 172 prohibits sales or gifts of liquor "within one mile of the grounds of the University of California at Berkeley." The premises in question in a 1963 case were at 3053 Telegraph Avenue, nine-tenths of a mile from recently-acquired university land on which the university had erected dormitories. This acreage was separated from the traditional "main campus" by public streets which were continued under the ownership and control of the city and not of the university.

---

[3] *Lybarger* v. *Husovich*, 119 Ohio App. 87, 196 N.E. 2d 795 (1963).

It was argued that "disconnected parcels of property should not be considered parts of the Campus," and pointed out that the university owned several such at various distances from the main campus, including at least one (for the housing of married students) which was outside the city of Berkeley and in another municipality on its periphery. Nevertheless a court of appeal held that liquor could not lawfully be dispensed at the Telegraph Avenue premises; but this decision was reversed by the California supreme court, holding that the statute should be construed as applying only to the "main Campus."[4]

The reasoning was that this rule would "ensure a workable basis of computation and result in greater certainty—and hence, fairness— in the administration of the law." Moreover, said the court, the statute is penal, and the courts should not "build up a penal law by judicial grafting upon legislation," but should give the defendant the most favorable reasonable construction. Also, Business and Professional Code section 24052 and Penal Code section 172 f., dating respectively from 1959 and 1961, stipulated that "the extension of the boundaries of any institution mentioned in Section 172 shall not affect licenses issued and in effect at the time the boundaries are extended, and such licenses are transferable from one person to another for use on the premises for which issued."

Xavier University in New Orleans has a dormitory on its campus known as Mercedes Hall, for the housing of women students. Both a Louisiana statute (LSA - RS 26:280) and an ordinance of the city of New Orleans prohibit liquor-selling (by any new applicant for a license for the operation of a new business) within 300 feet of any "playground, church, public library, or school, except a school for business education conducted as a business college or school."

The court of appeals concluded that a proposed establishment to be called "College Lounge and Bar," at 7338 Washington Avenue, within 300 feet from Mercedes Hall, could not be licensed:[5]

> A dormitory, erected to provide housing for students attend-
> ing the university, forms an integral part thereof. Thus the pro-

---

[4] *Walsh* v. *Department of Alcoholic Beverage Control,* 59 Cal. 2d 757, 31 Cal. Rptr. 297, 383 P. 2d 337 (1963).
[5] *Xavier University* v. *Thigpen,* (La. App.), 151 So. 2d 550, 49 A.L.R. 2d 1103 (1963).

hibition against establishing a bar within 300 feet of a school applies with equal facility to a campus dormitory.

Brushed aside were the arguments that Xavier University was not a "citizen" and thus not competent to bring the adverse action, and that the university was not a "school" within the intent of the statute.

A Washington statute (RCW sec. 66.44-190, enacted 1933, amended 1957) prohibits sales of intoxicating liquors on the grounds of the University of Washington and within a specified area surrounding it. Owners of certain premises within that area contended that this law is discriminatory because it does not apply to similar areas surrounding other institutions of higher learning in the state of Washington.

The state supreme court conceded that this is a special law, but not of the type forbidden by the Washington Constitution (Article 2, section 28), and held that it does not deprive of equal protection in violation of the state constitution or of the Fourteenth Amendment of the federal Constitution. The court quoted the rule from 30 *American Jurisprudence* 615:

> The state, in the exercise of its police power, may enact a valid law forbidding the sale of intoxicating liquors in a particular locality, where, in the opinion of the legislature, the peace and good order of the society so require.

Justice Rosellini took note of the old California case of *Ex parte Burke*, 160 Cal. 300, 116 P. 755 (1911), in which a general statute carefully phrased to apply only to Stanford University was sustained as constitutional. "Here, as there," said he, "there has been no showing that there is any other university of the same class in the state, and the evidence . . . indicates that there is none. This a fact so well known as to be within the judicial knowledge of the court."[6]

This is interesting as a judicial rebuke to the too-easy assumption that all colleges and universities are so much alike that a statute applicable to one must apply to all. It evidences a keen judicial insight into the nature of higher education.

A conflict between Rule 61.1 of the California Department of Alcoholic Beverage Control and Section 172 e of the Alcoholic Beverage Control Act has led two separate California courts of appeal to declare Rule 61.1 invalid and void. This rule provided that:

---

[6] *"U" District Building Corporation* v. *O'Connell*, 63 Wash. 2d 756, 388 P. 2d 922 (1964).

No on-sale general license or on-sale beer and wine license
shall be issued within one mile of a university unless the Department is satisfied that the location of the premises is sufficiently distant from the campus and the nature of the licensed business is such that it will not be patronized by students. Any
premises licensed under this rule must be operated as a *bona
fide* public eating place as defined in Sec. 23038 of the Alcoholic Beverage Act.

But section 172 e of the act says the foregoing provisions . . .

Shall not apply to sale by an on-sale licensee within premises
licensed as *bona fide* public eating places . . . and shall not . . .
preclude licenses for *bona fide* public eating places within the
areas prescribed.

George and Stella Jackson operated a restaurant on El Camino
Real about 100 feet from Stanford University's married couples' housing units. It was a "family" restaurant, about 25 per cent of its
business being with students. It had been given an on-sale beer
license in 1961, but its application for an on-sale beer and wine license
had been refused in 1963, the objectors being Stanford University and
several Palo Alto residents. This denial had been reversed by the Alcoholic Beverage Control Appeals Board in an opinion holding Section 61.1 invalid. The superior court declined to issue a writ of mandate to compel the board to reverse its decision, and this judgment
was affirmed by the court of appeal.[7] Thus the requested license was
issued.

A few months earlier, in a case involving an eating-place within
200 feet from the campus of the University of Southern California,
in which the issues were exactly the same as in the foregoing case,
another court of appeal had held Section 61.1 invalid and void.[8]

College Athletics Carry a Load of Tribulations

Two recent decisions concern (1) a libel suit by a member of a
university football team against the publisher of a magazine story
alleged to have falsely and libelously described the team as having
used stimulating drugs before a game, and (2) a criminal prosecution

---

[7] *Harris* v. *Alcoholic Beverage Control Appeals Board*, (Cal. App.), 45 Cal.
Rptr. 450 (1965).
[8] *Harris* v. *Levin*, (Cal. App.), 39 Cal. Rptr. 192 (1964).

for conspiracy and bribing of college basketball team members at various colleges and universities.

Alleged Libelous Publication Regarding Football Players. The popular magazine *True* carried in one of its 1958 issues an article entitled "The Pill That Can Kill Sports," concerning alleged use of amphetamine and other similar drugs by athletes. A member of the 1956 football team of the University of Oklahoma sued the publisher for damages in Oklahoma courts, averring that the story was libelous *per se*, and imputed a crime to him. The trial court directed a verdict for the plaintiff, and the jury awarded him $75,000 actual damages.

The article in *True* had said in part: "You can go to jail for selling amphetamine to a truck driver or injecting it into a racehorse, yet this same drug is being handed out to high school and college athletes all over the country.

"The amphetamines are administered to athletes by hypodermic injection, nasal spray, or in tablets or capsules . . .

"Speaking of football teams, during the 1956 season, while Oklahoma was increasing its sensational victory streak, several physicians observed Oklahoma players being sprayed in the nostrils with an atomizer. And during a televised game, a close-up showed Oklahoma spray-jobs to the nation. 'Ten years ago,' Dr. Howe observed acidly, 'When that was done to a horse, the case went to court. Medically, there is no reason for such treatment. If players need therapy, they shouldn't be on the field.' "

But Dennit Morris, the Oklahoma player who was the successful plaintiff in the libel suit, contended that the substance in the atomizers was only "spirits of peppermint," a mild and harmless application used for relief of "cotton mouth" resulting from prolonged or extreme physical exertion.

The Oklahoma supreme court, by a divided vote, held the article was defamatory on its face and *per se*, and affirmed the judgment for the plaintiff.[9] The opinion for the majority was written by Chief Justice Williams, and three other justices who concurred in it also dissented in part, but not on issues which would change the outcome,

---

[9] *Fawcett Publications, Inc.* and *Mid-Continent News Company* v. *Morris*, (Okla.), 377 P. 2d 42 (1962). Appeal dismissed for want of jurisdiction, and *certiorari* denied, 376 U.S. 513, 84 S.Ct. 964, 11 L.Ed. 2d 968 (1964); petition for rehearing denied, 377 U.S. 925, 12 L.Ed. 2d 217, 84 S.Ct. 1218 (1964).

and their opinions were not written into the published record. Justice Halley dissented, seemingly with much cogency, saying in effect: "Nothing in the article is libelous to Dennit Morris. Nowhere does it name him, say he partook of amphetamine, or that he would have been violating the law if he had. Failure of the trial court to require the plaintiff to plead and prove special damages was reversible error."

In this same decision the codefendant, Mid-Continent News Company, distributor of *True* in Oklahoma, was held not liable. Twelve other members of the same football team filed separate actions for damages. One of these was removed to the U.S. District Court, and subsequently a motion to remand it to the state court was denied on the ground that "the law of Oklahoma as determined in the *Morris Case* is binding upon the federal court," and this judgment was affirmed by the United States Court of Appeals in *Dodd* v. *Fawcett Publications, Inc., et. al.*, (U.S.C.A., 10th circ.), 329 F. 2d 82 (1964). The litigation will probably continue further.

Criminal Prosecution for Conspiracy and Bribery of College Basketball Players. Some of the activities of a wide-flung ring of underworld gamblers were uncovered in North Carolina courts in a recent case involving alleged bribery of North Carolina State College basketball team members in eight games played at various locations in North Carolina and South Carolina between December 1959 and January 1961.

It seems there were five principal characters in the gambling ring, two of whom lived in the Bronx (New York City) and three in St. Louis. They were operators in a conspiracy to bribe basketball players in many colleges. They usually bribed one player in each big game with $1,000 to "shave points" or "throw the game." The two Bronx characters seem to have supervised the operation in the Carolinas. They were indicted, tried, convicted, and sentenced to prison terms in North Carolina. Their convictions were affirmed by the supreme court of North Carolina in a 12,000-word opinion by Justice Parker, affirming in part and reversing in part the trial court judgment.[10] It is not practicable to reproduce or digest here the numerous technical issues of evidence and criminal procedure upon which the various counts in the several indictments were held good or bad.

---

[10] *State* v. *Goldberg and Lektometrios*, 261 N.C. 181, 134 S.E. 2d 334 (1964). *Certiorari* denied, 377 U.S. 978, 84 S.Ct. 1884, 12 L.Ed. 2d 747 (1964).

Forgery by Nonstudent of Application and Receipt
for Transcript of Recent Graduate

A case difficult to classify arose at San Diego State College. A young man with a prison record and an education limited to high school made a clumsy and unsuccessful attempt to obtain from the college a copy of the transcript of a recent (1957) graduate in business administration. His efforts included a request in person, one or more telephone calls, and the forging of the graduate's signature on an application for transcript and on a receipt for transcript. His early attempts aroused the suspicion of the registrar, so that on the occasion of his visit to sign the receipt she had alerted policemen who were present without his knowledge, and who placed him under arrest as he was forging the signature.

He was convicted by the trial court jury of (1) forging the application with intent to defraud its true owner and the college, (2) forgery of the receipt, and (3) personation of another. The court fined him $1,000 plus $50 penalty, and placed him on probation for five years. The court of appeals affirmed this, in an opinion by Presiding Justice Griffin, in which the other two justices, Caughlin and Brown, concurred. Some of Justice Griffin's words:[11]

> In a limited sense, there was an intent to defraud the college of the transcript, for the college would not otherwise give it up to the forger. In a wider sense, the forger is violating the college rules that restrict the circulation of such transcripts. It is well settled that the fraud may be against the public.
>
> It makes no difference that the college personnel had detected the fraud and would not be deceived. All that the statute requires is an intent to defraud. The record does not show the nefarious purpose toward which the transcript would have been utilized. It is not difficult to speculate on its possible wrongful use . . . the securing of employment under false pretenses is an example.
>
> The forging of the request and receipt, made for the purpose of securing the transcript, might well result in a possible dismissal of some college employee in issuing the transcript to one not authorized to receive it; and negligent release of the transcript might well subject the school to suit by Mr. A (to whom the transcript belonged) for a violation of his right of privacy. This would particularly be true if the forger intended to

---

[11] *People* v. *Russel*, 214 Cal. App. 2d 445, 29 Cal. Rptr. 562 (1963).

use the transcript in a way that would cause embarrassment, pecuniary loss or injury to the reputation of Mr. A.

These reflections cast some fresh light into an area in which but little litigation has occurred, but in which the rights of increasing millions of persons are involved.

Automobile Liability Insurance Policies in Cases Where Student's Vehicle Is Driven by Person Other Than Owner

Some automobile liability insurance policies extend coverage to accidents occurring when the vehicle is being driven by someone other than the owner, with the owner's permission. Question seems frequently to arise as to whether under the particular facts there was actual permission, or implied permission, or no course of action which would support any claim of permission at all.

In a Wisconsin case, the son of a Packard dealer in Kenosha who was a 1955 graduate of the University of Wisconsin returned to Madison in 1957 for a visit with some of his former friends and college-mates. He became intoxicated and had to be put to bed in a fraternity house (of which he was not a member). He gave the keys to his car to one of his friends and instructed him to drive the car to the fraternity house parking lot, which he did, leaving the keys in the car. Later in the evening two other friends took the car, while the owner was still incommunicado, and became involved in an accident in Janesville wherein one of them was injured. Under these circumstances, the court decided, the use of the car was not with the implied consent of the owner, and the accident was not covered by his liability insurance policy.[12]

In New Hampshire, a Dartmouth College student with his car was attending a party at the Snow Crest Inn near Hanover. Having allowed a fellow-student to take his car to drive to Hanover, he later took his girl companion into the parking lot, found the car of another fellow-student (Straus) with the keys in it, and took it to drive, with the girl, to Hanover in search of his own car. On this trip an accident occurred, in which the young woman was injured. Here the court

---

[12] *Main v. Cameron,* 13 Wis. 2d 15, 108 N.W. 2d 142 (1961).

noted that though both the owner of the car and the driver at the time of the accident were Dartmouth students, they were not fraternity brothers, and had no classes together or other common college activities, and there was no history of previous use of the vehicle with permission. Hence there was no implied consent, and the insurance company was not liable for a judgment against the driver, under its policy issued to the owner (Straus), even though Straus said he would probably have given his consent if asked.[13]

A Texas case of 1964 is to the same effect. There was, said the court of civil appeals, no implied permission for one college student to use another student's automobile, where the owner and the driver were not friends or fraternity brothers and there had been no course of conduct between them to indicate mutual acquiescence. In such circumstances the insurance company is not liable under its policy issued to the owner, although the policy covers cases in which the vehicle is being used by another person with the owner's consent.[14]

---

[13] *Fireman's Fund Insurance Company* v. *Brandt*, (U.S.D.C., N.H.), 217 F. Supp. 893 (1962).
[14] *Globe Indemnity Company* v. *French*, (Tex. Civ. App.), 382 S.W. 2d 771 (1964).

CHAPTER 5

CHARITABLE TRUSTS FOR STUDENT AID; OTHER TYPES AND INCIDENTS OF STUDENT AIDS

THE PRINCIPLES governing the validity and operation of charitable trusts for student aid are the same as for charitable trusts in general, and for trusts for the general or restricted purposes of nonprofit educational corporations. Cases concerning these latter are grouped in Chapter 19. Only the occasional case involving a charitable trust for the aid of students is placed in this present chapter, in order to juxtapose it with other chapters relating to students.

Other cases in this chapter relate to frugal management of a private trust for an individual's college education, and the status of United States Naval ROTC payments to students, under the Internal Revenue Code.

Creating Valid Charitable Trust

A Quaker farmer in southwestern Ohio (Warren County) bequeathed his small estate to his sister and brother until the death of the last survivor, and thence to a trust which would provide for the execution of four purposes: (1) perpetuating Turtle Creek Graveyard, (2) preserving Turtle Creek Meeting House, (3) maintaining and improving his 42½-acre Home Place, as an adjunct to (4) helping educate "worthy young men and/or worthy young women in Veterinary Science and/or General Sanitation." Beneficiaries were to be selected "in the order of nearness of their legal residence to the said Home Place." The fourth purpose was given bottom priority: "After the First, Second, and Third Purposes as above stated are accomplished for the year which is then current, or if for any lawful reason any one or more of said Purposes cannot be so accomplished, then and in that event all remaining income from said property for said year shall be expended to help educate . . . (as above)." The will requested the court to appoint a trustee.

The probate court evidently doubted that all the four purposes were charitable, and if not, whether they could be separated; and whether the four purposes, if not severable, would collectively constitute a charitable trust; and for these and other reasons concluded in the negative and declared the decedent had died intestate and the estate must go to his heir-at-law.[1] This was reversed and remanded by the Ohio court of appeals, which held that the first and fourth purposes created a valid charitable trust.[2]

It followed that the attorney general would be a proper party to any further proceedings, and the Ohio Charitable Trust Act would be applicable.

Operation of Charitable Trust for Student Aid

The founder and first president of the Alumnae Association of the Newport Hospital School of Nursing in Rhode Island bequeathed about $60,000 in her residuary estate to the association "to provide scholarships for persons who desire to make nursing their profession and who have the intention and purpose to become good bedside nurses."

Details were left to be worked out by the association. It asked the Rhode Island supreme court for approval of some features of its tentative plans. It was within the scope of the trust, said Justice

---

[1] The details of the probate court litigation are reported in *Baily* v. *McElroy*, (Ohio Prob.), 186 N.E. 2d 213 (1961), and 186 N.E. 2d 219 (1962).

[2] *Baily* v. *McElroy*, 120 Ohio App. 85, 195 N.E. 2d 559 (1963).

Joslin, to make awards to *graduate nurses* to further their professional education; and he also approved the scheme of having the awards made by a committee of the association appointed by its president pursuant to a vote of its board of directors. (This, he said, was a matter of the internal affairs of the association.)

Question was also put to the court as to whether expenditure of the principal of the trust as well as expenditure of the income was authorized; but since the question was neither briefed nor argued, and the plans as presented to the court did not contemplate any expenditure of principal, but only use of income, the court declined to answer, evidently preferring to postpone determination of that issue until such time as plans for the use of principal might be proposed.[3]

Doctrine That Gift to College for Student Aid
Does Not Create Technical Trust

The will of a Wisconsin decedent establishing a trust fund stipulated first that two-thirds of the fund would go to the Beloit Foundation to be administered as a loan fund for students of Beloit College and the University of Cincinnati, preferably those from Beloit and Rock County, Wisconsin; but in the event of the foundation's refusal of the gift, then it would go to Beloit College and the University of Cincinnati in equal shares, to be administered for the same purposes. In any event, the other third of the fund was to go to the Beloit Foundation for such charitable purposes as the foundation might from time to time determine, with permission to use the income, and, at its discretion, portions of the principal, for such charitable purposes.

The foundation refused the gift of the student loan fund, and the Wisconsin supreme court rendered a declaratory judgment holding that that part of the fund must go to the two institutions of higher education, in accord with the testator's clearly expressed intent.[4] Then Justice Heffernan, for seemingly obscure reasons, gratuitously

---

[3] *Alumnae Association of Newport Hospital School of Nursing* v. *Nugent*, (R.I.), 219 A. 2d 763 (1966).

[4] *In re Estate of Earl E. Berry; Board of Trustees of Beloit College* v. *Farrow*, 29 Wis. 2d 506, 139 N.W. 2d 72 (1966).

expatiated at length on his conclusion that the gifts to the two educational institutions did not create "technical trusts," but were instead "outright gifts," quoting 2 Trusts, *Restatement*, page 1093:

> Where property is given to a charitable corporation, a charitable trust is not created, even though by the terms of the gift the corporation is directed . . . to use the property only for a particular one of its purposes.

There is ample authority, as has often been shown, for holding exactly the opposite. One must recognize, however, that the two lines of opinion exist; and one must, no doubt, grant appropriate deference to the authenticity of the *Restatement;* but it seems simpler and more accurate to say that any gift to a charitable corporation carries with it a species of trust obligation. This view was well set forth in an extensive note in the *Harvard Law Review* as early as 1951:[5]

> Thus the decision as to whether to apply trust rules should not be foreclosed by the characterization of the interest of the corporation as either absolute or in trust. The difficulty seems ultimately one of semantics: Is the danger that the use of the word trust" would cause an application of all the rules normally associated therewith so great as to outweigh the economy of mental effort in using a term which is in general valid, though modification of certain of its consequences would be necessary?

Not only in the Wisconsin case just cited, but also in a 1961 North Dakota decision the no-trust idea appears, though the North Dakota court seems to rely not on the debatable clause of the *Restatement* so much as on a strict reading of the state statutes. John E. Myra bequeathed his residuary estate of more than $300,000 to his sister merely as intermediary trustee until a charitable corporation could be formed as directed by the will, to become permanent custodian of the fund. The corporation had three "trustees" who were to direct its operation for the charitable purposes for which it was formed. The will clearly indicated an intent that the fund should be a perpetual charitable trust, with income to be used for only "charitable, character-building, and educational purposes."

The state supreme court decided that the corporation "does not hold the property in trust in the true sense of the term. It holds the

---

[5] "The Charitable Corporation." *Harvard Law Review* 64: 1168-1181 (May 1951).

property as its own to be devoted to the purposes for which it was formed." The district court had no authority to supervise the administration of the corporation under the North Dakota statutes on trusts (Chapter 59-04); but the court hastened to add:

"This opinion is in no way intended to limit or qualify the rights of the Attorney General to visitation of nonprofit corporations under other provisions of our statutes, nor is it intended to be a restriction upon the powers of the district court to supervise the administration of property held in trust by a charitable corporation."[6]

The no-trust concept had also been declared in a 1955 Massachusetts decision in which the court relied on *Scott on Trusts*, Sections 96.3 and 348.1, and upon Chapter 11 of the *Restatement: Trusts*. It also cited the cases of *Brigham* v. *Peter Bent Brigham Hospital*, (U.S.C.C.A., 1 Cir.), 134 F. 513 (1904), and *St. Joseph's Hospital* v. *Bennett*, 281 N.Y. 115, 22 N.E. 2d 305, 130 A.L.R. 1092 (1939), which are among the underpinnings of the doctrine.

Antoinette Rehmann Perrett of Rockport, Massachusetts, bequeathed the residue of her estate to the American Institute of Architects, a nonprofit membership corporation chartered in New York and having its headquarters in the city of Washington. Her will expressly stated that the bequest was to be held in trust to establish and maintain scholarships and fellowships for advanced study by deserving architects and students. It referred to the gift as an "endowment fund" (which is, by definition, a perpetual trust), and stipulated that if the A.I.A. ever became unwilling or unable to administer the fund, then it should be transferred to some other organization best fitted to maintain the fund and carry out its purposes.

In the face of this language the court declared: "The Institute takes this gift not upon a technical trust but rather upon a quasi trust. Title to the gift vested in the institute upon a restriction that it be used in the manner and for the purposes expressed in the will."[7] This seems near to a nullification of the testator's expressed intent, or a judicial rewriting of the will. We reserve our heavier guns for Chapters 11 and 12, *infra*, where the issue reappears in different words. Here we turn to other types of student aids.

---

[6] *In re Myra Foundation*, (N. D.), 112 N.W. 2d 552 (1961).
[7] *American Institute of Architects* v. *Attorney General*, 332 Mass. 619, 127 N.E. 2d 161 (1955).

*Guardian of Minor College Student Is Advised by Court
to Borrow from New York Higher Education Assistance
Corporation to Pay Tuition*

In New York a minor student was the beneficiary of a court-controlled bank deposit for the purpose of financing her college education. Her guardian applied to the court for permission to withdraw $580 to pay tuition fees. Justice J. Irwin Shapiro denied the application, pointing out that the funds in the bank were earning 4¼ per cent interest, while money for college expenses could be borrowed through the New York Higher Education Assistance Authority at a cost of only 3 per cent, and "Interest and principal are repayable in installments becoming due only after the student is graduated."[8]

The favorable terms described seem to be very similar to those provided for in the Guaranteed Student Loan Program of the act of Congress known as the Higher Education Act of 1965. How large this program will become seems to be at present a matter of some uncertainty; but if it does attain impressive proportions, apparently it may be taken advantage of, even by students amply able to finance their own education, or by students of affluent parents unwilling to finance their children's college education. It will apparently be profitable to keep their money productively invested, while borrowing the money for college expenses on much more favorable terms. Only families having net incomes before taxes in excess of $15,000 a year are excluded from this benefit under the Higher Education Act of 1965.

*Educational Expenses Paid by Navy Department in
Behalf of Naval ROTC Student Are in Nature
of Nontaxable Scholarship or Gift*

The general rule regarding the taxability under the federal income tax act of the various payments to students is that a scholarship or fellowship, which is by definition a payment given with no requirement that the recipient render any service as a *quid pro quo*, is nontaxable; while the various types of assistantships and traineeships

---

[8] *In re Bano*, 46 Misc. 2d 7, 258 N.Y.S. 2d 665 (1965).

carrying compensation for definite services to be rendered constitute taxable income.

A full-time student at Cornell University, a member of the Naval Reserve Officers' Training Corps, was the beneficiary during the year 1958 of payments on his behalf by the Navy Department of $1,480 for tuition and fees, and $20 for books. During the same year he also participated in a naval training cruise, for which he received pay for services, travel, meals, and lodgings, totaling $946. During the year his parents supported him to the extent of $1,500, and claimed him as a dependent on their income tax return, on the ground that they had provided more than one-half of his support during the year. The Internal Revenue Service disallowed this exemption, pointing out that the boy had received more from the Navy Department than he had from his parents. The parents countered that the total of $1,500 for tuition and books constituted a gift or scholarship under Section 152 (d) of the *Internal Revenue Code* of 1954, and was nontaxable. No, said the revenue officer, this payment was actually for service rendered and to be rendered, because all recipients were required to sign a statement agreeing to serve on active duty as a naval officer for three years after graduation.

The United States tax court decided in favor of the parents, saying in part:

> Although it may be conceded that the Navy Department initiated its program of educational grants to aid in its officer procurement program, it chose to do so by providing education to students in their individual capacity. . . . It is apparent that the education involved in the present case is a basic college training and not specific training for any duties to be performed for the Navy. . . . We think that the primary purpose of the payments was . . . to further the education of Charles. The fact that the Navy would also benefit inadvertently by obtaining an officer with a college level of education would not destroy the essential character of the payment as a scholarship.

The decision of the tax court was subsequently affirmed by a United States court of appeals, which said:[9]

> If the fact that the United States would benefit from the training in question were itself sufficient to preclude a tuition grant from being a "scholarship," no governmental grant could

---

[9] *Commissioner of Internal Revenue v. Ide*, (U.S.C.A., Pa.), 335 F. 2d 852 (1964).

> qualify. For it is only to serve some public purpose that the government may expend public funds. . . . We cannot adopt an interpretation of the present regulation which might well have so questionable a consequence.

The last two decisions in this present chapter may be the fore-runners of many future decisions called forth by incidents of the administration of the several recently-enacted acts of Congress providing for various forms of student aids out of public funds.

In the more familiar field of testamentary trusts for student aid, two recent cases appear at Footnotes 2 and 4 in Chapter 16, *infra*, because the issue involved is the applicability of the Oregon state inheritance tax.

PART TWO

THE FACULTY AND
OTHER EMPLOYEES

Members of the Faculty: Contracts; Promotion; Tenure

The Loyalty Oath Furor

Other Litigation Touching Faculty Members

Nonacademic Employees

Members of the Governing Board; the President;
Central Administrative Officers

CHAPTER 6

MEMBERS OF THE FACULTY:
CONTRACTS; PROMOTION; TENURE

SUCH FAMILIAR SUBJECTS as (1) inception of the contract, (2) promotions in rank, (3) termination of the services of nontenure and tenure teachers, and (4) the interpretation of group insurance contracts, among others, appear in this chapter.

Inception of the Contract

The elementary fact that the governing board (of a public institution at least) ordinarily does not and can not delegate its authority to make contracts for personal services, was again illustrated. This means nearly universally that a written offer and acceptance between a department head or other administrative officer of the college or university and a prospective member of the faculty are only a tentative agreement, and do not become a binding contract until approved or ratified by a vote of the governing board. In briefer words, the governing board itself ordinarily enters into the contract as the party of the first part (employer), and does this only by formal vote in a duly called meeting.

Frances Brown was employed as an instructor in speech at Eastern Montana College of Education at Billings during the academic

77

year 1961-62. Early in that academic year both her department head and her division head assured her that she would be appointed for the summer session of 1962, and agreed with her that her salary would be $1,300 for that period of two months. On March 27, 1962, the vice president of the college informed her that she would not be employed for the summer session nor for the succeeding academic year.

No rights of permanent tenure were involved. The regulations of the college stipulated that notice of nonrenewal of an annual contract should be given by April 15. That was done in this case. The sole question was: Did the division and department heads have authority to bind the college by contract? There was no evidence of any action by the governing board, and no proof of any delegation of authority in this matter; and the Montana supreme court, reversing a lower court judgment for the teacher, concluded that under Montana statutes and precedents, "no implied power could have been delegated to create a contract such as asserted here."[1] Justice Adair dissented without opinion.

As reported in the opinion of the court, the testimony of the president of the college is a correct description of the usual situation, in public institutions at least: "President Steele testified he was authorized by the Board to seek out and get instructional staff. He also said that he delegates the interviewing of applicants to heads of departments, and he, in turn, recommends to the Board the hiring. He testified flatly that the Board does the hiring. He admitted that he never specifically told heads of departments that they did not have authority to hire; but also, that he had not considered it necessary." It should not be necessary, for every department head is obligated to know the extent of his own authority in matters as important as this; and in dealing with any public institution, a prospective contractor is bound to know the extent of the authority of the person with whom he deals. Too many teachers and department heads are ignorant of these elementary principles.

Alleged Denial of Promotion Because of Religious Discrimination

Queens College of the City University of New York has been

---

[1] *Brown v. State Board of Education*, 142 Mont. 547, 385 P. 2d 643 (1963).

plagued with protracted controversy because certain members of the faculty have persistently asserted that they were denied promotions in rank for which they were qualified, and that others were promoted ahead of them because of prejudice against them as members of the Roman Catholic faith.

As early as 1958 the State Commission Against Discrimination, a governmental agency of the state of New York, resolved to initiate a formal study and investigation of the charges. In 1960 it reported: "There has been resistance to the employment and promotion of Catholics in teaching positions at Queens College" in a number of specific instances.

This precipitated two distinct lines of litigation: (1) an action by the Board of Higher Education of the City of New York, under the Civil Practice Act, sections 1283 *et seq.*, for an order prohibiting SCAD from taking any action with respect to the matter at Queens College or at any other educational unit under the jurisdiction of the board; and (2) an action by Associate Professors Josef V. Lombardo and Joseph P. Mullally, under Article 78 of the Civil Practice Act, for an order to annul the determination of the board of higher education which was alleged to have refused the petitioners promotion to the rank of Professor because they were Catholics.

As to the first of these (in which the board of higher education contended that SCAD had no jurisdiction in this matter), Justice Arthur Marrowich of the local supreme court granted the prohibitory order against SCAD, holding that the statutes clearly exclude educational corporations not organized for private profit from the jurisdiction of SCAD.[2]

The history of the legislation, he thought, showed that this exclusion was probably made (in the act of 1945 creating SCAD) in deference to the fact that the state board of education has statutory supervisory authority over educational corporations; but this jurisdiction insofar as it appertains to the adjudication of disputes is not necessarily exclusive, but may be concurrent or parallel. Thus, the present action of the city board of higher education need not be

[2] *Application of Board of Higher Education of City of New York*, 26 Misc. 2d 989, 213 N.Y.S. 2d 132 (1961); modified and affirmed in 16 A.D. 2d 443 (1962); modified and affirmed in 14 N.Y. 2d 138, 199 N.E. 2d 141 (1964).

brought before the state commissioner of education, though it could have been initiated in that manner.

The main point was that the board of higher education is not an "employer" within the meaning of the statutes governing SCAD. The five-judge appellate division modified the order, and, as modified, affirmed it. Here the holding was that SCAD could not take any action in this matter except "investigations, studies, recommendations, programs, conciliation efforts, reports and proceedings as conformed to the statute."[3] This would exclude any enforcement actions by SCAD.

The decision was by a divided court, with Presiding Justice Breitel writing the opinion of the majority, joined by Justices McNally and Eager. Justices Stevens and Steuer dissented, arguing principally that the city board of higher education, though it is a separate corporation, is a state agency under the state board of education; and the statute against discrimination applies to state agencies. Justice Steuer added that his view of the statute would give SCAD no power to initiate investigations and studies except upon receipt of a formal complaint. When the case went up to the court of appeals the decision was again modified, to the substantial effect that "The Commission on Human Rights (formerly SCAD) has jurisdiction and power to eliminate and prevent discrimination in employment in all public agencies, including public educational institutions within the control of the Board of Higher Education of the City of New York." The opinion was by Judge Bergan, with three colleagues concurring, and with a strong dissent by Judge Dye, in which Judges Fuld and Van Voorhis joined.

As to the suit brought by Professors Lombardo and Mullally, Justice Vincent A. Lupiano of the local supreme court defined the issue:

> Were respondent's (Board of Higher Education's) determinations denying petitioners (Lombardo and Mullally) preferment the result of honest evaluations of the objective criteria of professional qualification and competence exclusively, or were they the tainted fruit of judgments distorted by religious bias? This is a grave issue. Immediately to mind come the repeated pronouncements of this State, constitutional and statutory, depre-

---

[3] Board of Higher Education of City of New York v. Carter, 16 A.D. 2d 443, 228 N.Y.S. 2d 704 (1962); modifying and affrming 26 Misc. 2d 989 (1961).

cating and interdicting discrimination amongst men because of race, creed, color, religion or national origin. . . .

And to divert for a moment, we may recall the recurring desperate attempts in some quarters to justify such discrimination through theological sophistry or spurious esoteric theories of religious, cultural, or ethnic superiority.

He concluded by ordering a trial of the facts by a jury. This was reversed by the unanimous appellate division; and on appeal to the New York court of appeals the judgment of the appellate division was affirmed.[4] Thus the conclusion was that no triable issue had been presented.

Parts of the opinion of Justice Breitel for the unanimous appellate division are here quoted:

> Promotion in the advanced ranks of the instructional staff is determined by the exercise of administrative discretion, using faculty committees for recommendations and based upon the records and evaluation of candidates, with internal procedures for review of candidacies, including ultimate review by the Board. Although various hearings were granted petitioners, none is mandated by law. As a consequence, the only aspect of the matter subject to judicial review is whether the action of the Board was arbitrary or capricious.
>
> . . . .
>
> Promotions in the advanced academic ranks are not determined solely by lapse of time and record qualifications consisting of advanced degrees and written works . . . The more elusive qualifications of teaching ability, administrative capacity and creative inspiration are relevant.
>
> The Board's bylaws provide the standard for promotion: "For promotion or appointment to the rank of professor, the candidate must possess the qualifications for an associate professor, and in addition a record of exceptional intellectual, educational or artistic achievement. There shall be evidence of his continued growth." It should be readily evident that such qualifications are not mechanically measurable nor susceptible to visual comparison with conclusive result.
>
> . . . .
>
> The record is replete with evidence of consideration by the College committees and the Board of all the proper factors to be evaluated, and, consequently, it is difficult to sustain the accusation that either committees in the College or the Board acted arbitrarily. Whether sporadic instances of resistance or dis-

---

[4] *Application of Lombardo*, 246 N.Y.S. 2d 631, 13 N.Y. 2d 1097, 196 N.E. 2d 266 (1963); affirming 18 A.D. 2d 444, 240 N.Y.S. 2d 119 (1963), which had reversed 37 Misc. 2d 436, 235 N.Y.S. 2d 1010 (1962).

crimination exist, assuming this could be proven, is not relevant
to the right of petitioners to relief in the very individual and
personal matter of advanced academic promotion.

Had there been a showing of systematic exclusion or restriction, or a generalized pattern of unlawful discrimination directed to petitioners, it might be another matter. (There were
some isolated incidents of discrimination described by petitioner
Mullally, but they occurred years ago, and he achieved advances
and promotions despite these incidents.)

The situation becomes even more confusing on the Board's
demonstration, not disputed by petitioners, that persons of petitioners' own religious persuasion were indeed promoted, were
represented on the College committees, were on the Board sub-
committee which investigated their charges, and, of course, were
represented on the Board itself. In short, there is nothing to
support the bare conclusions of petitioners and, thus, they do
not succeed in even raising an issue of fact requiring trial.

The decision of the court of appeals affirming the foregoing
unanimous judgment of the appellate division was supported by five
of the seven judges of the court of appeals (Judges Dye, Fuld, Van
Voorhis, Burke, and Foster) without writing an opinion, evidently
being fully satisfied to adopt the opinion of Justice Breitel of the appellate division; but Judge Scileppi wrote and filed a dissent, in which
Chief Judge Desmond joined him.

The tenor of the dissent, exemplified by some excerpts, is offered
here to enable the reader to strike his own balance between the conflicting views:

> In this day and age, bias and prejudice are not often express-
> ly declared, but rather, concealed. Where they do exist they
> probably would be manifested either by conduct and/or action.
> Thus a person claiming discrimination would normally be con-
> fronted with the problem of proving that certain conduct or
> acts are motivated by bias or prejudice. Certainly, a showing
> "of systematic exclusion or restriction" is one method of prov-
> ing unlawful discrimination. It is not, however, the only method.
> Essentially, the issue is one of fact, to be determined on the basis
> of all the facts in each case . . .
>
> I am not suggesting that every bare charge of discimination
> should be tested by a trial; however, in this case we are confront-
> ed by allegations of specific instances tending to show the exist-
> ence of bias and prejudice. In addition, there are the findings of
> the State Commission for Human Rights (new name for the
> former SCAD) to the effect that key personnel at Queens Col-
> lege have resisted the employment and promotion of Catholic
> teachers, evidenced in a number of specific instances. Although
> these findings are not binding on the courts, they tend to

demonstrate the existence of a triable issue here. Simply stated, I believe petitioners are entitled to their day in court.

Faculty Salaries and Fringe Benefits

Barnes and Bender, teachers in Mount San Antonio College in California, a public junior college, and respectively holders of the M.A. and Ph.D. conferred by San Gabriel College in June 1959, were paid during the academic year 1959-60 according to the Mount San Antonio salary schedule recognizing such degrees. The same schedule provided that "After June 30, 1959 only degrees from accredited institutions will be accepted." For the year 1961-62 recognition of degrees from nonaccredited institutions was entirely withdrawn, and this meant an automatic drop in salary for Barnes and Bender. They won a suit for a writ of *mandamus* to restore them to their highest previous slots in the salary scale.

The court of appeal, holding that the writ should be granted, said:[5]

> The Board can not pick out some teachers in a particular category, and without a change in duties or functions, classify that group for salary purposes different from others in the same category; nor can it reduce salaries in an arbitrary, capricious, or unreasonable manner.

It seems probable that the Mount San Antonio board lost the case on account of insufficiencies in its pleadings. It failed to allege that its 1959 classification of these two teachers had been a mistake, and offered no evidence that San Gabriel College was in fact of non-accreditable academic standing. If these matters had appeared in the pleadings, the outcome might have been different.

A professor at Vanderbilt University was, among other duties, charged with oversight of the Arthur J. Dyer Observatory, an appurtenance of the university located about nine miles from the main campus. He was required to live in a house on the observatory grounds, and commuted in his automobile between the observatory and the campus. One of his "fringe benefits" from the university was coverage under a group travel accident insurance policy.

He was killed in an automobile accident while driving his car on

---

[5] *Barnes* v. *Board of Trustees of Mount San Antonio College District*, (Cal. App.), 32 Cal. Rptr. 609 (1963).

a triple mission: (1) to do a stint at the local broadcasting station (a weather report), (2) to get a piece of observatory equipment from the home of a research associate who had borrowed it, and (3) to pick up a visiting professor at the airport and take him to the observatory. All this was clearly within the nature of his duties, and within the scope of the insurance policy as written; and when his widow sued the insurance company she was awarded a judgment for $50,000, which was affirmed by a Tennessee court of appeals. Judge Humphreys, with his two colleagues concurring, noted that the fact that the university did not compensate him specifically for the expenses of his local travel was of no consequence in the case, and deplored the attempt of insurance company attorneys to introduce oral testimony to vary the terms of the contract, in violation of the parol evidence rule. If this were permitted, he said, it would be bad for all parties and ultimately bad for insurance companies.[6]

Under Contract Between University and Medical Insurance Organization, Participating Physician May Not Charge Fees Higher Than Schedule in Contract

Effective July 1, 1960, Harvard University contracted with Massachusetts Medical Service, Inc. (Blue Shield), to pay monthly to that organization 108 per cent of the amounts paid by it to participating physicians for services rendered to Harvard's covered employees. In 1964 the supreme judicial court of Massachusetts held that this is a valid contract, and in no sense a "reinsurance agreement" which Harvard University is not authorized to make. The subject is governed by statute (GL Ch 176 B).

In this case the plaintiff was a "participating physician" under contract with Blue Shield, who treated a Harvard employee in January and February 1961, and charged $300. Blue Shield paid $191 and the patient paid the physician the balance of $109. The review board in the state department of insurance ordered the physician to return to the patient the money charged in excess of the amount paid by Blue Shield in accord with its fee schedule which was a part of his contract

---

[6] *Newark Insurance Company* v. *Seifert,* (Tenn. App.), 392 S.W. 2d 336 (1964).

with it. This was affirmed successively by the trial court and the supreme judicial court. A "participating physician" is bound by the fee schedule in effect when his services were rendered.[7]

Termination of Nontenure Contract

A teacher currently employed in the New York City Public Schools was also a part-time lecturer in biology in the Evening and Saturday Division of Hofstra College, a private institution, from 1958 to 1962, being reappointed for each semester. In 1962, after receiving complaints from students about her teaching and her personality traits, the dean notified her department head that she "was not to teach after the Fall semester." On December 15 she made a written request for a hearing before a faculty committee, as provided in the rules of Hofstra College for tenure teachers. This was denied, and she then sued under the Civil Practice Act, Article 78, sections 1283 ff., for an order annulling her dismissal and restoring her position. The College declined to answer and moved that the case be dismissed on the ground that the facts alleged were insufficient to entitle the plaintiff to the relief sought, and that Article 78 was not applicable to a private college.

Apparently without full knowledge of the facts and law of the case, the trial court directed the college to answer on the merits within eight days, and spoke heatedly of the matter:

> As recently as October 1962 petitioner had been promoted, and the head of her department rated her as "excellent" academically and spoke in complimentary terms of her performance as a teacher. To allow accusations by students who are permitted to hide behind a "screen of anonymity" to stand unchallenged, and to refuse to one so accused an opportunity to refute the accusations, violates our basic concepts of democratic justice and academic freedom.

On appeal, the appellate division unanimously reversed the judgment and ordered the petition dismissed *in toto*, on the ground that the teacher had no claim to tenure at Hofstra; upon the expiration of her short-term contract the college did not offer to renew it, and

---

[7] *Rose* v. *Board of Review in Division of Insurance*, 346 Mass. 581, 195 N.E. 2d 82 (1964).

was within its rights. No charges were made against her. She was not dismissed. In these circumstances she was not entitled to a hearing.[8]

Probationary Faculty Members in California

There are two 1966 California decisions, in both of which the courts declined to disturb determinations of educational governing boards to terminate the service of probationary members of the faculty in time to forestall their acquiring permanent tenure, for causes deemed sufficient by the boards.

Two teachers were employed from year to year on the faculty of San José State College during the three years immediately preceding June 30, 1962. They would have acquired tenure if employed for a fourth year. On April 5, 1962, they were notified in writing by the president that they would not be so employed. Later they sued for *mandamus* to compel the board of trustees and chancellor of state colleges, and the president of San José State College, to restore them to the faculty as of September 1, 1962, and to recover salary from that date.

They contended that the termination of their employment was solely for improper reasons: namely, their activities in the California State College Federation of Teachers, and (2) their alleged exposé of an agreement among the several state college presidents not to admit "Southern sit-in students." In short, their dismissal was an abuse of discretion. However, they had had an administrative hearing before the chancellor of state colleges, in which it appeared that their termination was for legitimate reasons based on the welfare of the students and the institution, upon the recommendation of the appropriate department heads and deans; and the record of this hearing was before the court. Judgment was against them in each of the three echelons of California courts. Justice Burke of the supreme court wrote an opinion in which all the justices concurred, in which he said: [9]

> Nothing in the record would warrant a conclusion that the decision not to reemploy plaintiffs turned on other than the customary academic and professional reasons. No cause of action is

---

[8] *Barone* v. *Adams*, 20 A.D. 2d 790, 248 N.Y.S. 2d 72 (1964); reversing 39 Misc. 2d 227, 240 N.Y.S. 2d 390 (1963).
[9] *Stanton* v. *Dumke*, 49 Cal. Rptr. 380, 411 P. 2d 108 (1966).

stated when, as in this case, an administrative hearing has been accorded, the record of which demonstrates that the charges of impropriety are illusory.

A teacher in his third probationary year at Coalinga Junior College was notified by the board of trustees on May 11, 1964, that he would not be re-employed for 1964-65. The board gave him a written statement of causes, held a hearing July 9, 1964, and made findings of fact and voted to dismiss him. His petition for *mandamus* to compel the board to rehire him was denied in the trial court, and the judgment affirmed in the court of appeal, on the ground that refusal to re-employ a probationary teacher, for cause related to the welfare of the school and the students, is not subject to judicial review.[10]

Some excerpting and paraphrasing of the findings of fact made by the board of trustees regarding the merits of this teacher follow:

> (1) His philosophy with respect to grading is unsuitable for the junior college level and is contrary to accepted practices . . . in that he has an extremely "tough" attitude toward his students which causes excessive dropouts during the semester and between semesters; his severity of grading, his tough philosophy, his sarcasm towards his students, particularly those who may disagree with his philosophy, results in many students either failing to take his courses or failing to complete them, resulting in said students missing an important basic course.
> (2) He proved ineffective as a counselor, with extremely poor rapport with his students. . . . he would never be suitable for counseling.
> (3) He has a general reputation among students, faculty, and the community as a contentious person, which lessens their respect for him, thereby reducing his effectiveness as a teacher.

Damages for Breach of Contract When Dismissal Is Without Just Cause

Pan American College at Edinburg received a National Science Foundation grant for research in astronomy and astrophysics, with Professor Paul Engle as director of the project. As a research associate in this project, Dr. Hector R. Rojas, a resident of France, was first employed for one year terminating May 31, 1963. This contract was renewed, to expire May 31, 1964.

---

[10] *Raney* v. *Board of Trustees of Coalinga Junior College District*, (Cal. App.), 48 Cal. Rptr. 555 (1966).

Soon after the renewal a strong personal animosity developed between Engle and Rojas. On September 21, 1963, in response to a letter from Engle, Rojas wrote, "Because you are not astronomer at all, and anymore I will not accept from you any instruction regarding what to do or what not to do in the research project."

Thereafter the college not only allowed Rojas to continue his work, but furnished him with a new and better office. On October 25, 1963, just outside Rojas' office, a fist-fight between Engle and Rojas occurred, in which both were knocked to the ground. There were no eyewitnesses, and the two principals gave flatly conflicting testimony as to which had been the aggressor and which had acted in self-defense. On this point an adult student was permitted to testify that Engle's reputation for veracity was not good.

The president of the college dismissed Rojas, and this action was confirmed by the board of regents, apparently without giving him a hearing. Rojas later sued for damages for breach of contract; and in the district court the question was put to a jury: "Was there just cause for the dismissal?" The verdict of the jury was: "No." The court awarded Rojas a judgment for $5,100 (the total of his unpaid salary) and $434 for traveling expenses for his return to France, as stipulated in his contract.

The statutory power of the board of regents to "dismiss an employee whenever in their judgment the best interests of the College require it" was unsuccessfully pleaded when the case went up to the court of civil appeals. There was no evidence or allegation, said that court, that the regents considered the best interests of the college, rather than a mere wish to placate Professor Engle. Thus the judgment was affirmed.[11]

Termination of Employment by Abolition of Position

A statistician employed since 1957 in the J. Hillis Miller Health Center at the University of Florida was notified in June 1963 that his job would be abolished, terminating his employment as of June 30, 1964. He contested the matter. His termination was sustained by a faculty committee appointed by the president of the university, whereupon he asked for a hearing before the board of control.[12] The board

---

[11] Pan American College v. Rojas, (Tex. Civ. App.), 392 S.W. 2d 707 (1965).

appointed a commissioner to study and report on the case, and after receiving his recommendations the full board conducted a hearing and voted to uphold the termination.

Soon thereafter the statistician filed with the state board of education a petition for review of the determination of the board of control. Before he had received an answer from the state board of education he also asked the district court of appeal for a writ of *certiorari*. The court refused the writ on the simple ground that he could not be heard until he had exhausted his administrative remedies; *i.e.*, until the state board of education had acted on his case.[13]

The published court record affords no clues as to his status as a member of the faculty of the university or as an employee of the state, no inkling of the causes for the university's action, and therefore no exposition of the merits of the case.

Dismissal of Tenure Professor in Private College

In 1959 a professor at Findlay College in Ohio was placed on tenure. In 1961, without following the prescribed procedure, the president of the college gave him one hour in which to decide whether to accept a letter of dismissal or to resign. He denied the charges (the record affords no inkling of the charges), accepted the letter of dismissal, and notified the board of trustees that he would contest the dismissal. The board affirmed the action of the president, and declared that by not requesting a hearing the professor had waived his right to one. He then asked the court to enjoin the dismissal. The court refused an injunction, citing the familiar but somewhat outmoded rule that a court of equity will not order specific performance of an employment contract for personal services. This decree was affirmed in the court of appeals.[14]

Under this reasoning tenure professors would apparently have little or no remedy other than a suit for damages. The case is reported

---

[12] The statewide board governing all state universities in Florida from 1905 through 1964. On January 1, 1965, it was superseded by a new board of regents with similar powers, pursuant to a legislative act of 1963 and a constitutional amendment adopted in November 1964. The statutes gave the state board of education general supervisory authority over the board of control.

[13] *Hoffman* v. *Board of Control*, (Fla. App.), 172 So. 2d 874 (1965).

[14] *Felch* v. *Findlay College*, Ohio App. No. 640 (1963).

to have been certified to the Ohio supreme court, but subsequently settled and dismissed by agreement of the parties. An anonymous commentator in a law review has presumably correctly written that the court should have ordered the board of trustees to give the professor a hearing before a faculty committee, and, if appealed therefrom, before the board of trustees itself.[15]

"The Loyalty Oath Furor" is the subject of the next following chapter. Miscellaneous litigation affecting faculty members is reserved for Chapter 8.

---

[15] "Judicial Review of the Tenure Contract of a Professor in a Private College." *Ohio State Law Journal* 25: 289-298 (Spring 1964).

CHAPTER 7

THE LOYALTY OATH FUROR

THE ACTION by a large group of professors and other staff members of the University of Washington against the requirement of special oaths of loyalty was left in the predecessor to this volume at the point where a second appeal to the United States Supreme Court was dismissed for want of a substantial federal question, with Justices Black and Douglas dissenting, in 1962.[1]

Loyalty Oath Statutes of Washington
Declared Unconstitutional

Subsequently a suit was brought by 64 professors, other staff members, and students of the University of Washington, before a three-judge United States district court pursuant to 28 U.S. Code, sections 2281 and 2284, to have two "oath statutes" of the state of Washington declared unconstitutional and to enjoin their enforcement.

Chapter 377, Washington Laws of 1955, had been at issue in the earlier litigation. It applied to all state employees, including teachers. Chapter 103, Laws of 1931, was also an oath statute applicable only

---

[1] *Nostrand* v. *Little*, 58 Wash., 2d 111, 361 P. 2d 551 (1961); appeal dismissed, 368 U.S. 436, 82 S.Ct. 464, 7 L.Ed. 2d 426 (1962). Discussed at pages 102-103 in *The Colleges and the Courts Since 1950*.

to school, college, and university teachers. The oath form concocted for use by members of the teaching faculty at the University of Washington was based on both of these statutes, with a dash of the Subversive Activities Act of 1951 in the background:

> I solemnly swear (or affirm) that I will support the constitution and laws of the United States of America and of the State of Washington, and will by precept and example promote respect for the flag and the institutions of the United States of America and of the State of Washington, reverence for law and order and undivided allegiance to the government of the United States.
>
> I further certify that I have read the provisions of RCW 9.81.010 (2), (3), and (5); RCW 9.81.060; RCW 9.81.070; and RCW 9.81.083, which are printed on the reverse hereof; that I am not a subversive person as therein denned; and I do solemnly swear that I am not a member of the Communist party or knowingly of any other subversive organization.
>
> I understand that this statement and oath are made subject to the penalties of perjury.

The complaint before the three-judge federal court was that the 1955 act (references to the Revised Code of Washington in the second part of the oath) infringed upon First and Fourteenth Amendment freedoms and was unduly vague, so as to create a wide zone within which it would be impossible for the oath-taker to locate the line between compliance and violation. Thus mere uncertainty and caution would operate to restrict his freedoms much farther than intended. The court did not sustain this plea.

As to the further allegation that the 1931 act was unconstitutionally vague on its face, the court held that although the challenge raised a substantial constitutional issue, adjudication in a federal court was not proper in the absence of proceedings in the state courts which might resolve or avoid the constitutional issue. Accordingly the action was dismissed.

Appeal to the United States Supreme Court resulted in that tribunal's entering a note of probable jurisdiction "because of the public importance of this type of legislation and the recurring serious constitutional questions which it presents." Accordingly the high court reviewed the case and *reversed the judgment* in 1964.[2] Thus

---

[2] *Baggett* v. *Bullitt*, 377 U.S. 360, 84 S.Ct. 1316, 12 L.Ed. 2d 377 (1964); *reversing* (U.S.D.C., Wash.), 215 F. Supp. 439 (1963), after probable jurisdiction noted, 375 U.S. 808, 84 S.Ct. 60, 11 L.Ed. 2d 46 (1963).

Washington joins a few other states wherein oath statutes have been invalidated by the United States Supreme Court. The reasoning of the majority of the justices in this instance is of very great interest. The opinion was by Mr. Justice Byron White, with six justices concurring. Justices Clark and Harlan dissented, in an opinion written by Clark.

Opinion of United States Supreme Court
in Baggett v. Bullitt (1964)

Setting the tone of his opinion, Justice White wrote:

> A law forbidding or requiring conduct in terms so vague that men of common intelligence must necessarily guess at its meaning and differ as to its application violates due process of law.

Here he cited, among other decisions, the case of *Cramp* v. *Board of Public Instruction*, 368 U.S. 278, 82 S.Ct. 275, 7 L.Ed. 2d 285 (1961), wherein a Florida teachers' oath law was held unconstitutionally vague by the United States Supreme Court in an opinion written by Mr. Justice Potter Stewart.

To demonstrate the vagueness of the 1955 Washington statute, Justice White asked many questions, among which were:

> Does the statute reach endorsement or support for Communist candidates for office? Does it reach a lawyer who represents the Communist Party or its members, or a journalist who defends constitutional rights of the Communist Party or its members, or any one who supports any cause which is likewise supported by Communists or the Communist Party? . . . This statute is unconstitutionally vague.

Among many penetrating questions he put were these:

> Is it subversive activity, for example, to attend and participate in international conventions of mathematicians and exchange views with scholars from Communist countries? What about the editor of a scholarly journal who analyses and criticizes the manuscripts of Communist scholars submitted for publication? Is selecting outstanding scholars from Communist countries as visiting professors and advising teaching, and consulting with them at the University of Washington a subversive activity if such scholars are known to be Communists, or regardless of their affiliations, regularly teach students who are members of the Communist Party, which by statutory definition is subversive and dedicated to the overthrow of the Government?

The Washington statute of 1955, said Justice White:

goes beyond overthrow or alteration by force or violence. It extends to alteration by "revolution" which, unless wholly redundant and its ordinary meaning distorted, includes any rapid or fundamental change. Would, therefore, any organization or any person supporting, advocating or teaching peaceful but far-reaching constitutional amendments be engaged in subversive activity? Could one support the repeal of the Twenty-Second Amendment, or participation by this country in a world government?

He continued: "We also conclude that the 1931 oath offends due process because of vagueness. . . . :

> The oath may prevent a professor from criticizing his state judicial system or the Supreme Court or the institution of judical review. Or it might be deemed to proscribe advocating the abolition, for example, of the Civil Rights Commission, or the House Committee on Un-American Activities, or foreign aid.
>
> We cannot say that this oath provides an ascertainable standard of conduct or that it does not require more than a State may command under the guarantees of the First and Fourteenth Amendments. . . .
>
> We are dealing with indefinite statutes whose terms, even narrowly construed, abut upon sensitive areas of basic First Amendment freedoms. The uncertain meanings of the oaths require the oath-takers—teachers and public servants—to "steer far wider of the unlawful zone" than if the boundaries of the forbidden areas were clearly marked. Those with a conscientious regard for what they solemnly swear or affirm, sensitive to the perils posed by the oath's indefinite language, avoid the risk of loss of employment, and perhaps profession, only by restricting their conduct to that which is unquestionably safe. Free speech may not be so inhibited.

In a footnote to his opinion, Justice White added an apposite quotation from the opinion of the court in the 33-year-old case of *Stromberg* v. *California*, 283 U.S. 359, 51 S.Ct. 532, 75 L.Ed. 1117 (1931):

> The maintenance of the opportunity for free political discussion to the end that government may be responsive to the will of the people and that changes may be obtained by lawful means, an opportunity essential to the security of the Republic, is a fundamental principle of our constitutional system. A statute which upon its face . . . is so vague and indefinite as to permit of the punishment of the fair use of this opportunity is repugnant to the guaranty of liberty contained in the Fourteenth Amendment.

The dissent by Justice Tom Clark, in which Justice Harlan joined, is based chiefly on the belief of these two justices that the 1964 decision in *Baggett* v. *Bullitt* is an overruling of the opinion of the court in the 1951 case of *Gerende* v. *Board of Supervisors of Elections*, 341 U.S. 56, 71 S.Ct. 565, 95 L.Ed. 745 (1951), a brief opinion sustaining the constitutionality of Maryland's *Ober Act*, with which the Washington Act of 1955 is said to be identical or practically so.

Said Justice Clark: "It is unfortunate that Gerende is overruled so quickly. Other state laws have been copied from the Maryland Act—just as Washington's 1955 Act was—primarily because of our approval of it, and now this Court would declare them void. Such action cannot command the dignity and respect due to the judicial process."

From another point of view it might perhaps be noted that the time elapsed between the two decisions was about 13 years. At the beginning of that period the nation was in the grip of a wave of postwar and cold war hysteria. At the end of the period the tenor of public opinion had tended to become somewhat more rational. Possibly the change, and also the experience of almost a decade and a half, not only justified the court in taking a different position, but made it seem imperative.

In that view, if the decision has the practical effect of inducing a trend toward invalidating war-produced loyalty oath laws in many states, and of effectively discouraging "witch-hunting" legislation, it may represent a landmark of progress toward ridding the nation of a curious type of legislative product which is at once futile for the purposes for which it was intended and dangerous to constitutional liberties.[3]

Georgia Teachers' Oath Statutes Unconstitutional

Georgia Act 224 of 1949, as amended 1950, (and Resolution 54 of Georgia Statutes, 1935) required all teachers in public schools, colleges, and universities to refrain from subscribing to or teaching "any theory of government or of economics or of social relations inconsistent with the fundamental principles of patriotism and high ideals of Americanism," and carried a penal provision that any violation of

---

[3] An informed commentary is by Arval A. Morris. "The University of Washington Loyalty Oath Case." *American Association of University Professors Bulletin* 50: 221-231 (September 1964).

the oath to that effect would constitute a misdemeanor and subject the violator to immediate summary discharge from his teaching position. Another provision required every person on the payroll of the state to swear that he "has no sympathy for the doctrines of Communism and will lend neither aid, support, advice, counsel nor influence to the Communist Party or to the teaching of Communism."

Attacked on several grounds by the Georgia Conference of the American Association of University Professors, these statutes were held unconstitutional by a three-judge federal court composed of Circuit Judge Griffin B. Bell and District Judges Hooper and Morgan, in a 1965 decision. The anti-Communist oath was void for vagueness (on reasoning similar to that of the United States Supreme Court in *Baggett* v. *Bullitt*, cited in Footnote 2, this chapter). The penal provision was a denial of due process under the Fourteenth Amendment, and the prohibition involving discussion of "any theory of government . . ." was a denial of the First Amendment right of freedom of speech. The decision was further supported by a 1961 decision of the United States Supreme Court invalidating a Florida school teachers' oath act (*Cramp* v. *Board of Public Instruction of Orange County, Florida*, 368 U.S. 278, 82 S.Ct. 275, 7 L.Ed. 2d 285).

Concluding, the three-judge federal court said: "The sum of our holding is that the plaintiffs may be required to swear to uphold, support and defend the Constitution and laws of Georgia and of the United States and that they are not members of the Communist Party. They have not objected to doing so. The balance of the oaths described in these statutes are void."[4]

Arizona Oath Act Declared Unconstitutional by United States Supreme Court in April 1966

A young husband and wife, both Quakers, and both teaching in public junior high schools in Tucson, decided in 1961 that their consciences would not allow them to subscribe to the oath which was required of public employees by the Arizona anti-Communist and anti-subversive statute. The act provided for prosecution of any violator

---

[4] *Georgia Conference of American Association of University Professors* v. *Board of Regents of the University System of Georgia*, (U.S.D.C., Ga.), 246 F. Supp. 553 (1965).

and immediate termination of his pay as a public employee. For nearly five years this husband and wife continued in their teaching positions without pay, during which time they lived with extreme economy and received some $20,000 in contributions from Quaker and other civil rights organizations. Meantime they pursued court action for declaratory relief.

A judgment adverse to the teachers by the Arizona supreme court[5] was vacated and remanded by the United States Supreme Court in 1964,[6] for "reconsideration in the light of Baggett v. Bullitt." Later in the same year the Arizona supreme court held that the oath statute was not void for vagueness, with Justice Bernstein dissenting.[7] In 1965 the United States Supreme Court granted a petition for certiorari and transferred the case to its appellate docket.[8]

The case next came before the court in 1966, resulting in a judgment wholly favorable to the teachers and declaring the Arizona statute unconstitutional because its language provided no exception for persons who might knowingly associate with an organization without being in accord with the organization's unlawful ends. "The hazard of being prosecuted for knowing but guiltless behavior . . . is a reality," said the court. The majority opinion was written by Mr. Justice William O. Douglas, with four justices concurring. A dissenting opinion was entered by Mr. Justice Byron K. White, joined in dissent by Justices Clark, Harlan, and Stewart.

The reasoning of the majority included a good deal of emphasis on the menace of vagueness:[9]

> Petitioner . . . decided she could not in good conscience take the oath, not knowing what it meant and not having any chance to get a hearing at which its precise scope and meaning could be determined.
>
> . . . .
>
> Would a teacher be safe and secure in going to a Pugwash Conference? Would it be legal to join a seminar group predominantly Communist and therefore subject to control by those who are said to believe in the overthrow of the government

---

[5] Elfbrandt v. Russell, 94 Ariz. 1, 381 P. 2d 554 (1963).
[6] Same, 378 U.S. 127, 84 S.Ct. 1658, 12 L.Ed. 2d 744 (1964).
[7] Same, 97 Ariz. 140, 397 P. 2d 944 (1964). Rehearing denied.
[8] Same, 382 U.S. 710, 86 S.Ct. 116, 16 L.Ed. 2d 321 (1965).
[9] Elfbrandt v. Russell, 86 S.Ct. 1238, Supreme Court of the United States, April 18, 1966.

by force and violence? Juries might convict though the teacher did not subscribe to the unlawful aims of the organization. And there is apparently no machinery provided for getting clearance in advance.

. . . .

This Act threatens the cherished freedom of association protected by the First Amendment. . . . Public employees of character and integrity may well forego their calling rather than risk prosecution for perjury or compromise their commitment to intellectual and political freedom: "The Communist trained in fraud and perjury has no qualms in taking any oath; the loyal citizen, conscious of history's oppressions may well wonder whether the medieval rack and torture wheel are next for the one who declines to take an involved negative oath as evidence that he is a True Believer."

. . . .

A law which applies to membership without the "specific intent" to further the illegal aims of the organization infringes unnecessarily on protected freedoms. It rests on the doctrine of "guilt by association" which has no place here.

Complicated Maze of "Antisubversive" Statutes in New York Declared Unconstitutional by United States Supreme Court in January 1967

The statutes of New York are generously peppered with "antisubversive" sections and clauses directed at teachers, university professors, and other public employees. Five members of the faculty of the State University of New York at Buffalo (which was the private University of Buffalo prior to 1963) brought a class action under United States Code Annotated, Sections 2281 and 2284, to convene a three-judge federal court to pass on the constitutionality of three of these gems: Sections 3021 and 3022, New York Education Law; Section 105, New York Civil Service Law; and Section 244 of Article XVIII of the Rules of the Regents of the University of the State of New York and State Board of Education; *and* the certificates and oaths required thereunder.

District Judge John O. Henderson dismissed the complaint, declaring that no substantial federal question was presented; but this judgment was reversed and remanded by the United States court of appeals through the voice of Circuit Judge Thurgood Marshall, who intimated that the opinions in *Baggett* v. *Bullitt* and *Wieman* v. *Updegraff*, 344 U.S. 183, 73 S.Ct. 215, 97 L.Ed. 216 (1952), the latter being the decision in which the Oklahoma teachers' oath statute was held unconstitutional and void, afforded ample indication that federal questions of importance are concerned. Accordingly, convening of a three-judge court was ordered.[10]

It turned out that the judgment of the special three-judge court was adverse to the plaintiffs.[11] The Supreme Court of the United States consented to review it, reversed the judgment, and remanded it to the district court. The decision of the high tribunal was by a vote of five to four, with the majority opinion written by Mr. Justice Brennan, with whom Chief Justice Earl Warren and Justices Black, Douglas, and Fortas concurred. The dissent was by Justice Tom Clark, with Justices Harlan, Stewart, and White joining.[12]

A key paragraph in the majority opinion:

> Our nation is deeply committed to safeguarding academic freedom, which is of transcendent value to all of us and not merely to the teachers concerned. That freedom is therefore a specific concern of the First Amendment, which does not tolerate laws that cast a pall of orthodoxy over the classroom.

Another:

> Because First Amendment freedoms need breathing-space to survive, government may regulate in the area only with narrow specificity. New York's complicated and intricate scheme plainly violates that standard. When one must guess what conduct or utterances may lose him his position, one necessarily will "steer far wider of the unlawful zone."

And another:

> The theory that public employment may be denied altogether or may be subjected to any conditions, regardless of how unreasonable, has been uniformly rejected. . . .
> Mere knowing membership without a specific intent to further the unlawful aims of an organization is not a constitutionally adequate basis for exclusion from such positions as those held by the appellants.

---

[10] *Keyishian* v. *Board of Regents of University of State of New York*, (U.S.C.A., N.Y.), 345 F. 2d 236 (1965); reversing 233 F. Supp. 752 (1964).

[11] *Keyishian* v. *Regents*, (U.S.D.C., N.Y.), 255 F. Supp. 981 (1966).

[12] Probable jurisdiction noted, 384 U.S. 998, 86 S.Ct. 1921, 16 L.Ed. 2d 1012 (1966); *reversed*, (U.S. S.Ct.), 35 U.S. Law Week 4152 (January 23, 1967). The American Association of University Professors, as *amicus auriae*, filed a brief against the constitutionality of the statutes at issue.

Again:

> The regulatory maze created by New York is wholly lacking
> in "terms susceptible of objective measurement. . . ." Vagueness
> of wording is aggravated by prolixity and profusion of statutes,
> regulations and administrative machinery, and by manifold cross-
> references to interrelated enactments and rules.

"We therefore hold that Section 3021 of the *Education Law*
and Subsections (1) (A), (1) (B), and (3) of Section 105 of the
Civil Service Law as implemented by the machinery created pursuant
to Section 3022 of the *Education Law* are unconstitutional."

By no means discarding the doctrine that the state has a right
to act for its own preservation by protecting its classrooms from
those who would destroy it, the majority justices remarked, "There
can be no doubt of the legitimacy of New York's interest in protecting its educational system from subversion," and left the clear
implication that new statutes, if drafted in terms sufficiently specific
and clear, might stand. (A realistic feel for the current climate of
public opinion makes it seem unlikely that any new antisubversive
statutes will be enacted soon.)

The dissenting justices viewed this latter feature of the majority
opinion with apparent disdain. "The state's right of self-preservation,"
said they, "has been swept away." And in a tone perhaps a trifle
platitudinous—perhaps in this context a bit alarmist:

> Our public educational system is the genius of our democ-
> racy. The minds of our youth are developed there, and the
> character of that development will determine the future of our
> land. Indeed, our very existence depends upon it.

Within three years the nation's highest court has struck down loyalty oath legislation in three states: Washington, Arizona, and New
York. In each case the majority opinion was written by a different justice: White, Douglas, Brennan. In all three cases Justices Clark and
Harlan dissented, and were joined in the *Elfbrandt* and *Keyishian* cases
by Justices Stewart and White. Justice White wrote the majority
opinion in the *Baggett* case, and the dissenting opinion in *Elfbrandt*.
Justice Clark wrote the dissents in *Baggett* and *Keyishian*. Chief
Justice Warren and Justices Black, Brennan, Douglas, and Fortas or
his predecessor Goldberg were on the side of the angels in all three
cases.

Although all three decisions were less than unanimous, it may be said without disparaging the views of the dissenting justices that the idea of state statutes providing compulsory "loyalty oaths" for teachers in schools, colleges, and universities has received three staggering blows from which it will probably not recover. Born of the hysteria of war or "cold war," popular support for this type of legislation is unquestionably declining. Comprehension of its folly and futility continues to increase on the part of the bench, the bar, and the public.

New Hampshire's Loyalty Oaths Now in Question

On December 31, 1966, George Pappagianis, Attorney General of New Hampshire, gave an opinion at the request of the secretary of state to the effect that two New Hampshire statutes prescribing oaths for teachers and civil employees, including the Subversive Activities Act of 1951, are unconstitutional; he recommended that an advisory or declaratory opinion of the supreme court of New Hampshire be sought. The oath required by the act of 1951, it was said, is virtually identical with the oath statute of the state of Washington which was declared void by the United States Supreme Court in *Baggett* v. *Bullitt*.

Charge of Falsifying Oath Under California's
Levering Act Is Not Sustained Against Junior
College Teacher

The Fullerton Junior College District employed an instructor in welding as a probationary teacher in 1961. Scarcely had he begun his work until an anonymous investigation of his alleged subversive history and tendencies was begun. Eventually he was charged with having falsely sworn that he had not been a member of the Communist Party within the past five years, as required by the Levering Act oath for teachers. At a school board inquiry (which was not a hearing on his dismissal, but only a proceeding for information) he testified that he knew the person who had denounced him, but refused to divulge the name because he did not want to be an "informer"; and that the act did not require this. At the inquiry he stated that he wished to be cooperative, and asked to be told the reasons for asking for the name he refused to divulge. No reason was forthcoming, and he was given no guidance.

His story was that he had joined the Communist Party in 1938 and left it in 1951. He sought readmission in 1957, but was rejected. In 1958 he joined with four others in writing an article for *The Militant* (a Communist organ) asserting the claims of the five for recognition as party members, but the party never reinstated his membership, and told him he had not been a member since 1951.

His dismissal on the charge of falsifying the oath was sustained by the local superior court, but the California court of appeal reversed the judgment, holding it not supported by the evidence. The facts showed he had not been a member of the party since 1951, and he was correct in his belief that the statute did not require him to divulge names.[13]

---

[13] *Fullerton Junior College District of Orange County* v. *Phillips*, (Cal. App.), 41 Cal. Rptr. 608 (1964).

CHAPTER 8

OTHER LITIGATION TOUCHING
FACULTY MEMBERS

SOME OF THE DIVERSE MATTERS included here are (1) use of copyrighted materials by teachers, (2) rights in patents and trade secrets, (3) determinations as to what expenses of college or university academic staff members are deductible for purposes of the federal individual income tax, and (4) a case involving libel of a university football coach by the publisher of a popular magazine nationally circulated.

Under each of these rubrics only one or a few recent decisions appear. The reader will understand that this chapter is hence not to be mistaken for a treatise on patents and copyrights, or the federal income tax, or the law of libel. It merely notes a few recent cases.

Use of Copyrighted Materials by Teacher

The head of the vocal department of the Clarinda, Iowa, Junior College and High School in 1958-59, who also apparently served as choir leader or instructor in the First Methodist Church of Clarinda, found that his school library contained about 25 copies of the published copyrighted version of a hymn entitled *My God and I*. He made a re-arrangement of the music and reproduced 48 copies of the hymn on one of the school's duplicating machines. He had this performed once by the high school choir of 84 voices, and once by the church choir.

In June 1959 he wrote to the publisher, one Wihtol, doing business in California as "The Kama Company," informing him of his new arrangement and offering to "get the score ready for your perusal next Fall, if you are interested." On July 28 the publisher wrote him, saying he was guilty of infringement of copyright, entailing a statutory fine of $250 to $5,000, and offered to settle for $250. A month later he forwarded 44 copies of his re-arrangement to the publisher, who brought an infringement suit against him in the United States district court January 15, 1960, asking for pecuniary damages and an injunction against further infringement.

The district court held that there had been no infringement; the use of the music solely for testing and experimentation with the school and church choirs was within the meaning of "fair use," which is said to be

> based upon the principle that subsequent workers in the same field are not deprived of all use thereof, as, otherwise, the progress of science and the useful arts would be unduly obstructed.

The court prudently added:

> Whether a particular use of a copyrighted article, without permission of the owner, is a fair use, depends on the circumstances of the particular case, and the court must look to the nature and objects of the selections made, the quantity and value of the material used, and the degree in which the use may prejudice the sale, diminish the profits, or supersede the objects of the original work.

Taking a skeptical view of the plaintiff in this case, the court noted that the letter of July 28 was apparently for purposes of extortion, because the plaintiff must have known that the criminal sanctions (actually imprisonment for not more than one year and/or a fine of $100 to $1,000, and not as stated in the letter) required a *willful* infringement for *profit*, of which there was no evidence. The applicable section of the U.S. Code making infringement a misdemeanor contains a proviso:

> That nothing in this title shall be construed as to prevent the performance of religious or secular works such as oratorios, cantatas, masses or octavo choruses by public schools, church choirs, or vocal societies, rented, borrowed or obtained from

some public library, public school, church choir, or vocal society, provided the performance is given for charitable or educational purposes and not for profit.

Moreover, the plaintiff's tearful testimony about the poverty of his wife and child at the time he originally wrote the song was presumably false, because investigation disclosed that at that time he had no child and was not living with his wife. Nevertheless, he appealed his case, and the United States court of appeals flatly reversed and remanded the decision.

Circuit Judge Sanborn, for the court of appeals, concluded that the defendant teacher had infringed the copyright. The judge held that damages, within the statutory limits, must be allowed by the trial court, and that the plaintiff publisher had a right to have his plea for an injunction considered and ruled upon by the trial court.[1]

Further, said Judge Sanborn, the church, as an employer of the teacher, was jointly liable with him under the doctrine of *respondeat superior*; and the public school district, as his chief employer, escaped only because it was an agency of the state of Iowa, and as such could not be sued in federal courts by a citizen of another state, because of the prohibition in the Eleventh Amendment.

To justify these harsh conclusions, the judge said: "It must be kept in mind that the applicable law is purely statutory and that the Copyright Act has little elasticity or flexibility."

Can a Note-Taker or Transcriber of a Professor's Lecture Have His Notes or Transcription Copyrighted?

A national newspaper reported in mid-May 1966 that at the University of California at Los Angeles a local optometrist and his wife had operated a business since 1962, in which they hire students to sit in on selected university courses and transcribe or take full notes on the lectures, after which the optometrist copyrights the notes, prints them, and sells them to students at 25¢ per lecture or $5 for a semester course.

Two members of the faculty in anthropology, Dr. B. J. Williams and Dr. Herman Bleibtreu, are reported to have instituted a suit

---

[1] *Wihtol* v. *Crow*, (U.S.C.A.), 309 F. 2d 777 (1962); reversing (U.S.D.C., Ia.) 199 F. Supp. 682 (1961). Also appears in 147 *United States Patent Quarterly* 106.

in the local court against the optometrist (Dr. J. Edwin Weisser), with the main object of obtaining a court order to prevent him from copyrighting their lecture materials. It was said that the court issued a temporary restraining order against the note-taking, pending a hearing on the case.

On the Law and the Ethics of Patents and Trade Secrets

Professor Jay W. Forrester of the Massachusetts Institute of Technology is credited with having invented the "magnetic core computer storage system" in 1949. He was then a research engineer at the institute, and is now professor of industrial management.

There was a conflicting claim to prior invention of the same device by Jan A. Rajchmann, an employee of Radio Corporation of America. In litigation involving the licensing agreements under which International Business Machines Corporation engages in large-scale manufacture of computers in which the device is used, a "consent decree" was arrived at in 1964 in the United States district court for the southern district of New York, whereby International Business Machines Corporation agreed to pay the Massachusetts Institute of Technology $13 million for a paid-up license to use Forrester's invention.[2]

The esoteric complexities of the claims involved do not lend themselves to simple and brief narration. On the broader subject of university patent policies there is fortunately available a recent comprehensive book-length digest and survey published by the National Academy of Sciences and National Research Council.[3]

Scientists sometimes transfer from university employment to private employment with industrial concerns, and vice versa. They also sometimes move from employment with one industrial concern to another, to obtain higher salaries or various other advantages. In

---

[2] *Research Corporation and Massachusetts Institute of Technology* v. *Radio Corporation of America*, (U.S.D.C., N.Y.), Civil Action No. 61, Civ. 1280; Civ. 1538; *Research Corporation and Massachusetts Institute of Technology* v. *International Business Machines Corporation*, Civil Action No. 62, Civ. 2593 (April 10, 1964).

[3] Archie M. Palmer, *University Research and Patent Policies, Practices, and Procedures.* Washington: National Academy of Sciences, 1962. 291 pp.

such instances questions of ethics arise as to the right of the scientist to take with him and use for the benefit of his new employer any "trade secrets" of his former employer, of which he gained knowledge while in that employment.

It is clear that the scientist-employee should consider himself ethically bound not to disclose trade secrets which had been created wholly by others and to which he himself had contributed nothing. The question of his responsibility regarding secret processes which he himself had invented or developed while engaged in his former employment is perhaps more difficult.

There is the case of the young chemist who made a meteoric rise in the field of space-suit technology, during six years of employment with the B. F. Goodrich Company. He then left to enter employment with International Latex Corporation, a competing concern. He was reported as evidently having no moral compunctions against disclosing Goodrich trade secrets after leaving Goodrich employ, and was quoted as saying that loyalty and ethics had their price; and insofar as he was concerned, International Latex was paying the price.

In an action to enjoin him from disclosing trade secrets which were the property of the B. F. Goodrich Company, a United States court of appeals said:[4]

> Public policy demands commercial morality and courts of equity are empowered to enforce it by enjoining an improper disclosure of trade secrets.

Another case involving Columbia University as defendant was a suit for a temporary injunction to forbid the university from "unfair competition by the misappropriation of an unpatented trade secret belonging to the plaintiff." It seems that during the 1950's certain scientific and engineering employees of the university's development laboratory (the Lamont Geological Observatory) were engaged in geophysical oceanographic research and the development of devices for gaining knowledge of the ocean floor by recording the echoes of sound waves traveling to the sea-bottom and returning to the surface. This required the production of sound under water, either by means of explosives (expensive and dangerous) or by some other means.

---

[4] *B. F. Goodrich Company* v. *Wohlgemuth*, (U.S.C.A.), 137 *U.S. Patent Quarterly* 387 and 804 (1965).

The idea of producing the sounds by the release of compressed air seemed practicable and desirable, and the president of the plaintiff corporation claimed he had invented an "air-gun" and demonstrated it secretly to three representatives of the university in 1961.

By that time he had apparently left the employ of the university to form a "spin-off" private corporation. He offered to sell a license to manufacture his device to the university, but the university expressed no interest, saying it was developing such a device in its own laboratories. In the ensuing years the university fabricated a score or more of these devices for use in its oceanographic research for the United States Navy.

Expressed in an amalgam of engineering patois, scientific jargon, and government gobbledegook, the description of the hardware at issue was:

> An unpatented underwater pneumatic acoustical repeater for use in submarine geophysics, the seismological branch of ocean-ography, for the purpose of developing a profile picture and topography of the ocean floor and the stratification and thickness of the sediments beneath it.
>
> Aside from commercial application, such and similar devices are an essential implement in the university's performance of oceanographic research since November 1960 for the Navy Department, looking to improvements in the techniques of under-sea warfare, subsurface deployment and navigation of submarines and methods of locating and destroying enemy craft.

The United States district court denied the injunction, observing that every allegation in the complaint was flatly refuted by the university's answer; that granting the injunction would cause the university great financial hardship and add to the danger of its research at sea with specially-equipped vessels; and that the plaintiff had prejudiced its claim by *laches* (delaying approximately five years before seeking relief).[5]

Sale of Copyrights and Patents: Federal Income Tax Treatment

Copyrights and patents are species of property, seemingly closely related; but under existing federal statutes and regulations authors,

---

[5] *Bolt Associates, Inc.* v. *Trustees of Columbia University in the City of New York,* (U.S.D.C., N.Y.), 249 F. Supp. 612 (1966).

musicians, and artists are not permitted to treat receipts from sales of their own copyrights as capital gains (taxable at substantially lower rates than ordinary business income), while inventors are assured of the right to report sales of their patents as sales of capital assets, even when the proceeds are in the form of royalties. A 1964 case illustrates this.

One Puschelberg was co-inventor of a disposable blood filter, with Dr. Warren B. Cooksey, a physician. They sold a license to manufacture, use, and sell the device to a third party; and contemporaneously all three agreed that Puschelberg would manufacture the filters and supply them to the licensee at 8 cents per unit. Obviously the proceeds would, for purposes of Puschelberg's federal income tax, have to be divided into one part for the sale of his patent rights and one part for his price as manufacturer—the former being a sale of a capital asset and the latter being ordinary business income. The United States district court decided that 4.3 cents per units was a fair manufactured price for the filter, and the remaining 3.7 cents per unit could properly be allocated to "purchase of the invention," and reported as a capital gain. Accordingly, Puschelberg and his wife were allowed to recover taxes overpaid in a previous tax period when the entire proceeds were taxed as ordinary income. This judgment was affirmed by the United States court of appeals, in an opinion by Circuit Judge Shackelford Miller.[6]

Professors' Federal Income Tax: Educational Expense Deductions Permissible and Not Permissible

The general tendency of the Internal Revenue Service has been to maintain that expenses incurred by a professor or instructor for his own further education, by means of attendance at university summer sessions or by educational travel or other means, are not deductible as "business expenses" unless a showing is made that the specific activity was a legal or official requirement which the individual concerned must perform in order to continue in his current employment.

Thus educational expenses incurred other than on pain of losing one's job were not deductible; and they would not be deductible for

---

[6] *Puschelberg* v. *United States*, (U.S.C.A., Mich.), 330 F. 2d 56 (1964).

the professor who was incurring expenses for his own professional growth, or in the hope of increasing his chances of promotion, or other like purposes. Generally the same principles apply to foreign travel by professors. A 1962 decision illustrates.

A university professor of mathematics was under contract for twelve months of work each year, with every third summer as "sabbatical leave." In 1955 he occupied the period of leave with a trip to Europe, and contended that the expenses of the trip should be deductible. An adverse judgment by the United States tax court was affirmed by the federal court of appeals:[7]

> The taxpayer's activities on his trip abroad were not different from those reasonably expected of any other tourist of his age on a sightseeing trip abroad; no report thereof was required or submitted to the university; many of his fellow faculty members did not travel during their sabbatical summer (and in no known instance has one ever been discharged for that reason); the taxpayer was not required to travel in Europe or elsewhere during the year in question to retain his position.
>
> Assuming, as did the Tax Court, that foreign travel would be culturally broadening and therefore of benefit not only to the taxpayer individually but also to the university because of the potential increase in his teaching accomplishment, and that the taxpayer might thereby qualify for promotion, no justification for the claimed deduction as ordinary and necessary business expense appears.

A classically long-drawn litigation was that of Dr. Ephraim Cross, a teacher of Romance languages at City College in New York, who claimed that a deduction of $1,300 for expenses of a summer trip to Europe was improperly denied him on his income tax return for 1954, and that in consequence $519.62 in taxes was erroneously and illegally collected. The teacher sued to recover. A United States district court once ruled in his favor, but this was reversed by the United States court of appeals in 1964; and at last, in 1966, the federal district court rendered judgment against him.[8] The conclusion was that "It appears . . . that since no express requirement of taxpayer's employer is claimed for his trip, in order to prevail he is required to

---

[7] *Denneby* v. *Commissioner of Internal Revenue*, (U.S.C.A., 309 F. 2d 149 (1962); affirming 36 Tax Court 1195 (1961).

[8] *Cross* v. *United States*, (U.S.D.C., N.Y.), 250 F. Supp. 609 (1966); following (U.S.C.A.), 336 F. 2d 431 (1964), which reversed (U.S.D.C., N.Y.) 222 F. Supp. 157 (1963).

show that his travels were undertaken *primarily* for the purpose of maintaining or improving his skill as a teacher of Spanish, French, . . . and Romance linguistics. I find that Professor Cross has not sustained his burden of proving this fact by a fair preponderance of the credible evidence." The court thought the trip was primarily a personal vacation.

There are sets of facts in which a teacher is able to prove that his expenses for education are unavoidably necessary to enable him to continue in his present position, and are thus properly deductible under Section 162 (a), 1a and 1b, Internal Revenue Code of 1954. (The full text of these sections is quoted in *United States* v. *Michaelson,* cited in the next footnote herein.) In that case the regulations of the Washington State Board of Education stipulated that a teacher holding a provisional certificate could not continue teaching for more than five years without completing his fifth year of education and thereby obtaining a standard certificate.

A female teacher holding a provisional certificate enrolled as a student in a night school for a course in law, and the state board of education accepted the credits as satisfying the fifth-year requirement. In this situation she was allowed to claim deduction of the cost of books, tuition, and supplies for the night school course as an ordinary and necessary business expense.

The same was true of the summer school expenses of a female teacher in Oregon under an emergency teaching certificate who was required to take summer courses, and the courses selected by her also served to assist her in eventually securing a permanent certificate. The Washington and Oregon cases were consolidated and argued and decided together in the federal courts.[9]

Chief Judge Powell of the federal district court remarked in the course of the opinion:

> The importance of encouragement of individuals interested in self-improvement should not be minimized. Certainly rapid write-offs of investments in buildings, deductions for advertising and deductions for expenses of those in higher brackets, are no more important to them than a smaller deduction is to one who has limited funds, as the taxpayer here.

---

[9] *United States* v. *Michaelson, (and Commissioner of Internal Revenue* v. *Johnson),* (U.S.C.A.), 313 F. 2d 668 (1963); affirming (U.S.D.C.), 203 F. Supp. 830 (1961), which affirmed 28 U.S. Tax Court 1164 (1957).

This socially enlightened view from the bench is a welcome deviation from the hard-nosed "get-the-revenue" attitude often adhered to, and perhaps partly understandably, by revenue officers and sometimes by judges.

The tightest interpretation is that educational expenses will be deductible only if necessary to retain the taxpayer's present position, and not if for the purpose of obtaining a new position or a promotion. However, there are exceptions wherein both motives appear to be inseparable.

For example, a graduate of Rensselaer Polytechnic Institute in 1957 with the degree of B.S. in electrical engineering immediately accepted employment as a patent trainee in the Patent Training Center of the International Business Machines Corporation in Washington, D.C., and concurrently studied law in the evening law school of the George Washington University. IBM *required* him, as a condition of his employment as trainee, to study law, obtain a degree of LL.B., and gain admission to practice before the United States Patent Office. He completed these requirements in 1961, and was immediately transferred to Poughkeepsie, N.Y., and given an increase in pay of $1,000 per year.

In these circumstances the United States district court held him entitled to a refund of $107 for taxes paid in the tax year 1958, when he was denied deduction of his $540 tuition fee paid to the law school. The court was merely giving a literal interpretation to Treasury Regulation 1.162 - 5 (b), which says in part: "The fact that the education undertaken meets express requirements for the new position or substantial advancement in position will be an important factor indicating that the education is undertaken primarily for the purpose of obtaining such position or advancement *unless* such education is required as a condition to the retention by the taxpayer of his present employment."[10]

Two earlier cases indicated that unanimity among the judges of the United States tax court has not always been attainable on various aspects of this issue, and that harmony between the tax court and the United States court of appeals has not always existed. In one of these, the taxpayer was holding a temporary appointment as a tutor in Queens College (now a unit of the City University of New York)

---

[10] *Williams* v. *United States*, (U.S.D.C., N.Y.), 238 F. Supp. 351 (1965).

and had been made to understand unequivocally that he would have to make progress toward the doctorate in order to hold his position as a tutor—yet a majority of the tax court held that his expenses for furthering his own education toward that end were not deductible. Judge Raum, however, entered a dissent, in which he was joined by Judges Tietjens and Withey. Said he. "I find it very difficult to see why such expenses do not qualify as 'ordinary and necessary business expenses.' " On appeal the United States court of appeals adopted the dissenting opinion of Judge Raum of the tax court, and reversed the tax court decision.[11]

A little later there was the case of Harold H. Davis, a full professor on tenure at Pomona College, having taught English at that college since 1927. In 1956 he made a trip of six weeks' duration to England for research on a book not expected to be profitable, but to add to his scholarly repute. The expense involved was about $2,000. The tax court held it not deductible because it was apparently not required of him in order to retain his current employment. He also sought to deduct the expense of building a room on his house for use as a study, and about $3,000 a year for its operation and maintenance. This, too, was disallowed; and mention was made of the fact that Pomona College furnished him with a "cubicle in Holmes Hall" for office use.

This tax court opinion was by Judge Fay, with a majority concurring, but with five dissenters. Judge Fisher dissented without opinion, and Judge Scott dissented as to the trip to England only, without writing his reasons. Judges Bruce, Forrester, and Train joined in a lengthy dissent by Judge Raum, in which he said:[12]

> The test is not whether the expenditure is *required*, but rather whether it is *appropriate* or *helpful* and proximately related to the taxpayer's trade or business.

This is at least an urbane and reasonable statement; but, as just observed, it is not subscribed to by all the judges. Even more depressing was the fact that in mid-1966 efforts seemed to be on foot to revise the regulations of the Internal Revenue Service to make it more difficult for professors and teachers to obtain "ordinary business

---

[11] *Marlor* v. *Commissioner of Internal Revenue,* (U.S.C.A., N.Y.), 251 F. 2d 615 (1958); reversing 27 Tax Court 618 (1956).

[12] *Davis* v. *Commissioner of Internal Revenue,* 38 U.S. Tax Court 175 (1962).

expense" deductions of their outlays to further their own education. In the later half of the year 1966 it was reported that the Internal Revenue Service was proposing new regulations which, if adopted, would place educational expense deductions on new and somewhat different bases, which would probably make it more difficult to obtain an allowance of such deductions than hitherto. In the *New York Times* for September 1, 1966, a story entitled "Personal Finance: U.S. Proposal on Education Expenses Would Eliminate Special Tax Advantage," in the business section and under the by-line of Sal Nuccio, indicated that "Under the recently issued regulatory proposals, education expenses no longer would be deductible from taxable income under any circumstances, if the training even incidentally qualifies the taxpayer for a new specialty, job, trade, or business, or if the schooling leads to a degree, diploma or comparable certificate." At that time it could not be known whether the new stringent proposals would be adopted and put into effect.

University Football Coach Awarded Damages for Libel by Publisher of Popular Magazine

Writers on the staff of the *Saturday Evening Post* produced for the issue of March 23, 1963, an article entitled "The Story of a College Football Fix—How Wally Butts and Bear Bryant Rigged a Game Last Fall." The story alleged that Butts, coach of the University of Georgia team, had given information on Georgia plays to Bryant, coach of the University of Alabama team, in advance of the Alabama-Georgia game played in Birmingham in September 1962.

Butts, a man in his fifties holding the post of university athletic director at the University of Georgia, at the height of his career and having good prospects for possible advancement to a larger institution or other larger responsibilities, sued the publisher for damages for libel. Publication of the articles, he said, had halted all his current negotiations for future employment in college or professional football, and in effect destroyed or diminished his prospects.

A jury in federal district court returned a verdict in his favor, and awarded him $60,000 actual damages and $3,000,000 punitive damages, whereupon the defendant publisher moved for a new trial on the ground that the award was grossly excessive. The order of the court was that the new trial be granted "unless the plaintiff, within

20 days shall in writing remit all the punitive damages awarded above the sum of $400,000; the award of $60,000 for general damages to remain undisturbed."[13]

In the opinion of the court, "The article was clearly defamatory and extremely so" because it unequivocally charged that Butts was a corrupt person who "betrayed or sold out his students." The charge was not substantiated in court. One of the writers had specifically quoted several informants in support of his story, but most of these persons denied under oath that they had ever given him any such information. Thus the story appeared to be a libelous publication based on charges unsupported by the evidence.

Striking Faculty Members Sue for Damages for Alleged Fraudulent and Libelous Listing of Their Names

At St. John's University in New York City, operated by the Vincentian Order and said to be the largest Roman Catholic university in the world, faculty members serve under contracts expiring each year. Late in 1965 strenuous demands by a number of faculty members for a larger faculty voice in the management of the university led to an announcement that 31 faculty members would be dropped at the expiration of their short-term contracts. This precipitated a strike, beginning early in January 1966, of a number of faculty members, mostly members of the United Federation of College Teachers, under the leadership of the Rev. Peter O'Reilly, chairman of the St. John's chapter of the federation, to protest the dismissals and to disassociate themselves from the university unless and until reforms were made.

Later, when the university's *Undergraduate Bulletin 1966-67* came off the press it contained the names of the strikers as faculty members for that year. Thereupon 24 whose names were thus listed brought suit in Manhattan supreme court, asking damages of $100,000 each, contending that the listings are knowingly fraudulent and that they

---

[13]*Butts* v. *Curtis Publishing Company*, (U.S.D.C., Ga.), 225 F. Supp. 916 (1964); affirmed in (U.S.C.A.), 351 F. 2d 702 (1965), with Circuit Judge Rives dissenting. Meantime, in 242 F. Supp. 390 (1964), motion for new trial denied, on ground that university athletic director is not a "public officer or official" within the meaning of the United States Supreme Court decision in New York Times v. Sullivan.

libel and defame the individuals named, and "hold them up to contempt, reproach, and ridicule" because they had notified the university that they had no intention of returning "under present circumstances." The complaint was scheduled for hearing before Justice Charles E. Tierney.

CHAPTER 9

NONACADEMIC EMPLOYEES

IN THIS AREA actions under workmen's compensation laws arise with considerable frequency. Two such cases in the present chapter concern (1) a football player as a compensable employee of a college, and (2) a laborer who was injured while working on a college building, but actually at the time in the employ of a contractor, and not of the college. There is also the unusual case of a "field representative" of a medical college who was concurrently self-employed part-time, and who unsuccessfully sought damages for libel by a business competitor who wrote a letter to an officer of the college describing the activities of the field representative in uncomplimentary terms. The impact of labor legislation providing for recognition of labor organizations and for the right of collective bargaining also receives some attention.

College Football Player as Compensable Employee
Under Industrial Accident Insurance Act

The California State Polytechnic College sent its football team by nonscheduled air transportation to a scheduled game in Ohio in October 1960. This case concerns the claim for death benefits by the widow of a member of the team who met death when the plane crashed on the return trip. The California Industrial Accident Commission denied her claim on the ground that the deceased was not an employee of the college in the sense intended in the statute. This order was annulled and remanded by a California court of appeal.[1]

The decedent had been an outstanding high school athlete, and had been recruited in 1956 by the Polytech coach. During the fall term of that year he played on the team and lived on the campus. He was given work in the college cafeteria, his pay being applied to his room rent. In the summer of 1957 he married and thereafter lived in Paso Robles, about 25 miles away, and commuted to the campus (in San Luis Obispo). In the fall of 1957 he did not play football. Instead, he worked in a flour mill managed by his father and earned $500 during the football season. In the spring of 1958 he returned to football practice, saying the coach had promised to give him $50 at the beginning of each school quarter and $75 rent money during the football season. This was done for the next three years, except the $75 was raised to $100.

The $50 checks were by the treasurer of state on behalf of the college, and were marked "scholarship." The others were drawn by the coach on a special bank account contributed by the Mustang Booster Club and used to provide additional inducement to married students. Apparently the Mustang Booster Club also contributed the $150 per year paid by the state. During 1960 the decedent worked part-time for the athletic department of the college, liming the football field, on an hourly pay basis. On this state of facts, the court of appeal said:

> The uncontradicted evidence was that to receive an athletic scholarship a student must maintain a 2.2 grade average while carrying 12 units, must be a member of an athletic team, and be recommended by the coach to the scholarship committee. He recommended only those who were on the team.
>
> . . . .
>
> The only inference to be drawn from the evidence is that decedent received the "scholarship" because of his athletic prowess and participation. The form of remuneration is immaterial.
>
> A court will look through form to determine whether consideration has been paid for services.

---

[1] *Van Horn* v. *Industrial Accident Commission and California State Polytechnic College*, 219 (Cal. App.) 2d 457, 33 Cal. Rptr. 169 (1963).

Careful to decide only the case before it and not to lay down a sweeping dictum, the court added a delimiting paragraph:

> It cannot be said as a matter of law that every student who receives an "athletic scholarship" and plays on the school athletic team is an employee of the school. To so hold would be to thrust upon every student who so participates an employee status to which he has never consented and which would deprive him of the valuable right to sue for damages. Only where the evidence establishes a contract of employment is such an inference reasonably to be drawn.

But here, "There is no uncertainty in the record. The fact that the funds were contributed by the Mustang Booster Club is not determinative of who is the employer." Citing the two recent Colorado cases[2] that are in point, the court added that "Student teachers and student nurses have been held to be employees" and in support of this statement cited 22 Cal. Comp. Cas. 212 and 9 Cal. Comp. Cas. 295.

Thus the deceased football player was held to have been an employee of the college, and if his death was the result of a hazard of his employment his widow would be entitled to an award.

Workman Injured on Job at College Not Covered by Workmen's Compensation Act

At the Oklahoma College for Women, a painter, while working on a college building as employee of a contractor, was injured by falling from a scaffold and sought an award under the Oklahoma Workmen's Compensation Act. The trial court ordered the award to be granted, but this judgment was reversed by the state supreme court. In the opinion by Justice Irwin, it is held that the college is not covered by the Workmen's Compensation Act, and is not required to be; and painting, said the justice, is a job incidental to the governmental function of maintaining the college, and the college is protected by the doctrine of "governmental immunity," which was not questioned. No particular significance seems to have been assigned to

---

[2] *University of Denver* v. *Nemeth*, 127 Colo. 385, 257 P. 2d 423 (1953); and *State Compensation Insurance Fund* v. *Industrial Commission*, 135 Colo. 570, 314 P. 2d 288 (1957); both discussed at pages 128-129 in *The Colleges and the Courts Since 1950.*

the fact that the injured painter was not an employee of the college, but of a contractor.

A peculiar conjunction of statutory provisions and the facts of this case is so rare as to be almost amusing. The Workmen's Compensation Act expressly covers persons performing hazardous work at "state penitentiaries and reformatories, state mental hospitals, and state schools for the mentally retarded . . ." Actually, in the present case, a class for mentally retarded children was being conducted in the building on which the plaintiff painter was working at the time he was injured. Justice Irwin emphatically disposed of this coincidence: "There are no statutory provisions which remotely suggest that the College is or could be considered a school for mentally retarded. The fact that the College may have been conducting a class for mentally retarded children, does not constitute such institution a school for the mentally retarded."[3]

Alleged Libelous Communication Regarding University "Field Representative"

It seems that one Wallingford was employed as "Field Representative of the Department of Post-Graduate Medical Education, University of Kansas Medical Center," and that he was a private vendor of hearing aids on his own account. A district representative of the Zenith Radio Corporation, which is a competitor in the hearing aids field, wrote to the head of the department of hearing and speech at the University of Kansas Medical Center, reporting that Wallingford was using a University of Kansas station wagon to visit his private clients and demonstrate his hearing aids, thus confusing or deceiving them by causing them to believe mistakenly that his hearing aids were a product of or were indorsed by the University of Kansas Medical Center.

Wallingford sued the corporation for libel in the U.S. district court for northern Illinois, and from an adverse judgment appealed to the federal court of appeals, where Circuit Judge Duffy found that the letter in question was not libelous *per se* under Kansas law,

---

[3] *Melrose v. Oklahoma College for Women*, (Okla.), 393 P. 2d 878 (1964).

and affirmed the judgment of the district court.[4] Wallingford was operating in northern Illinois, and thus diversity of citizenship put the case within federal jurisdiction. The case is of a type in which federal courts interpret and follow the law of the state concerned.

Contract Photographer Fails to Obtain Recourse from Publisher Whom He Accuses of Unworkmanlike Job

A case which defies classification here because it does not involve a university employee as a party is that of a photographer who had done contract photographic work for Southern University at Baton Rouge for several years prior to 1963. He made the photographs for the University Yearbook (*The Cat*) for that year, and thereafter sued for recourse against the publisher of the book, alleging that the reproduction of the pictures was so poorly done that he had been unable to obtain any further contracts with the university.

Two officials of the university deposed that his misfortune was in no way based on the reproduction of his pictures in *The Cat* for 1963, but instead upon his habitual failure to meet agreed deadlines for furnishing pictures, and frequent failure to appear at the appointed time to take photographs of students and groups. This, they said, had delayed delivery of the 1963 *Cat* until after the end of the academic year. They also testified that the university's photographic department complained that many of his pictures were inferior on account of such defects as being out of focus, showing students with eyes closed, and not having good color tones; and for these reasons alone his contract was not renewed after 1963.

The court granted the defendant publisher's motion for summary dismissal of the complaint, on the ground that there was no privity of contract between the plaintiff and the defendant, and no evidence of any connection between the quality of the publisher's work and the university's refusal to deal further with the plaintiff photographer.[5]

---

[4] *Wallingford* v. *Zenith Radio Corporation*, (U.S.C.A.), 310 F. 2d 693 (1962).
[5] *Williams* v. *Taylor Publishing Company of Dallas, Texas*, (U.S.D.C., La.), 238 F. Supp. 587 (1965).

Labor Organizations and Collective Bargaining for
University and College Employees

The extent to which universities and colleges, public or private, are subject to the provisions of the acts of Congress relating to the regulation of industrial and labor relations, and to the jurisdiction of the National Labor Relations Board, seems to depend on whether the activities in which particular institutional employees are engaged may be deemed to have a substantial effect upon interstate commerce. Generally, this tends to be construed more and more liberally in favor of the national jurisdiction. There is no large body of judge-made law on the subject, and comparatively few pertinent decisions of the National Labor Relations Board.

In 1951 the board declined to take jurisdiction in a dispute involving clerical employees of the libraries of Columbia University;[6] but in 1954 it asserted jurisdiction in a labor dispute involving the employees of the Lincoln Laboratory, a nonprofit corporation associated with the Massachusetts Institute of Technology, doing research and development work exclusively for the federal government. This was on the new theory that at least some of the work was of so great value to the national defense that this alone justified taking jurisdiction.[7]

The same reasoning was employed to justify intervention in 1963 in a dispute involving certain employees of the Woods Hole Oceanographic Institution at Woods Hole, Massachusetts.[8] But in a 1965 dispute regarding employees of a computer center operated by the Massachusetts Institute of Technology, the board took a somewhat different view and declined jurisdiction, even though some of the work was sponsored by commercial organizations and some of it was related to the national defense. The reasoning seemed to be that the work was in large part and primarily so closely integrated with the instructional program of the institute itself that intervention could not properly be justified either on the ground of interstate commerce or defense-related importance.[9]

---

[6] *Trustees of Columbia University*, 97 N.L.R.B. 424 (1951).
[7] *Massachusetts Institute of Technology*, 110 N.L.R.B. 1161 (1954).
[8] *Woods Hole Oceanographic Institute*, 143 N.L.R.B. 568 (1963).
[9] *Massachusetts Institute of Technology*, 152 N.L.R.B. 64 (1965).

Regardless of the minutiae of specific cases, and of the seemingly vacillating jiggles in the curve, it should not be forgotten that the wave of the future is toward recognition everywhere of labor organizations and of the right of collective bargaining.

Status of Clerical Employees of New York State Community Colleges

Certain typists, clerks, and stenographers of a dozen years' standing as employees of public two-year colleges in the city of New York actually hold positions which were initially established by Chapter 525 of the Laws of 1952, at a time when none of these colleges was under the administration of the Board of Higher Education of the City of New York, which governed the four senior colleges often called the "city colleges" (City College, Hunter College, Brooklyn College, Queens College). In 1955 the Staten Island Community College was the first two-year college to be brought under the jurisdiction of the board of higher education.

Section 6214 of the Education Law provided for titles and salary schedules for "college office assistants" and "college secretarial assistants" under the board. This section was amended in 1959 (Chapter 600) to *except* community colleges administered by the board, and again in 1964 to *include* them. Meantime in 1964 the board adopted its first bylaws applicable to community colleges, "the effect of which was to adopt the titles and salary schedules established under the career and salary plan of the city of New York." A small group of employees whose service had spanned this period of vast confusion sued for a declaratory judgment entitling them to compensation for past and future services as "college office assistants" and "college secretarial assistants."

Their action failed, because the court noted that in 1964 bills intended to give them this same status were vetoed by the Governor; and, said the court: "The educational and experimental qualifications for the positions of college office assistant and college secretarial assistant in the four-year colleges under the board of higher education, set out in its bylaws pursuant to subdivision 3 of Section 6202 a, Education Law, differ from and are greater than those for the positions for which the petitioners qualified."[10]

A recent unsuccessful effort to get a court order which would have had the effect of covering nonacademic employees of the California state colleges into the general civil service system of the state is not discussed here, but reserved for treatment in Chapter 11 (Footnotes 6 and 7) because it is of far-reaching import in maintaining and developing optimum operating relationships between state institutions of higher education on the one hand, and various noneducational state administrative agencies on the other hand.[11]

Desegregation of Nonacademic Employees

The Hampton Training School for Nurses owns and operates the Dixie Hospital. It was maintaining a cafeteria and dining room for all employees, but white employees were allowed to eat in the large room adjacent to the cafeteria line, while Negro employees, though allowed to select their food in the same cafeteria line, were required to carry their trays a considerable distance down the hall to a small and crowded dining room reserved for Negroes only.

Three Negro nurses were discharged for violating the rule by eating in the "strictly white" dining room. They brought an action for re-instatement with back pay since the time of their discharge, under the Civil Rights Act of 1958 (42 United States Code Secs. 1981, 1983). Summary judgment against them was rendered in the United States district court, on the ground that their discharge was before the handing down of certain court decisions interpreting the statute, which could not be retroactive. On appeal, Circuit Judge Sobeloff, for the unanimous five circuit judges *en banc*, demolished that argument by pointing to a recent declaration by the United States Supreme Court: "Until a case has been finally adjudicated on direct appeal it is controlled by the most recent statutory and decisional law." [380 U.S. 127, 85 S.Ct. 806, 13 L.Ed. 2d 792 (1965).] Ac-

---

[10] *Arnow* v. *Board of Higher Education of City of New York*, 25 A.D. 2d 511, 267 N.Y.S. 2d 55 (1966).

[11] *California State Employees' Association* v. *Board of Trustees of California State Colleges*, (Cal. App.), 47 Cal. Rptr. 63 (1965); discussed in Chapter 11, *infra*.

cordingly the court ordered the nurses re-instated with back pay since the date of their discharge.[12]

---

[12] *Smith* v. *Hampton Training School for Nurses*, (U.S.C.A., Va.), 360 F. 2d 577 (1966); reversing (U.S.D.C., Va.), 243 F. Supp. 403 (1965).

CHAPTER 10

MEMBERS OF THE GOVERNING
BOARD; THE PRESIDENT;
CENTRAL ADMINISTRATIVE
OFFICERS

THE QUESTION OF THE COMPATIBILITY of being a member of a university or college governing board and simultaneously holding some other state or local public office is not new. In at least two instances (in Michigan and Arkansas) the office of a member of the state legislature has been declared incompatible with that of a member of the governing board of a state institution of higher education; and such a board member can not lawfully take or hold the office unless he resigns his seat in the legislature.[1]

Incompatibility of State College Board Membership
with Concurrent Membership in State Legislature

In Arkansas, Article V, section 10 of the state constitution stipu-

---

[1] In *Attorney General ex rel. Cook* v. *Burhans,* 304 Mich. 108, 7 N.W. 2d 370 (1942), discussed at page 34 in *The Colleges and the Courts, 1941-45,* it was held that the election of a state senator to the Board of Regents of the University of Michigan was void.

lates that "No Senator or Representative shall, during the term for which he shall have been elected, be appointed or elected to any civil office under this State."

Thus when a member of the state legislature was appointed a member of the board of trustees of Southern State College at Magnolia and undertook to serve as such, a taxpayer's suit was brought to enjoin him as the holder of two incompatible officers from holding one or the other, and for an accounting of any moneys received unlawfully while holding both. He was able to respond that he had received no pay or reimbursement of any kind for service on the board of trustees, and this simplified the matter somewhat.

The local chancery court refrained from deciding the matter, on the ground of lack of jurisdiction; but the state supreme court concluded that jurisdiction was in the chancery court and transferred the case back with instructions to enjoin the legislator from holding membership on the board of trustees of Southern State College during the term for which he was elected a member of the legislature. No accounting was required, in the absence of any evidence of fraudulent intent.[2]

Passing the Torch When a Governing Board is Renamed and Reconstituted

In Florida a statute of 1963 provided that the board of control, governing, under the general supervisory authority of the state board of education, all state universities in Florida, should be superseded on January 1, 1965, by a board of regents, contingent upon the adoption of a constitutional amendment in November 1964. The amendment was adopted.

The term of the outgoing governor, Farris Bryant, extended several days beyond January 1, 1965, prior to the inauguration of his successor, Haydon Burns. This circumstance gave Governor Bryant the opportunity and the duty of appointing the members of the new board of regents. Could he appoint them for full terms (terms of from one to nine years, so as to overlap) as provided in the statute? Governor Burns asked the state supreme court for an advisory opinion on this question.

---

[2] *Starnes* v. *Sadler*, 237 Ark. 325, 372 S.W. 2d 585 (1963).

The first issue to be settled was that of whether the members of the board of regents are state officers as contemplated by Section 27 of Article III of the constitution of Florida. To this the court responded affirmatively, and remarked that it is not a new question, because soon after the creation of the board of control by the legislature in 1905, the court had said:[3]

> The fact that there is no salary or emolument affixed to such office does not make it any the less a civil office, since salary or emolument, like an oath of office, is an incidental to the office, merely, and not a necessary element in the determination of its character.

Accordingly, the governor had the power to fill a vacancy "by appointment in accordance with law, and if such appointment is made when the Senate is not in session, the maximum term that it can be made for is to the last day of the ensuing session of the state Senate, or until a successor shall be appointed and confirmed by the Senate, whichever occurrence is first." The appointments of members of the board of regents by the predecessor governor were validly made for the period beginning January 1, 1965, "but expire on the last day of the ensuing session of the Senate . . . and any language in a commission purporting to extend an appointment beyond such date is ineffectual and void."[4]

Thus the new appointees of the outgoing Governor Farris could at best hold office for only a few weeks, unless reappointed by the incoming Governor Burns. Actually it seems that most of the Farris appointees resigned even before the expiration of their limited terms and were replaced by Burns appointees.

It should be noted here that while the device of long and overlapping terms tends to prevent any one governor from dominating the board by packing it with his own appointees, nevertheless the creation or reconstituting of such a board gives one governor the power to appoint the entire membership. This is an open temptation to any ambitious governor to increase his patronage by accomplishing a reorganization during his own tenure, and is one of the unsolved problems of state government.

The question of whether members of university and college gov-

---

[3] *In re Advisory Opinion to the Governor*, 49 Fla. 269, 39 So. 63 (1905).
[4] *In re Advisory Opinion to the Governor*, (Fla.), 171 So. 2d 539 (1965).

erning boards are "state officers" or "constitutional officers" or "civil officers" has been before the courts of at least half a dozen other states, and the decisions have been far from uniform. The question is more than merely academic. It is briefly discussed at pages 92 and 93 of Elliott and Chambers' *The Colleges and the Courts* (1936),[5] and the concluding sentence there, written 30 years ago, will bear repeating:

> While members of state institutional governing boards are generally recognized as public officers, yet numerous decisions exhibit a tendency to distinguish them at several points from the state officers of the traditional political departments, and to accord them a special status, the characteristics of which are determined with deferential regard to the usages of colleges and universities and with solicitude for the welfare of such institutions. It is not far-fetched to say that this indicates a recognition of higher education as a public function deserving of the exercise of social invention for the sake of its protection and advancement.

For a 1966 New Mexico decision differentiating the status of the governing board of a public junior college from that of "elective public officers" mentioned in Article VII, Section 2, constitution of New Mexico, see *Daniels* v. *Watson*, (N.M.), 410 P. 2d 193 (1966), cited and discussed in Chapter 11, *infra* herein.

Rule of Board of Trustees of State University of New York Regarding Selection of President

Selecting the president is often said to be the most important single duty of the governing board. In 1963 the Board of Trustees of the State University of New York adopted a rule that "No member of the administrative staff or faculty of any state-operated college or university in the State University of New York may be appointed to the chief administrative position of that same institution." Four months later it adopted Rule 63-208, extending the same prohibition to the local public two-year colleges. Section 355 of the New York Education Law gives the trustees of the State University power to "approve the appointment of the head of each statutory or contract college

---

[5] New York: Carnegie Foundation for the Advancement of Teaching, 562 pp. Now out of print, but available in university and college libraries, presidents' offices, state supreme court libraries, and large city public libraries.

and community college by the respective boards of trustees or other governing bodies of such institutions."

Three faculty members of the New York City Community College of Arts and Sciences asked the local supreme court for an order vacating the rules of the board of trustees above quoted, alleging that they were arbitrary and unreasonable. Justice Sydney F. Foster dismissed the petition, saying:

> A rule or policy is not arbitrary if any reasonable basis can be envisioned to support it. Here the respondent Board could conclude, within the exercise of fair discretion, that since the head of a college occupies an administrative position he should not be subjected to possible jealous factions in the faculty under him, or perhaps disloyalty from those with whom he has lately associated. The whole issue is one of educational administration, and the courts will not substitute their judgment for that exercised by the officials to whom administrative power has been delegated by the legislature.

Thus the court refrains from appraising the expediency, propriety, or wisdom of the rule, but merely concludes that since a reasonable basis for it seems possible, it must be left within the discretion of the Board of Trustees of the State University of New York.[6]

There is a strong and commendable tradition that a university governing board, whether governing one institution or wielding authority over many institutions, as here, should exercise its powers with the utmost restraint. The question remains very much open, then, as to whether the rule in question, applied uniformly to some 59 public institutions, is advisable.

University President's Right of Privacy

Another decision concerning a university president is that of the New York court of appeals regarding the rights of Father Theodore M. Hesburgh, president of the University of Notre Dame, as joint petitioner with his university for an injunction to prevent the release and circulation of the book and motion picture film entitled "John Goldfarb, Please Come Home." Father Hesburgh's averment was that the producers of the novel and the play used his name and

---

[6] *Kugler* v. *Board of Trustees of the State University of New York*, 45 Misc. 2d 239, 256 N.Y.S. 2d 409 (1964).

identity for purposes of trade and without his consent, in violation of Sections 50 and 51 of the New York Civil Rights Law. By a vote of four to two of the judges, with the chief justice not participating, the court denied the injunction, with the two dissenters writing a trenchant opinion in strong support of the pleas of Father Hesburgh and the University.[7]

The case is discussed in greater detail in Chapter 12, *infra*, under the subcaption "Protection of the Corporate Name and Symbols of a Private University or College."

Is University Psychiatrist Liable in Damages to Former Student Who Alleges Unfavorable Psychiatric Report in University Files Has Injured Him?

In the predecessor of this volume were two cases in which a former student of the University of Texas unsuccessfully sought recourse against the university and several of its administrative and medical officers for having adjudged him to be mentally disturbed and having procured his temporary commitment to the Austin State Hospital.[8]

The same plaintiff appeared in a third action in 1965, asking some $90,000 damages against the university psychiatrist, who he alleged had improperly diagnosed his condition in a letter retained in the university files, without having previously examined him, and had thereby unlawfully and wilfully or maliciously placed false information in his record which had acted as a detriment to his employability. Dismissal of the case in the trial court was affirmed by the court of civil appeals, where it was said:

> A possible new allegation of wrongdoing on the part of the appellee (psychiatrist) is that he had written a letter stating that appellant "was suffering either from a pre-senile psychosis or an early cerebral arteriosclerotic change," though he had not examined appellant and therefore could not have validly made such a diagnosis. Copies of the letter were retained in the files

---

[7] *University of Notre Dame du Lac* v. *Twentieth Century-Fox Film Corporation*, 259 N.Y.S. 2d 832, 15 N.Y. 2d 940, 207 N.E. 2d 508 (1965); affirming 22 A.D. 2d 452, 256 N.Y.S. 2d 301 (1965).

[8] *Morris* v. *Nowotny*, (Tex. Civ. App.), 323 S.W. 2d 301 (1959); *certiorari* denied, 361 U.S. 889, 80 S.Ct. 164, 4 L.Ed. 2d 124 (1959); and *Morris* v. *University of Texas*, (Tex. Civ. App.), 348 S.W. 2d 644 (1961); discussed at pages 137 and 345 in *The Colleges and the Courts Since 1950*.

at the University where prospective employers have access to them; and prospective employers had seen the letter and consequently had not employed him or had discharged him after employment.

Apparently these averments were found not to be supported by evidence of specific instances in the pleadings. Hence the issues of fact and law were not tried.[9]

---

[9] *Morris* v. *Roussos*, (Tex. Civ. App.), 397 S.W. 2d 504 (1965).

PART THREE

GOVERNMENT AND CHARITY

The Legal Status of Public Universities and Colleges

Private Universities and Colleges: Nonprofit Charitable Corporations

Cooperative Interactions Between Public and Private Agencies in Higher Education

Exemption from Property Taxes

Property Taxation of Other Types of Educational Agencies

State Taxes Other Than Property Taxes

Federal Taxation

CHAPTER 11

THE LEGAL STATUS OF PUBLIC UNIVERSITIES AND COLLEGES, INCLUDING TWO-YEAR COLLEGES

IN THIS AREA the cases may be said to fall into two general types: (1) those relating to the autonomy of the institutions (the courts are frequently asked to intervene in appropriate cases to prevent the operations of state universities from being hamstrung or brought to a standstill by overconstrictive administrative interpretations of constitutions or statutes, or by overzealous state fiscal officers); and (2) litigation concerned with the birth-pangs of local public community colleges or other incidents of their relationships to local civil subdivisions or established educational agencies in their respective states. It is well known that these two-year institutions are being established at the rate of 20 to 30 per year, and that the amount of relevant litigation is considerable.

North Dakota State Board of Higher Education
Held Subject to Detailed Legislative Control

Chapter 155 of the 1965 Session Laws of North Dakota authorized the sale of bonds and directed that "The proceeds . . . are hereby appropriated to the State Board of Higher Education for use in the construction and equipping of facilities authorized by this Act at state institutions of higher education as determined by the Board and in accordance with such schedule of priorities as may be prescribed by such Board."

The state supreme court thought this was a classical case of unconstitutional delegation of legislative power, and held it void:[1]

> In this case the Legislature has not determined the question of the necessity of any particular type of building, at any particular institution, nor laid down any rule to guide the Board in determining these questions. It has authorized the construction of facilities at some or all of the institutions. It has attempted to delegate to the Board the power to determine what facilities shall be constructed at the different institutions, and the amount, if any, to be expended at each. This, we find, is an unconstitutional delegation of legislative authority. . . . It is not necessary to pass on the other challenges to the constitutionality of the Act.

Among the "other challenges" was the apparently valid one that the act authorized the establishing of "student facilities fees" to pay half the amortization cost, and thus violated Section 148 of the North Dakota constitution, which provides for "a system of free public schools extending through all grades up to and including the normal and collegiate course." The board had already fixed this fee at $15 per year per student; and one of the plaintiffs in this suit was a taxpayer who had two sons attending the University of North Dakota, each of whom had been required to pay the fee of $7.50 per semester.

The upshot of the decision is that, although the North Dakota State Board of Higher Education was created by a constitutional amendment in 1938, it is adjudged to be in the category of higher educational governing boards which are *established* or *otherwise mentioned* in the state constitutions, but *not given a sphere of autonomy* independent of the authority of the state legislatures. About half the 50 state universities receive some sort of mention in the state constitutions, but scarcely more than half a dozen of them (Michigan, Minnesota, California, Idaho, Colorado, Nevada, Arizona, Georgia) have a judicially guarded sphere of independence from the legislature and from the state administrative and fiscal offices.

---

[1] *Nord* v. *Guy*, (N.D.), 141 N.W. 2d 395 (1966).

Justice Knudson, writing the opinion of the North Dakota court, apparently chose the view that the present board has no wider powers than its predecessor, the state board of administration, which had been created by the legislature. He adhered tightly to *stare decisis* by relying heavily upon two decisions of the same court of a generation ago, in one of which a legislative act of 1927 (intended to authorize the construction of self-liquidating dormitories) was held invalid because it did not limit the amount to be spent for any particular building, and because all details regarding the number and character of the buildings to be erected were left to the discretion of the board of administration.[2]

In the second of these old decisions, a new act, drafted to obviate the objections of the court and enacted in 1929, was subsequently sustained by the court.[3] Thus the decision of 1966 is consistent with the court's precedents, regardless of any doubts that may arise regarding its construction of the constitutional amendment of 1938 and subsequent relevant legislation.

Illinois State Building Authority (Acting for State Universities) Is Not Subject to Certain Restrictions of State Purchasing Act

The Illinois State Purchasing Act (Illinois Revised Statutes, 1963, Chapter 127, Paragraph 132.6) requires that state agencies soliciting bids for the construction of buildings must advertise for *separate* bids for plumbing, air conditioning, electrical wiring, and heating, for each project, in contradistinction to a *single* bid for all types of work involved in the project. The University of Illinois followed this required practice in soliciting bids on Phase II of its Chicago Circle Campus in Chicago, but rejected all bids in August 1965 because they aggregated some 51 per cent above estimated costs. The University board of trustees did not advertise for bids a second time, but turned that responsibility over to the Illinois State Building Au-

---

[2] *Wilder* v. *Murphy*, 56 N.D. 436, 218 N.W. 156 (1928).
[3] *State ex. rel. Kaufman* v. *Davis*, 59 N.D. 191, 229 N.W. 105 (1930).

Both these cases are cited and discussed briefly at page 483 in *The Colleges and the Courts* (1936), by Edward C. Elliott and M. M. Chambers, New York: Carnegie Foundation for the Advancement of Teaching, 1936. 562 pp.

thority, a separate public corporation which is authorized to finance buildings by borrowing and to amortize the cost by leasing them to the state agencies using them. The building authority thereupon promptly advertised for *single bids* for all of the work and was ready to proceed with the construction when, in a suit brought by certain disgruntled electrical contractors, the circuit court of Cook County erroneously held that the building authority was subject to the Purchasing Act requirement prohibiting the taking of *single bids*. This threatened to halt further progress until a decision of the Illinois supreme court in January 1966 set matters aright.

Justice Underwood, for the supreme court, held that the building authority is not a "state agency" within the meaning of the Purchasing Act, and that it does not expend or encumber state funds "by virtue of annual or biennial appropriations from the General Assembly." Hence there is no legal objection to its use of the *single bid* method of letting contracts.[4]

He pointed out that the building authority, created by an act of 1961 (IRS Chapter 127, Paragraph 213.1) had been judicially declared to be a separate corporate entity, distinct from the state, and that its power to borrow and spend did not create debts against the state or violate the debt referendum section of the state constitution.[5]

For a somewhat similar New York decision regarding the independent character of the New York Dormitory Authority as a "public benefit corporation," compare the case of *Schumacher and Forelle, Inc.* v. *Johnson,* 47 Misc. 2d 65, 261 N.Y.S. 2d 943 (1965), cited and discussed in Chapter 21, *infra* herein. For litigation involving the site of the Chicago Circle Campus of the University of Illinois, see also *Harrison-Halsted Community Group, Inc.* v. *Housing and Home Finance Agency,* (U.S.C.A. 7th Cir.), 310 F. 2d 99 (1962), in Chapter 22.

California Constitutional Prohibition of Civil Service
Encroachment upon State Colleges

In California, a constitutional amendment of 1934 (Article XXIV,

---

[4]*Electrical Contractors' Association of City of Chicago* v. *Illinois Building Authority,* 33 Ill. 2d 587, 213 N.E. 2d 761 (1966).
[5]*Berger* v. *Howlett,* (Ill.), 182 N.E. 2d 673 (1962).

section 4, subdivision a) exempts employees of the "state teachers colleges" from civil service.

At that time these colleges were governed by the state board of education through its division of state colleges and teacher education. Employees in that division were under civil service.

In 1960 the Donahoe Act abolished that division and transferred its functions to the new Board of Trustees of State Colleges. Some of the employees were transferred from the old central office to the new, but gave up their civil service status. As to the campus employees of the colleges themselves, they have consistently been ruled exempt from civil service in a series of at least five opinions of the Attorney General, spread over a quarter of a century from 1938 to 1961.

Now comes an effort to impugn the transaction of 1960 by maintaining that it is unlawful to reduce the coverage of the civil service system by abolishing jobs and transferring their functions; and that even the campus employees of the state colleges should be under civil service because in 1934, when the amendment was adopted, they were actually employees of the division (central office) and not of the "state teachers colleges" in the language of the amendment. (They were at that time appointed by the state director of education, but only on the recommendation of their respective college presidents.)

The pleading was dismissed in superior court, and this disposition was affirmed in the district court of appeal, in an opinion by Justice Devine in which his two colleagues concurred.

To sustain the plea would be in effect to say the amendment of 1934 was meaningless and useless from the moment of its adoption, the court pointed out. Said the forthright Justice Devine: "A person generally is considered employed by the institution for which he works."

Showing a keen understanding of public higher education, he then quickly refuted the contention that the size and offerings of the state colleges have expanded so greatly that they are no longer the institutions meant by the words "state teachers colleges":[6]

> It cannot be gainsaid that the institutions have grown enormously, as what has not? Their curricula are vastly expanded, and

---

[6] *California State Employees' Association* v. *Board of Trustees of California State Colleges*, (Cal. App.), 47 Cal. Rptr. 73 (1965).

their organization is much more centralized. But they do educate teachers, together with aspirants to other vocations. But more than this, the colleges are part of the prized system of higher education. The exemption from civil service, it would appear, is not made because *teachers* were and are educated in these institutions of advanced learning, but because *people* were and are provided with higher education in these colleges, and because it has been thought that the whole system should be in control of persons responsible for proficiency in education.

The exemption has to do with the function of education, rather than with any particular profession for which the students may be trained. This appears from the cognate exemption, contained in the next preceding subdivision of the article in the Constitution, of all employees of the University of California.

The exception, constitutionally granted, should not be deemed lost merely because the functions of the teachers colleges have been greatly enlarged and the colleges' title has been changed.

The foregoing decision is a rebuke to more than one all-too-prevalent fuzzy thought, such as the idea that educational institutions should be run by remote control from central noneducational state offices, and the equally misguided notion that the larger and more complex a system becomes, the more tightly centralized its management must be.

A companion case, decided at the same time, challenged the right of the state colleges to employ architects other than those who are civil service employees. The court of appeal held that architects employed by the state colleges are within the same constitutional exemption as other nonacademic employees.

Moreover, said the court explicitly, it is not necessary, prior to such employment, to make any factual finding that the work could not adequately be performed by the state architect.[7]

A State University Can Lawfully Offer Course
Entitled "The Bible as Literature"

The University of Washington at Seattle has offered continuously since 1919 an elective course on "The Bible as Literature." Such offer-

---

[7] *California State Employees' Association* v. *Board of Trustees of California State Colleges,* (Cal. App.), 47 Cal. Rptr. 81 (1965). For other cases involving various aspects of the employment and status of nonacademic employees of universities and colleges, see Chapter 9, *supra.*

ings are common among state universities. In 1966 two Fundamentalist preachers, of the sect known as Bible Presbyterians—Thomas Miller of Seattle and Harold Webb of Tacoma, sued to compel the university to drop the course, contending that it was sectarian teaching in that it presented a one-sided, ultramodern, non-Fundamentalist viewpoint.

Their petition was dismissed by Superior Court Judge W. R. Cole of Seattle, who is reported in the press to have said: "I believe the Bible as literature is a proper subject in the humanistic field." Further, "This course . . . is an elective course. It is not required." It is understood that an appeal has been taken; but it is highly unlikely that this will result in any change in the decision. It is quite well established that public universities and colleges may teach the Bible as literature and that they may teach, and indeed must teach, in a secular and nonproselyting manner, such subjects as church history and comparative religions if they are to afford their students a grasp of history and philosophy.

Voluntary Extracurricular Student Religious Organizations Are Permissible in State Colleges and Universities

The Attorney General of New Jersey has ruled that there is no violation of the First Amendment to the United States Constitution involved in recognizing denominational clubs such as Canterbury Clubs, Lutheran Associations, Newman Clubs, Hillel Societies, and Westminster Clubs at the state colleges, and permitting them reasonable use of the college facilities for their activities.

He said with much cogency that "excessive application of the Establishment Clause effectively limiting or barring religious expression, might well be deemed to be violative of the Free Exercise guaranty"; and that "the duty to be neutral should not be taken to impose a requirement of abstention or abnegation."[8]

Relationship Between State University Teaching Hospital and Township Welfare Agency in Indiana

Frequently there are state statutes or other arrangements which

---

[8] New Jersey Attorney General's *Formal Opinion*, 1965, No. 1.

provide for the care of indigent welfare patients in state university hospitals maintained primarily as teaching facilities for schools of medicine, nursing, or other health professions.

Under such circumstances the hospital is playing a double role—that of a teaching facility of the university and that of a welfare agency of the state. Usually there is some prescribed method of reimbursing the hospital for the care of indigent welfare patients, either by payment by the state directly, or by its local subdivisions.

It seems that in Indiana the townships are responsible for these payments on behalf of indigent patients who are legally domiciled within their borders. A case arose in which an indigent person who had once resided and received welfare payments in a rural township, but had left that township and not subsequently established a "legal settlement" in any other local subdivision, eventually entered the hospital of the Indiana University Medical Center at Indianapolis and received care and treatment. When the University billed the township for this service, the township resisted payment on the ground that the recipient of the service was not "legally settled" within its borders at the time he received the service.

The decision of the court of appeal was that the township must pay, because for welfare purposes, once a person has established a legal settlement, he does not lose it until and unless he has established another legal settlement elsewhere.[9]

A Gift to a State University Should Create a Trust, Said Sveinbjorn Johnson

Apropos of the semisemantic squabble that has been in progress for 30 years since the appearance of the *Restatement: Trusts* prepared by the American Law Institute, as to whether a gift to a charitable corporation can create a technical trust or whether the charitable corporation takes as absolute owner, there is a bit of advice available from an eminent source regarding the same question applied to a state university.

In a letter of December 7, 1937, Sveinbjorn Johnson, distinguished

---

[9] *Trustees of Indiana University* v. *Montgomery Township of Owen County*, (Ind. App.), Division No. 2, (1964).

jurist and at that time professor of law and general counsel for the University of Illinois, wrote to Thomas E. Blackwell:[10]

> The paragraph from the *Restatement* may be a sound rule for the courts to adopt in appropriate factual situations. . . . The idea, however, that the donor of a fund to a state university who directs the investment of the principal and the use of the income for a stated purpose would view with equanimity the news that the donee treated the principal as well as the income as an unrestricted gift appears to me to be an unwarranted and unsafe assumption of complacency in the giver of the gift. If it were to be known that the University of Illinois, in situations of the type described, treated the gift as its absolute property and not encumbered in any sense with a trust, I am clearly of the opinion that friends who otherwise might have considered donations for purposes near their hearts would hesitate and probably place their bounty elsewhere.
>
> . . . .
>
> In any event, I do not know of a single gift of the type we are now discussing made to the University of Illinois which I could be willing to advise the Board of Trustees to treat as absolute and not impressed with a trust character. I should, . . . unless the circumstances be very clear to the effect that the gift is absolute, advise the Board to take the matter into court and obtain a formal adjudication which would protect that body against future challenge.

Fortunately there has appeared within the past decade at least one state supreme court decision that private gifts to public institutions of higher education are to be regarded with favor and construed liberally in favor of the donor's clear intent. The West Virginia supreme court of appeals has declared a bequest of a fund to the Bluefield State College as permanent endowment must be applied in accord with the testator's wish, and has ordered a recalcitrant state auditor to release the income of the fund to the college upon proper requisition from its governing board.[11] In this manner public confidence that private gifts to state universities and colleges are as inviolate as

---

[10] Quoted by Thomas E. Blackwell in his article, "The Charitable Corporation and the Charitable Trust." *Washington University Law Quarterly* 24: 1-45 (December 1938).

The much-mooted *Restatement* clause receives attention in Chapter 5, *supra*, and Chapter 12, *infra*, in connection with decisions concerned with it in varying circumstances.

[11] *State ex rel. West Virginia Board of Education* v. *Sims*, 143 W. Va. 269, 101 S.E. 2d 190 (1957). Discussed at page 159 in *The Colleges and the Courts Since 1950*.

gifts to private nonprofit organizations and institutions can be strengthened.

Authorization of Property Taxation for School Districts
Is Construed to Include Junior College Districts in Texas

In 1962 the Texas supreme court held, though not without a division of opinion, that the constitutional provisions authorizing *ad valorem* taxation for "school districts" whether "heretofore or hereafter formed" (Article V, section 3 b; Article VII, section 3) were broad enough to embrace public junior college districts within their meaning. Justice Norvell wrote for the majority of the court, and Justice Griffin contributed a separate concurring opinion. There was a lengthy dissent by Chief Justice Calvert, joined by Justice Walker, arguing that junior college districts are not school districts, but college districts; and that junior colleges in Texas are not tuition-free, as are public schools.[12]

Forming Public Junior College District in Oregon

Oregon statutes provide that at a specific stage in the process of bringing to life a new public junior college district, the state board of education must hold locally a public hearing on the matter of "fixing of boundaries of an area educational district for junior college purposes." At a later stage the action of the board is subject to approval in a popular election within the district.

A recent case turned upon the exact nature of the hearing required by law. Must it be an "adversary" hearing, with care taken to have opposing witnesses confront and cross-examine each other, and otherwise conducted with the formalities and safeguards of a court proceeding, or may it be merely an "auditive" hearing, in which persons present are given reasonable opportunity to state their views on either side of the issue, without the formalities of an exact stenographic record and other trappings of a full-scale judicial proceeding?

In this case the board's authorized representative held a duly pub-

---

[12] *Shepherd* v. *San Jacinto Junior College District,* (Tex.), 363 S.W. 2d 742 (1962).

lished hearing pursuant to ORS 341.730 and ORS 341.740, in which those present were permitted to express their views as to the desirability of establishing the district and as to the fixing of its boundaries. The only record was the *minutes* recording the name of each person who spoke, with a short summary of the views of each in a sentence or two. The board later issued an order fixing the boundaries of the district; and when a taxpayer therein asked the circuit court of Douglas County to invalidate it, the court reviewed the whole proceeding and reversed and remanded the board's order, because there was "no evidence which the court could review, and no evidence upon which the Board could have made its finding."

The supreme court of Oregon reversed this decision with some asperity, saying the whole matter was more appropriate for legislative than for judicial determination, and declaring that

> Residents and taxpayers do not have any personal or property rights in a particular school district boundary arrangement which are entitled to be asserted in an adversary proceeding in frustration of the board's (state board of education's) effort to carry out its policy-making function.

Hence the rather informal "auditive" hearing was sufficient to satisfy the requirements of the statute.[13]

Two Stillborn Junior College Districts in Wyoming

In an effort to reorganize and enlarge the Casper Community College District by creating it anew in expanded form, under Wyoming Statutes 1957, section 21-446, prior to its amendment by Chapter 223, Special Laws of 1961, it was found that the undertaking was definitely defeated by the fact that some of the school districts composing the proposed junior college district turned in majorities against the proposal at the popular elections which were then required as a part of the process.[14]

In Wyoming the state's part in the leadership and oversight of the network of public two-year colleges is through a body known as

---

[13] *Mohr* v. *State Board of Education*, 236 Ore. 398, 388 P. 2d 463 (1964).

[14] *Casper Community College District* v. *Natrona County High School District*, (Wyo.), 384 P. 2d 319 (1963).

the Community College Commission, which is in considerable degree virtually an agency of the University of Wyoming, with its membership including the executive officer and one member of the board of trustees of each approved community college district in the state. (Wyoming Statutes 1957, section 21-313.)

After the failure of an attempt to establish a Fremont County Junior College District under the statutes then in force, in January 1961 the board of trustees of the Fremont County Vocational High School District proceeded on their own initiative to organize by resolution the Fremont County Vocational Junior College, and hired teachers and other employees, invited students, and began negotiation with the Community College Commission and appropriate officials of the University of Wyoming regarding the accreditation of the new college and its representation on the commission.

Having been met with some coolness, the high school district eventually sued for a writ of *mandamus* to command the commission to declare its superintendent of schools, John W. Beng, and one member of its board of trustees, Carl Browall, full members of the Community College Commission. The writ was denied. Chief Justice Parker pointed out that a reading of the relevant statutes made it clear that *only* a school district or high school district *voting a special levy for the purpose* was authorized to establish and operate a junior college. This had not been done by the Fremont County district. Hence the resolution of its board of trustees of January 1961 was a nullity, and its "vocational junior college" had no legal existence.[15]

New Mexico Junior College Act of 1963 Is Constitutional

Under a junior college act of 1963, amended in 1964, New Mexico duly created a "New Mexico Junior College" in Lea County in 1964, with a 5-member governing board. A $3 million bond issue was approved, and the board organized itself and appointed a president of the institution in anticipation of opening its doors in September 1966.

The statute provided that initially the board members should be

---

[15] *State ex rel. Fremont County Vocational High School District* v. *Community College Commission*, (Wyo.), 393 P. 2d 803 (1964).

appointed; and moreover required that they be residents of the district and owners of real estate in the district. The constitutionality of the act was challenged because Article VII, Section 2 of the constitution of New Mexico stipulates:

> Every citizen of the United States who is a legal resident of the state and is a qualified voter therein, shall be qualified to hold any elective public office except as otherwise provided in this Constitution.

The state supreme court decided that a member of a junior college governing board is not such a public officer as is contemplated in the quoted section, and hence there is no conflict between the constitution and the junior college act. Furthermore, the court took occasion to make clear its view that junior college districts are not to be necessarily regarded as subject to all the constitutional provisions relating to schools and school districts. "The legislature did not intend the junior college districts to come within the general school system."[16] This view seems educationally wise as well as legally sound.

Relationships Between Community College and County on Which It Is Based in New York State

In 1961 New York Education Law, section 6305 (6), set forth three methods of disbursement of a county's contribution to the operating expenses of its county community college, and authorized the "local legislative board" to select any one of the three. The Oneida County Board of Supervisors selected "Plan C" and used it in disbursing funds to the Mohawk Valley Community College. Thereafter the board adopted a new county charter subject to approval by the voters in November 1961, and included in the new charter an express repeal of the resolution selecting "Plan C." The charter was approved at the polls.

The same new charter transferred the power to appoint the members of the community college board of trustees (until then residing in the county board of supervisors) to the county executive subject to confirmation by the board. Education Law, section 6305 (1), gave

---

[16] *Daniels* v. *Watson,* (N.M.), 410 P. 2d 193 (1966).

this power to "the local legislative board, or other appropriate governing agency."

Both of the just-described provisions of the new charter were challenged, and a declaratory judgment regarding the status of both was sought. The appellate division, in an opinion by Justice Del Vecchio, with the other four justices concurring, held that (1) "Plan C" must continue in force, because the statute authorized the choice among the three plans to be made by the board, and did not authorize the question to be submitted to the voters; and (2) the transfer of the appointing power from the board to the executive with confirmation by the board was valid and effective, because the statute gave it either to the board "or to some other appropriate governmental agency."[17]

Interpretation of Various Statutes in Different States

Three additional decisions of 1965 and 1966 do not seem to concern matters of unusual importance or principles of very wide applicability.

The Illinois Public Junior College Act, which became effective July 15, 1965, did not halt the building program of the Triton Junior College District (Northlake, Cook County), which had authorized the sale of $8,900,000 of site and building bonds at an election in March of that year. The successful suit for a writ of *mandamus* to compel the secretary of the district to sign the bonds was apparently a routine "friendly suit" to add to the attractiveness of the bonds by getting court "validation."[18]

The Clarendon Junior College District in Texas authorized its regents to levy a property tax up to 85 cents per $100 valuation, at an election in January 1964. The result of the election was contested on grounds too numerous to be recorded here, and an injunction was asked for to prevent the collection of the tax. The court of civil

---

[17] *Daugherty* v. *Oneida County*, 22 A.D. 2d 111, 254 N.Y.S. 2d 372 (1964).
[18] *People ex rel. Board of Education of Junior College School District No. 300*, 34 Ill. 2d 349, 217 N.E. 2d 1 (1966).

appeals, affirming the judgment of the trial court, decided that "the election was a true expression of the will of the voters."[19]

A California statute (Education Code, Section 25541.5) providing for the raising of special tax revenues to pay obligations incurred under interdistrict attendance agreements is literally construed to mean that the proceeds are to be used first for obligations incurred during the year when the revenue was raised, and that any excess may be used only for obligations of the following year. Hence such revenues can not be expended for obligations incurred in a prior year.[20]

Public Junior College History in Kentucky

The city of Paducah in western Kentucky established a locally supported and locally controlled public two-year college in 1932, which has been operated continuously since that year. In the 'Thirties the Ashland Independent School District, at the northeastward extremity of the state, also began to operate a junior college program. A Kentucky court of appeals decision of 1937 sustained the validity of legislation authorizing a second-class city to establish junior college instruction.[21] The Ashland program has continued to the present, and is the subject of litigation in a 1966 case.

Although in the 'Thirties some of Kentucky's moderately populous centers seemed eager to create local junior colleges, since World War II much of this enthusiasm seems to have waned, and the idea of the locally supported and locally controlled junior college has been largely supplanted by the policy of "educational colonizing" by the establishing of branches of the University of Kentucky in several appropriate places in various parts of the state. These are wholly owned and controlled by the university, and operated entirely at its expense.

The Ashland Community College is an exception. It has had a 7-cent local levy since 1937. In 1957 the Ashland Independent School

---

[19] *Sawyer* v. *Board of Regents of Clarendon Junior College,* (Tex. Civ. App.), 393 S.W. 2d 391 (1965).
[20] *West Valley Joint Junior College District of Santa Clara County* v. *Timpany,* 47 Cal. Rptr. 785, 408 P. 2d 113 (1965).
[21] *Pollitt* v. *Lewis,* 269 Ky. 680, 108 S.W. 2d 671, 113 A.L.R. 691 (1937).

District made an agreement with the University of Kentucky whereby the university would furnish the faculty and the curricular offerings, but the local levy would be continued unchanged, apparently chiefly to provide physical facilities. The district reserved the right to abrogate the agreement if and when it might appear that the district's needs were not being satisfactorily served by it. On December 31, 1964, after it had become apparent that the small downtown site and building could not meet the needs, a supplementary agreement was added, under which the district would furnish a larger new site, to become the property of the university, unencumbered. (The district and the university were in agreement concerning the desirability of acquiring a specific 43-acre site.) The district agreed to procure the establishment of a nonprofit corporation under Kentucky Statutes Chapter 273 to acquire title to the new site and to hold title to both sites and issue first mortgage bonds to finance the purchase of the new one. The district leases the new site, paying agreed rentals to the corporation, solely out of the proceeds of the 7-cent levy. Title to portions of the site on which the university erects buildings (not to exceed 80 per cent of it) will be transferred to the university as soon as each building is erected.

Local taxpayers sued for a declaratory judgment that the agreement was invalid and there was no necessity of continuing the local levy. In the trial court, judgment was against them on both issues, and this was affirmed by the court of appeals.[22] Commissioner Davis, writing the opinion for the court, concluded that the district did not unlawfully delegate or surrender its powers to maintain and operate a junior college, particularly because it reserved the right to terminate the contract. Nor does the contract require a perpetual levy of the special tax, as was contended. The commissioner believed that without the agreement the survival of a junior college at Ashland would have been doubtful, and was inclined to praise this example of intergovernmental cooperation.

---

[22] *Montague* v. *Board of Education of Ashland Independent School District,* (Ky.), 402 S.W. 2d 94 (1966).

CHAPTER 12

PRIVATE UNIVERSITIES AND
COLLEGES: NONPROFIT
CHARITABLE CORPORATIONS

IF A PRIVATE COLLEGE holds a charter as a nonprofit charitable corporation, and thus is a legal entity and an "artificial person," it is logical to think first of the source of its being and its continuing relationships with that source. Charters are granted by the states (and rarely by the federal government, as in the cases of the private universities in the District of Columbia).

Except where a charter has been granted without any reservation of the right to amend or repeal (as in the renowned Dartmouth College case), the state retains in theory a great deal of power over the corporation; but in nearly two centuries of practice the states have generally exercised only the lightest of surveillance over private colleges, leaving them largely free to manage their own academic and fiscal affairs. Under this policy some of the world's greatest universities have flourished, and hundreds of denominational and nonsectarian private colleges have played significant parts in the pageant of American progress.

From time to time some statutory regulations are imposed upon them for various reasons, chiefly to prevent fraud upon the public

through misinformation or through grossly unethical practices such as
the sale of diplomas or degrees. Some recent cases involving such
regulative measures appear.

Statutory Regulation of Private Institutions

A Connecticut statute of nearly 20 years' standing provides:

> Section 10-6. . . .(c). No person, school, board, association
> or corporation shall use in any way the term "junior college"
> or "college" or "university" in connection with an institution,
> or use any other name, title or descriptive matter tending to
> designate that it is an institution of higher learning with the
> power to grant academic or professional degrees, unless the insti-
> tution is operating under a license or a certificate of accreditation
> from the state board of education, or has been authorized to
> grant degrees in accordance with the provisions of this section.
>
> The provisions of this section shall not apply to any insti-
> tution of learning which used the term "junior college" or
> "college" or "university" in its name for a period of at least
> five years prior to October 1, 1947.

When a recent effort was made to enjoin a school in Bristol known
as De Witt Hall from operating in disregard of this statute, the trial
court granted the injunction, but this decree was reversed and remanded by the Connecticut supreme court of errors and appeals, with
direction to sustain the defendant's demurrer (plea of no cause of
action).

The last sentence in the quoted part of the statute, said the court,
makes the whole section unconstitutional and invalid, because there is
"no way of knowing whether a pre-1942 school might or might not
mislead the public in the future" and there is no reason sufficient to
support the discriminatory classification set up by the five-year loophole.[1]

The District of Columbia Code of 1901, amended in 1929 (Title
29, Sections 416-419) authorizes the board of education to issue
licenses to educational institutions to confer degrees. Such a license
was issued in 1951 to the National Art School, later renamed National
Art Academy, to confer the degree of Bachelor of Fine Arts. A

---

[1] *State of Connecticut* v. *De Witt School, Inc.,* 151 Conn. 631, 201 A. 2d
472 (1964).

dozen years later, after preliminary investigation and formal hearings, the board revoked the license for failure to comply with the standards prescribed by law.

In an action to review this determination, the United States district court for the District of Columbia conceived its duty to be to consider whether the board had made any error of law, whether its findings of fact were supported by substantial evidence, and whether its action was arbitrary or capricious. It decided that the board's decision should stand, and that the statute under which it was made was constitutional. It softened the blow, however, by commenting: "The school, although called the National Art Academy, is really a school for the teaching of commercial art and design. . . . the range of instruction is narrow. . . . The revocation of the power to grant the degree of Bachelor of Fine Arts is not to be taken as an indication that the school is not doing satisfactory or constructive work. It merely does not reach the high standard, or serve the big purposes of educational institutions that have the power to confer degrees."[2]

The power of the state to regulate the licensing of practitioners in the professions is often exercised in such ways as to affect significantly the conduct and fate of the professional schools, through what may be called a species of "indirect regulation." One of many examples is the Medical Practice Act of Louisiana, which, though exempting certain named specialties in the healing arts from its provisions, expressly requires chiropractors to meet all the requirements for the practice of medicine.

Certain chiropractors asked for an injunction to restrain the state medical examiners' board from enforcing this act against them, but the injunction was denied by the federal district court, with the following reasoning:[3]

> As broadly defined by its proponents, chiropractic is a healing art designed to relieve human ailments by manipulation and adjustments of the spine. It is chiropractic doctrine that most, if not all, human ailments result from a slight misalignment, or subluxation, of contiguous vertebrae. . . . The realignment of these subluxated vertebrae through manipulation of the spine

---

[2] *Kraft* v. *Board of Education for the District of Columbia*, (U.S.D.C., D.C.), 247 F. Supp. 21 (1965).

[3] *England* v. *Louisiana State Board of Medical Examiners*, (U.S.D.C., La.), 246 F. Supp. 993 (1965).

by the chiropractor removes the impingement and restores the
nerve function to the diseased parts of the body. . . .

. . . .

At the outset it should be noted that the laws of the State
of Louisiana do not prohibit the practice of chiropractic. The
question here is: May Louisiana require a chiropractor to obtain
what is in effect a medical education from an approved medical school before he may practice his profession in the state?
Suffice it to say that on this record we are unable to hold that
the Legislature of Louisiana has acted irrationally or unreasonably in the premises . . .

. . . .

There has been no showing here that the state has done
more than is necessary to protect the health of its citizens.
A difference of opinion as to whether one who purports to
practice a complete healing art should have a medical education
is not proof of unreasonable disregard of the plaintiffs' rights.

In California the state medical association, the state osteopathic association, and a private osteopathic college recently entered
into a merger agreement contemplating that the college would convert
to and become accredited as an allopathic medical college, and would
grant degrees of M.D. to licensed osteopaths in the state of California without examination or attendance at the college. These were
features of a plan which also contemplated that the college would be
acquired by the state and become a tax-supported public institution,
and that the two professions of allopathic and osteopathic medicine,
having hitherto had separate medical colleges, separate licensing, and
separate professional associations, would become united into one.

When the agreement regarding degrees was challenged on the
ground that it would violate the statutes prohibiting barter or sale of
medical degrees, a court of appeal held, in an 8,000-word opinion, that
it would not contravene the statute.[4] Other actions regarding other
aspects of the whole transaction include one to be noticed next herein.

*Alleged Breach of Trust When Private Osteopathic College
Agrees to Become Allopathic Medical School*

The College of Osteopathic Physicians and Surgeons was incor-

---

[4] *Osteopathic Physicians and Surgeons* v. *California Medical Association*,
224 Cal. App. 2d 378, 36 Cal. Rptr. 641 (1964).

porated in 1914, and after approximately 50 years of operation entered into the above-mentioned plan to convert itself into an allopathic institution and to seek membership in the Association of American Medical Colleges and the Council on Medical Education and Hospitals of the American Medical Association. These organizations are the voluntary accrediting agencies for medical colleges in the United States.

Three of the 26 trustees of the college opposed the plan and regarded it as a repudiation of the original charitable purpose of the nonprofit corporation, and, as such, a breach of trust. Accordingly they sued in the superior court of Los Angeles County to enjoin the breach of trust and for declaratory relief. The attorney general did not bring the suit on their behalf, and he was not a party to it. The majority trustees entered a demurrer (plea of no cause of action). The superior court sustained the demurrer and dismissed the case; but both the court of appeal and the California supreme court successively held that the dismissal was erroneous and must be reversed.[5]

The two upper-echelon courts were also in accord that the California Osteopathic Association was an indispensable party, because the college had contracted with it to execute the projected plan. This necessitated a reformation of the action, and no further report is presently available.

Judge Nourse, justice *pro tem* in the court of appeal, said:

> Each trustee has a duty to see that the funds of the corporation are not diverted to purposes other than those set forth in the articles of incorporation, and in the event that the attorney general fails to act, any trustee may do so.

In so holding, he ran counter to the 1954 decision of the court of appeal in *George Pepperdine Foundation* v. *George Pepperdine*, 126 Cal. App. 2d 154, 271 P. 2d 600 (1954), which was to the contrary but in a markedly different set of circumstances. For the state supreme court, Justice Traynor wrote the opinion "disapproving" the *Pepperdine* decision "to the extent that it is contrary." Four justices concurred, but Justice McComb wrote a dissent protesting the overruling of *Pepperdine*.

---

[5] *Holt* v. *College of Osteopathic Physicians and Surgeons*, 61 Cal. 2d 750, 40 Cal. Rptr. 244, 394 P. 2d 932 (1964); vacating (Cal. App.) 36 Cal. Rptr. 397 (1964), which reversed the superior court of Los Angeles County.

All Assets of a Charitable Corporation
Partake of a Trust Character

The perennial shadow-boxing about the long-disputed question of whether a private nonprofit college owns any of its property as "absolute owner" and not in any sense in trust, is perhaps not yet quieted; but plainly the usage is moving toward favoring more and more the concept of the charitable corporation as incapable of holding any assets in "absolute ownership," and the theory that all assets received by it from whatever source are automatically impressed with a trust character, though by no means always the highest-level trust characteristics which appertain to a "perpetual trust," "permanent fund," or "endowment."

The controversy, if real, is largely one of nomenclature in the last analysis. In recent years the courts of California have seemingly been leading in the advancement of the simpler and sounder concept. In a 1963 court of appeal decision regarding property tax exemption for a nonprofit charitable home for the aged, the court says unequivocally:[6]

> All property held by a benevolent corporation is impressed with the charitable trust, and the presumption follows that it will be so used.

The opinion also quotes from the California supreme court decision in *Pacific Home* v. *Los Angeles County*, (Cal.), 264 P. 2d 539 (1953), the words being those of Justice Spence:

> All the assets of a corporation organized solely for charitable purposes must be deemed to be impressed with a charitable trust by virtue of the express declaration of the corporation's purposes, and notwithstanding the absence of any express declaration by those who contribute such assets as to the purpose for which the contributions are made.
>
> In other words, the acceptance of such assets under these circumstances establishes a charitable trust for the declared corporate purposes as effectively as though the assets had been accepted from a donor who had expressly provided in the instrument evidencing the gift that it was to be held in trust solely for such charitable purposes.

---

[6] *Samarkand of Santa Barbara, Inc.* v. *County of Santa Barbara*, 216 Cal. App. 2d 341, 31 Cal. Rptr. 151 (1963).

Continuing to trace California precedents in point, the court of appeal also cited two other California decisions in support of its view.[7]

There seems to be substantial agreement among Thomas E. Blackwell in his *Washington University Law Quarterly* article of 1938 (cited in Chapter 11, *supra*); Alexander Lincoln in his *Virginia Law Review* article of 1939; and the anonymous contributor to the *Harvard Law Review* in 1951 (cited in Chapter 5, *supra*); and the California judges.

Both Blackwell and Lincoln included in their articles extensive listings of germane decisions in many states. At this point the conclusions of Lincoln, a learned Boston lawyer, seem appropriate:[8]

> From this review of the decisions it would seem that authority as well as reason supports the rule that where a gift is made to a charitable corporation for a corporate purpose the gift may be in trust if the donor so intended, that the question is one of the donor's intention and that there is little basis for the statement that as a matter of law the gift is necessarily absolute and not in trust.
>
> Even in New York and Maryland gifts for corporate purposes to charitable corporations, when authorized by statute to receive such gifts in trust, have been upheld as creating valid and enforceable trusts. In other states, where charitable trusts have always been valid or have been made so by statute, decisions in profusion have held such gifts to be in trust and have granted appropriate relief where a trust was intended by the donor. Some states have gone to the extent of holding that every such gift creates a trust, which if not express is implied. In only three states does the doctrine that the gift to a charitable corporation for a corporate purpose cannot create a trust appear to have been consistently followed.
>
> . . . .
>
> A searching inquiry might well be made as to the consequences reasonably to be anticipated from the adoption or rejection of the rule given in the *Restatement*. . . . It may be added, however, that general recognition of the rule that gifts to charitable corporations are subject to none of the restraints which equity imposes on a trustee, though directions are given for the investment of the principal and the use of the

---

[7] *Los Angeles County Pioneer Society*, 40 Cal. 2d 852, 257 P. 2d 1 (1953); discussed at pages 282-283 in *The Colleges and the Courts Since 1950*; and *In re Estate of Clippinger*, 75 Cal. App. 2d 426, 171 P. 2d 567 (1946).

[8] Alexander Lincoln, "A Question on Gifts to Charitable Corporations," *Virginia Law Review* 25: 764-795 (May 1939).

income for stated purposes, is apt to result in a material reduction in the amount of donations to such corporations.

These words, contemplating gifts to charitable corporations
(private colleges), are strongly reminiscent of those of Sveinbjorn
Johnson, contemplating gifts to state universities, as quoted in Chapter
11 herein.

Perhaps some of the edge is taken off the apparent controversy
by the view of the Missouri supreme court in a 1962 decision:

"Certainly many of the principles applicable to charitable trusts
are applicable to charitable corporations. In both cases, the Attorney
General can maintain a suit to prevent a diversion of the property to
other purposes than those for which it was given; and in both cases
the doctrine of *cy pres* is applicable."[9]

The facts of that case prevent it from having very direct rele-
vance at this point; but they carry such a distinctive aroma of a bygone
century that we digress, if it be a digression, to recite them here. The
St. Louis Mercantile Library Association is a charitable corporation
created by special act of the General Assembly in 1847. Its charitable
character is not vitiated by the fact that its library is not open to the
public, its members pay fees for the use of the library, and it restricts
its membership. It owns a solid old six-story-and-basement brick-and-
stone building at Broadway and Locust Streets. It uses only the top
floor and certain other small appurtenances. The rest of the building
was leased to the First National Bank in St. Louis in 1948. An extension of the lease carrying to the year 2019 is now in effect. The
rental is $59,000 a year for the approximately 70,000 feet of valuable
downtown floor space. The lease contains no escalator clause. It con-
templates extensive alterations of the space, but no provision for restor-
ation.

The suit was brought by five members of the association on behalf of all other members, to cancel the lease which they characterized
as *"ultra vires,"* unreasonable, voidable, and a breach of trust." Besides
its board of directors, the association had a board of trustees to
manage its real property. It was alleged that several members of

---

[9] *Voelker* v. *St. Louis Mercantile Library Association*, (Mo.), 359 S.W. 2d
689 (1962).

these boards had financial interests in the defendant bank, as did also several of their relatives by blood and marriage. The complaining members had brought the infirmities of the lease to the attention of the association's officers, directors, and members at an annual meeting, all of whom had refused to take any action. The court was convinced that the complaint stated no cause of action, but also took the trouble to explain that the complaining members had no standing to sue, because they had not the requisite pecuniary interest in the assets of the corporation. "Members of the St. Louis Mercantile Library Association have the right to participate in the charitable use, but that is not a pecuniary interest in its corporate assets." They have no right to sue the corporation in their own behalf alone. The attorney general is a necessary party to any such suit.

Protection of Corporate Name and Symbols of Private University or College

A *cause célèbre* of 1964 and 1965 was the petition of Notre Dame University and its president for an injunction against the release and distribution of the farcical film and novel, "John Goldfarb, Please Come Home," by the Twentieth Century-Fox Film Corporation. Both the book and the motion picture, it was alleged, involved (1) illegal misappropriation and commercial exploitation for private profit of the name, symbols, football team, high prestige, reputation, and good will of the University of Notre Dame with consequent dilution of their high value; and (2) use of the president's name and identity for purposes of trade and without his consent, in violation of Sections 50 and 51 of the New York Civil Rights Law.

The trial court granted a temporary injunction, but this decree was reversed by the unanimous five-judge appellate division, and the reversal was affirmed without opinion by the court of appeals, with two of the judges strongly dissenting.

To get the facts into the record, Presiding Justice Botein of the appellate division wrote a compact "sketch of a part of the plot" of the novel and movie. His sketch is a gem of its kind:[10]

---

[10] From the opinion of the court in *University of Notre Dame du Lac* v. *Twentieth Century-Fox Film Corporation*, 22 A.D. 2d 452, 256 N.Y.S. 2d 301 (1965); reversing 44 Misc. 2d 808, 255 N.Y.S. 2d 210 (1964).

A king of the Moslem faith, ruler of the mythical Arab country of Fawzia, has a son who has enrolled as a student in a Catholic college, the plaintiff Notre Dame—inferentially because it is the image and exemplar of supremacy in football. Enraged because his son has been denied a place on the football team, the king determines on vengeance by forming a team at Fawz U of his own subjects, which, he plans, will play the Notre Dame team and defeat it. To train his group of novices, the king impresses into service a former football star, known as Wrong-Way Goldfarb. Goldfarb, who is a Jew—to complete the plot's religious cycle—is an American aviator employed by the Central Intelligence Agency to fly over Russia but he has by mistake landed in Fawzia. The king demands that the United States arrange a game between Fawz U and Notre Dame as the price for allowing the United States to lease an air base in his country.

At the urging of the panic-stricken State Department, Notre Dame, after firm refusals, finally permits its players and coach to travel to Fawzia. There, on the eve of the game, they are dined by the king and witness an orgiastic entertainment provided by dancing girls from the royal harem. The culinary piece-de-resistance is spiced mongoose, renowned for its devastating effect on even more sophisticated digestive systems than those of American football players. The next day they engage in a wild burlesque of a football game with the Fawzians, losing it because of the distressing aftermath of the spiced mongoose and a variety of chicaneries practiced against Notre Dame by, among others, the chief of the Central Intelligence Agency, who acts as referee. Not the least credible incident of the game is the winning touchdown scored by the leading lady, an American reporter who enters the game at the last minute as a member of the Fawzian team. She is carried bodily over the goal line by a preposterous oil gusher which erupts on the football field.

After characterizing the novel and the photoplay as "broad farce" and "blunderbuss travesty," the court went on to say: "We may not import the role of literary or dramatic critic into our functioning as judges in this case. . . . Whether 'John Goldfarb, Please Come Home' is good burlesque or bad, penetrating satire or blundering buffoonery, is not for us to decide. . . . It is enough that the work is a form of expression 'deserving of substantial freedom—both as entertainment and as a form of social and literary criticism'; . . . and we are not prepared to hold that exercise of the freedom in the instant circumstances infringes on rights which equity should protect."

Unable to bring itself to the conclusion that the case was one in which an injunction should be issued, the court concluded by saying: "At bottom, it seems to us, the University's grievance, notwithstanding its disclaimer, sounds in defamation; and its remedy, if it can prove libel, is at law." This means, of course, that the proper action would be a suit at law for damages, to seek monetary indemnity upon proof of damage to the University's reputation and good will.

As to the alleged violation of the rights of privacy of Father Theodore M. Hesburgh, president of the university, by the unauthorized use of his name, the court noted: "In the book . . . he is referred to by name at page 108 and again at pages 115-116 as the University official with whom the State Department was in communication. In our opinion these isolated references are of that fleeting and incidental nature which the Civil Rights Law does not find offensive." And, "To the extent that Father Hesburgh's cause of action is based on the film, it fails for the additional reason that the film does not use his 'name, portrait, or picture,' the statutory test of identification. . . . We do not think the test is satisfied by the conjunction of the fact that the book names him and the fact that the cover pages of the paperback edition, which in no way refer to him or his co-plaintiff, laud the film."

When the case reached the New York Court of Appeals, the decision was affirmed without opinion by vote of Judges Dye, Fuld, Van Voorhis, and Bergan. Chief Judge Desmond took no part. Judge Burke entered a dissenting opinion, in which Judge Scileppi joined him.

Judges Burke and Scileppi unequivocally wrote, "The appellate division's decision is wrong on all points," and "Section 397 of the General Business Law and section 50 and 51 of the Civil Rights Law mandate a permanent injunction in the circumstances presented here, in favor of the plaintiffs."[11]

"There can be no question that the defendant's use of the University's property rights was for the purposes of trade—to render defendant's products 'marketable,' " said these two judges. As to the comments on the form of the action by the majority of the court, Judge Burke's words were biting: "Several Judges suggest that Father Hesburgh has a cause of action under the Civil Rights Law, but only one sounding in damages. The suggestion is no less than a de-

---

[11] Dissenting opinion of Judges Burke and Scileppi in *University of Notre Dame du Lac* v. *Twentieth Century-Fox Film Corporation*, 259 N.Y.S. 2d 832, 15 N.Y. 2d 940, 207 N.E. 2d 508 (1965); affirming 22 A.D. 2d 452, 256 N.Y.S. 2d 301 (1965).

mand that the court should decree a forced sale of Father Hesburgh's right to privacy and determine a license fee to be paid for the use of his name for a purpose he long ago rejected. A similar suggestion as to the University's cause of action is equally untenable and unjustified."

The difficulty which this type of case has presented to the New York courts is further illustrated by two others which bear at least a remote similarity to the *Notre Dame* case. In one instance Columbia University's top varsity tennis player visited the island of Jamaica in the West Indies and played a match, which he lost. A local newspaper published a truthful story of the match, including, of course, the players' names. A manufacturer of pajamas and various other intimate garments assembled a design for the cloth from which the garments were made, in a species of collage in which an irregular tear-sheet showing part of the newspaper story, including the Columbia player's name, appeared on the cloth as a part of the collage. The player brought an action for damages for libel for this unauthorized use of his name in a manner damaging to his dignity and reputation. The trial court dismissed his complaint, and the dismissal was affirmed by the appellate division, but by a vote of three to two of the justices.[12]

Justice Steuer, for the dissenters, said:

> It is clear that the plaintiff's name was used without authorization for a commercial purpose. Unless that use was incidental, a cause of action is indisputably alleged.
>
> As regards libel, . . . whether the opportunities for ribaldry coming from the association of the plaintiff's name with such garments would hold him up to ridicule presents a question of fact.

The implication is that the complaint should not have been dismissed, but scheduled for hearing in a trial of the facts.

In an earlier instance, a formula for the making of an extraordinarily nutritious bread had been developed in the New York State College of Agriculture which is administratively in the jurisdiction of the Board of Trustees of Cornell University, a private corporation. A commercial bakery was using the formula, and dispute occurred regarding the manner in which it could properly use the name and

---

[12] *Moglen* v. *Varsity Pajamas, Inc.*, 13 A.D. 2d 114, 213 N.Y.S. 2d 999 (1961).

symbols of Cornell University in advertising and selling the product. The university did not wish to deny that the formula had been invented in its laboratories, but it did not wish any impression to get abroad that the bread offered for sale was its own manufactured product. It did not want the bread to be "palmed off" as though every loaf had been manufactured at Cornell.

The trial court gave judgment for the university, in an order permitting the baker to use the words "Cornell Formula Bread" but prohibiting the words "Cornell Recipe Bread" which it had been using. The order also required that on the bread wrappers the name of the bakery corporation be displayed in letters twice as large as those used in "Cornell Formula Bread," and prohibited the placing of any phrase containing the word "Cornell" on a scroll, banner, pennant, or other similar device commonly used as a college symbol. The appellate division modified and affirmed this order, apparently retaining only the prohibition of the use of "Cornell" on any scroll or similar device imitating college practice. This was in turn affirmed by the court of appeals, but with two justices, Froessel and Van Voorhis, dissenting and voting to reinstate the original order.[13]

Notre Dame University is not without recent favorable experience in this general area. There is a "university ring" of a particular design embracing the university's corporate name and some of its official symbols, which the university allows to be sold only through its own agency. Sales are restricted to juniors, seniors, and alumni of the institution. When a private jewelry manufacturer obtained one of these rings through false representations, duplicated the design, and sold the rings through a private outlet without imposing the university's restrictions as to qualified buyers, the university sought and obtained in a federal court a permanent injunction forbidding him to manufacture or sell any ring bearing the corporate name of the University of Notre Dame or its official seal or other identifying symbols. This decree was affirmed by the United States court of appeals.[14]

---

[13] *Cornell University* v. *Messing Bakeries, Inc.*, 309 N.Y. 722, 128 N.E. 421 (1955); affirming 285 A.D. 490, 138 N.Y.S. 2d 280 (1955), which modified and affirmed 135 N.Y.S. 2d 101 (1954).

[14] *John Roberts Manufacturing Company* v. *University of Notre Dame du Lac*, (U.S.C.A.), 258 F. 2d 256 (1958); affirming (U.S.D.C.), 152 F. Supp. 269 (1957).

A spate of earlier cases concerning commercial pirating of university names is discussed briefly at pages 179 and 180 in *The Colleges and the Courts Since 1950*.

Passage of Many Decades Often Necessitates Reinterpretations of Charters of Nonprofit Educational Corporations

St. Lawrence University and Theological Seminary is the style of a single corporation chartered in 1856. It seems that in the early part of the present century it became desirable for the undergraduate segment of the institution to dissociate itself to some extent and at least make itself appear as a unit distinct from the theological seminary, in order to qualify for the receipt of philanthropic grants for which theological institutions were not eligible. For this purpose the charter was amended in 1910 to provide for a separate board of trustees for the theological seminary. It was also said that this ploy "freed the trustees of the University from the administration of the finances of the theological school." More than half a century later the (Universalist) Theological Seminary ceased operation for lack of students, and dispute arose as to whether its trustees were merely agents of the original corporation created in 1856 or whether they constituted a new and separate corporation dating from the amendment of 1910.

There was nothing in the language of either document to indicate that there was any intention to bring about a divorce between the university and the theological seminary by creating a new and separate corporation. The trial court decided:[15]

> The legislature did not amend the original Act for the purpose of creating a new corporation, but to permit the existing corporation to continue its original dual pursuits in a modified manner.

The Georgia Military Academy was founded many years ago by a gift of land from Colonel J. C. Woodward, under a deed providing for the reversion of the property to his heirs "if any of the afore-

---

[15] *St. Lawrence University* v. *Trustees of the Theological School of St. Lawrence University*, 49 Misc. 2d 1079, 269 N.Y.S. 2d 285 (1966).

mentioned properties herein conveyed cease to be used for the purposes set forth in the charter of the grantee corporation." Recently the academy sought and obtained a declaratory judgment holding that it could lawfully (1) abolish military training for its students, (2) admit girls and young women as students, and (3) change its corporate name to Woodward Academy, Inc.

Affirming the favorable judgment of the trial court, the Georgia supreme court concluded from a reading of the original petition for the charter and of the charter itself, that

> Nowhere is it said that grantee must conduct a military academy or must not admit girls and young women. If it had, clearly there would be a forfeiture of the estate. . . . We construe the charter as requiring that the property be used for a "charitable and educational institution," and giving the board broad powers as to the manner and method of operation, and that the reverter clause in the deed would not become effective if the governing board should admit girls and young women or should not furnish military training to its students, but only if the school should cease to function as a charitable and educational institution.

Justice Mobley wrote the opinion for the majority of the court.[16] Chief Justice Duckworth and Justice Grice dissented. That a school founded as a private southern military academy should be readily authorized to abolish military training and admit girls, and change its name to boot, seems indicative of an admirable sensitivity to social change on the part of the courts involved.

Private Charitable Institutions and Racial Desegregation: The Case of Girard College in Philadelphia

The story of Girard College, a home and elementary and secondary school for orphan boys established and endowed in the will of Stephen Girard, wealthy shipowner, merchant and banker of the late eighteenth and early nineteenth centuries, is sketched in part at pages 165, 166, and 381 in *The Colleges and the Courts* (1936), and at pages 172-174 in *The Colleges and the Courts Since 1950*. A spate of

---

[16] *Harris et al.* v. *Georgia Military Academy*, 221 Ga. 721, 146 S.E. 2d 913 (1966).

state and federal decisions during the late 1950's, after much con-
voluted litigation, produced the result that Negro orphan boys must
be refused admission to the school because Girard's will, written nearly a century and a half ago, had specified that the institution be for
white orphan boys; and the private charitable trust was not subject to
the anti-discrimination mandate of the Fourteenth Amendment.

Persistent efforts to gain admission for Negro orphan boys continued after that time, and on September 2, 1966, it appeared that the
goal had been won. On that day the press reported that District Judge
Joseph S. Lord III had ruled that if the plaintiffs (seven Negro orphan
boys) could prove from the facts that their exclusion was solely because of their race, "continued racial discrimination in the selection of
students for admission to Girard College will be enjoined."

Judge Lord is reported not to have made any ruling regarding the
applicability of the Fourteenth Amendment, but to have held that discrimination solely on grounds of race would be a violation of the
Pennsylvania Public Accommodations Act of 1939. He declared that
Girard College "is an educational institution under the supervision of
the commonwealth and is not in its nature distinctly private."

Attorneys for the plaintiff Negro boys argued that the trustees of
Girard College, "by stressing the word 'white' as used in the will and
at the same time relaxing the standards of poverty required for admission and by going as far abroad as Europe in their search for
white students, had lost sight of the true purpose of Girard College
—namely to combat poverty and ignorance, particularly in Philadelphia." There is indeed much evidence that this latter was exactly the
charitable intent of Stephen Girard.

Judge Lord is reported to have said the decision "does not mean
that a testator or settlor may not leave his property as he sees fit. It
does mean that disposition by will or trust must comply with the
applicable laws extant when the disposition was made and with laws
which the legislature may later enact." This seems in harmony with
the universally accepted principle that the privilege of disposing of
property by will is not an inherent right but only a gift of statute,
and also in harmony with the growing doctrine that not necessarily
every precatory word in a charitable trust instrument must stand inviolate forever, if and when great social changes over a long period of time bring it into conflict with current custom and law.

It is to be noted that the opinion of September 2, 1966, ordered no immediate affirmative remedy, but contemplated further proceedings based on additional submissions of facts in the pleadings. Press reports of some months later indicated that the decision had been reversed and remanded by the United States court of appeals, with instruction to consider and decide the impact of the Fourteenth Amendment.

Sweet Briar College in Virginia Achieves Desegregation

The will of Mrs. Indiana Fletcher Williams in 1899 devised the Sweet Briar plantation in Amherst County, Virginia, in trust to become a college "for the education of white girls and young women." In 1964 the college sued in a state court for permission to admit qualified Negro students. Its brief contended that social and legal changes since 1899 had made it impossible to operate a top-grade college on a segregated basis. The college would lose grants from the federal government and from private foundations, and moreover would be unable to attract many high-quality and high-principled teachers and students.

After nearly two years a Virginia judge released an informal opinion calling the suit "frivolous," whereupon the college instituted an action in federal district court asking that the segregation clause in the will of Mrs. Williams be declared no longer valid, and that the state be enjoined from enforcing it. The college board of trustees on May 28 ordered that a policy of no racial discrimination in admissions be begun immediately, and filed a copy of this order with the federal court. The court promised a decision as soon as a three-judge federal court could be convened, but by September 1, 1966, no decision had been announced. That a decision will be forthcoming, authorizing desegregation, can hardly be doubted.

The somewhat similar case of Rice University in Texas, as yet not finally determined, is discussed in Chapter 19, *infra*.

Incorporated Charitable Foundation Under Broadly-Phrased Charter May Establish and Finance Other Charitable Foundations

William H. Donner first founded the International Cancer Research Foundation. In 1945 its assets were turned over to the Donner

Foundation, Incorporated, a Delaware corporation. In 1950 he procured the incorporation of Donner Canadian Foundation under Canadian law, and it was endowed by a grant of $420,000 from Donner Foundation, Incorporated. Mr. Donner died in 1953, and disputes arose among the members of the Donner Foundation, Incorporated—the division being between his lineal descendants on one side and his adoptive daughters and some non-family-members on the other. By 1960 all agreed to split the foundation into two, with one faction in control of each. To this end the William H. Donner Foundation, Inc., was incorporated in the District of Columbia by the direct descendants, and the name of the Donner Foundation, Incorporated, was changed to Independence Foundation (to be in the hands of the adoptive daughters and non-family-members).

Independence Foundation then voted to transfer 55 per cent of its assets, amounting to about $25 million, to the new William H. Donner Foundation, Inc., as apparently had been substantially agreed upon in advance. The adoptive daughters resisted this, but were outvoted in the Independence Foundation and then sought the intervention of a Delaware court to enjoin the transfer. Their petition was dismissed by the supreme court of Delaware. Said Justice Wolcott: "A reading of the expressed purposes and objects of Independence makes it clear that the purpose of Independence is to give away its assets in order to achieve its broad object of promoting the well-being of mankind and alleviating human suffering." The certificate of incorporation authorized it to use both principal and income, and to establish and maintain charitable agencies and institutions. Accordingly, "this grant from capital to endow the William H. Donner Foundation, Inc. is within the powers conferred upon the Board of Directors of Independence."[17]

---

[17] *Denckla* v. *Independence Foundation*, 41 Del. Ch. 247, 193 A. 2d 538 (1963); affirming 181 A. 2d 78 (1962).

CHAPTER 13

COOPERATIVE INTERACTIONS
BETWEEN PUBLIC AND
PRIVATE AGENCIES IN
HIGHER EDUCATION

As NOTED IN THIS VOLUME'S PREDECESSOR, many forms of cooperation between governmental units and private colleges go on constantly without becoming subjects of litigation; and unquestionably their number and variety is increasing.

The firm tradition that governments at all levels habitually grant various exemptions from taxation to nonprofit educational institutions continues to be tested in the courts at its peripheries as new conditions arise. Accordingly, Chapters 14, 15, 16, and 17 treat a number of cases under the respective rubrics of (1) exemptions from property taxes, (2) property tax exemption of other types of educational agencies, (3) state taxes other than property taxes, and (4) federal taxation.

Meantime in this present chapter we look at recent litigation touching: (1) direct appropriation of public funds to denominational or sectarian colleges or universities, (2) the disposition of a bequest to a private university's endowment fund when the death of the testatrix did not occur until after the institution had been merged into the state university, and (3) the situation in which a new and prospectively large urban state university was established to absorb the plant and personnel of an urban private college. A fourth instance somewhat related to these categories was that of the legislation and litigation which culminated in the formerly private College of Osteopathy in California becoming the state-owned California College of Medicine, now the tenth campus of the University of California. This has already been discussed in Chapter 12, *supra*.

There is a fifth area which seems not to have been litigated—at least not in any widely significant case—within the past four years. This is the issue of the constitutionality, under both the federal and state constitutions, of the appropriations of tax-derived public funds for scholarships, fellowships, assistantships, traineeships, student loans, and student work-opportunities, all classified as aids to the student, but permitting the recipients to choose high-fee private colleges where their gains from these sources will be cancelled by high student fees.

This is in fact a thinly-veiled channeling of public funds to private colleges and universities—a very substantial form of financial aid to them, even if it must be called "indirect." It enables colleges that are academically and financially weak to fill their student rosters beyond the point of overflow and encourages those that are academically and financially strong to raise their charges for tuition, which has the well-known "ripple" effect of causing fees to move upward everywhere, and thus actually narrows the scope of higher educational opportunity in the nation.

Because its ultimate outcome may possibly affect drastically the public comprehension of this situation and cause attention to be drawn to it, the recent case having by far the farthest-reaching potentialities is the action brought in Maryland asking for a judicial declaration that Maryland's appropriations of funds for capital outlay to four allegedly denominational colleges contravene the First Amendment prohibition of "establishment of religion" and certain provisions of the Maryland constitution as well.

As background, it is well to note that Maryland is virtually the only state which currently makes direct appropriations to sectarian institutions.[1] Among the 50 states, 45 or more of the state constitutions have been interpreted as forbidding this practice. It was declared unconstitutional in Pennsylvania in 1921, after having been carried on for 40 years previous to that year.[2] However, as is well known, Pennsylvania continues to make substantial annual appropriations to a number of *nonsectarian* private universities and colleges.

Maryland also makes appropriations to *nonsectarian* private institutions of higher education, and this practice is not at issue in the current case. In fact, in 1952 it was expressly held not to be in violation of the Maryland constitution, by the Maryland court of appeals.[3]

State Financial Aid to Sectarian Institutions
Challenged in Maryland

It will be recalled that in a suit brought by taxpayers for a declaration that Maryland appropriations of public funds to four private and allegedly denominational colleges were in violation of the First Amendment to the United States Constitution, the judgment of the circuit court for Anne Arundel County was against the plaintiffs (as had been expected) but was appealed to the Maryland court of appeals.

The decision was reversed by the court of appeals June 2, 1966, holding that the appropriations to Western Maryland College (Methodist) and to the College of Notre Dame of Maryland and St. Joseph College (both Roman Catholic) were in contravention of the First Amendment prohibition of "establishment of religion"; but the ap-

---

[1] In 1955 the New Hampshire supreme court handed down an advisory opinion to the effect that a proposed bill to pay tax money to all hospitals operating schools of nursing (including sectarian hospitals) would not be unconstitutional. Chief Justice Kenison emphasized that the bill would provide public funds only for nurses' training and for no other kind of instruction or purpose. "If some denomination incidentally derives a benefit through the release of other funds for other purposes," he said, "this result is immaterial." Opinion of the Justices, 99 N.H. 519, 113 A. 2d 114 (1955); discussed at pages 189 and 190 in *The Colleges and the Courts Since 1950*.

[2] *Collins* v. *Kephart*, 271 Pa. 428, 117 Atl. 440 (1921); discussed at page 290 in *The Colleges and the Courts* (1936).

[3] *Johns Hopkins University* v. *Williams*, 199 Md. 382, 86 A. 2d 892 (1952); discussed at pages 186 and 187 in *The Colleges and the Courts Since 1950*.

propriation to Hood College was not. (The language of the First Amendment applies only to Congress, but it has long been held applicable also to the states through the Fourteenth Amendment.)

The distinction among the colleges in favor of Hood College was on the basis that although Hood College is loosely affiliated with the United Christian Church, the connection is comparatively attenuated and is not sufficient to bring the institution within the constitutional proscription.

The court thought best not to lay down any cut-and-dried across-the-board rule that would apply to all church-related colleges, but believed that in each instance the circumstances should be weighed and decided independently.

The opinion of the court was written by Chief Justice Prescott, with three justices concurring, and with Justice Hammond writing a dissent in part, in which Justices Horney and Marbury concurred.

The dissenters did not agree that any of the appropriations to any of the colleges were in violation of the Constitution. Dissenting Justice Hammond wrote:

> I think that the four grants under consideration were made pursuant to long-established practice to further a secular public purpose and that any aid or benefit flowing from them to religion would be slight, vague and purely incidental.

Thus the whole court upheld the appropriation to Hood College, but a majority of four of the seven justices struck down the appropriations to the other three colleges.[4]

Both parties to the litigation appealed to the Supreme Court of the United States, in the hope of obtaining a definitive interpretation of the "establishment of religion" clause of the First Amendment as applied to this case, and which would declare the law of the land, nationwide. The high tribunal declined to review the case. Accordingly, the Maryland court of appeals decision declares the law for Maryland only.

---

[4]*Horace Mann League* v. *Board of Public Works of Maryland*, (Maryland Court of Appeals, June 2, 1966). *Certiorari* denied, 35 U.S. Law Week 3174 (November 15, 1966).

Does Sale of Federally-Owned Land to Denominational College at Merely Nominal Price Violate First Amendment?

It was reported that the public school district of Portland, Oregon, and four individual taxpayers instituted a suit in March 1966 to prevent the sale of 24 acres of federally-owned land at 10 per cent of its fair value, to Concordia College, a Lutheran institution in Portland. The suit is said to be backed by the Oregon chapter of the American Civil Liberties Union. The argument is that the effect of the sale would be to contribute approximately $108,000 of public money to a college unquestionably having the advancement of religion as one of its primary purposes. Thus the sale would be in violation of the "establishment of religion" clause of the First Amendment to the Constitution of the United States.

State Acquisition of Private Universities and Colleges

To add to the cases in this category discussed at pages 191-194 in *The Colleges and the Courts Since 1950*, there are two: (1) a case concerning a bequest to the former private University of Buffalo when the death of the testatrix did not occur until after the university had been merged into the State University of New York; and (2) one concerning the acquisition by the state of Ohio of the plant of Fenn College, a private institution in Cleveland, to form the nucleus of the newly established Cleveland State University.

Bequest to Former Private University of Buffalo Goes to Its Successor, State University of New York at Buffalo

A will dated in 1955 recited: "I give and bequeath to the University of Buffalo fifty thousand dollars for its endowment fund." The testatrix died in February 1963. About five and a half months prior to that date the merger of the private University of Buffalo into the State University of New York had become effective, after which the old private corporation had no control of the institution.

Shortly before the merger, however, a new nonprofit private corporation, the University of Buffalo Foundation, Inc., was organized, and by agreement the State University of New York permitted it to receive and hold some $3 million of the endowment funds of the old University of Buffalo. The remaining $26 million of the endowment went to the State University of New York for the exclusive use of its Buffalo unit, as provided in the merger contract.

The dispute was as to whether the $50,000 bequest should go to the foundation or to the state university. In either event it would be held and used exclusively for the benefit of the successor to the named donee. The surrogate turned to Section 352, Subdivision 2, of the Education Law:

> Whenever such corporation (the State University of New York) acquires, absorbs, merges or consolidates with or becomes the successor to any higher educational institution, all the right, title and interest in real property held by such predecessor institution shall vest in and be held by the State of New York, and the State University of New York shall thereupon be deemed to be vested with and become the successor to all right, title, and interest in any personal property, or any beneficial interest therein, or any other rights and powers possessed by such institution, whether devised by gift, grant, devise or bequest, in trust or otherwise.

Surrogate William J. Reagan then concluded that it was possible to comply literally with the terms of the bequest by channeling it to the trustees of the state university as successor to the University of Buffalo, and hence all arguments about *cy pres* were irrelevant; and accordingly he issued his order to that effect, being careful to specify that the fund must always be for the exclusive use and benefit of the Buffalo unit, and never become a general fund of the state university.[5]

State of Ohio Acquires Fenn College in Cleveland as Nucleus of New Cleveland State University

The new Cleveland State University was created by Chapter 3344, Ohio Revised Code, enacted December 18, 1964. It is governed by a board of nine trustees, appointed by the governor.

Under an "Agreement of Transfer and Transition" Cleveland State University uses as its beginning nucleus the faculty, staff,

---

[5] *In re Dunbar's Will*, 41 Misc. 2d 1044, 247 N.Y.S. 2d 512 (1964).

and facilities of Fenn College, a private institution which originated in the early 1920's as an enterprise of the Cleveland YMCA. In the 'Thirties it was separately incorporated and in 1951 entirely severed from all connection with the YMCA.

The Fenn College Board of Trustees now turns its plant and facilities over to Cleveland State University. It receives from the state $260,000 and the expectation that the state will enormously expand the operation and will "continue, so far as practicable, the cooperative program of education" in engineering, with business and industrial employers.

The board of trustees will have its charter amended and become the "Fenn Educational Foundation" and "carry on as a nonprofit corporation supporting worthy educational, literary, charitable and scientific endeavors." The common pleas court issued a declaratory judgment regarding the rights of all parties, including private donors to the college.

Noting that "Those who have been generous to Fenn in the past have the assurance that their charitable intents will be perpetuated, and, although they have no legal title or interest in any of Fenn's assets, that their donations will continue to advance the cause of education," the court said the "doctrine of deviation" in the operation of charitable trusts is applicable here, and declared that the Fenn trustees had "full and complete legal authority and ample discretion to enter into the agreement and transfer most of their assets to the newly-created state university."[6]

New Jersey Acquires Seton Hall College of Medicine and Dentistry in 1965

Seton Hall College of Medicine and Dentistry was incorporated in 1954, and for 10 years had some of the characteristics of an "affiliate" of Seton Hall University at South Orange, New Jersey. Some of the tribulations accompanying its leasing of a physical plant in the Jersey City Medical Center were tranquilized by the decision in *Robbins* v. *Jersey City*, 23 N. J. 229, 128 A. 2d 673 (1957), which

---

[6] *Fenn College et al.* v. *Nance et al.*, (Ohio Com. Pl.), 210 N.E. 2d 418 (1965).

was discussed at pages 196 and 197 in *The Colleges and the Courts Since 1950.*

On May 3, 1965, the corporation sold all its assets to the New Jersey College of Medicine and Dentistry, a public corporation which had been created by a New Jersey legislative act of 1964 and authorized to buy. There was no transfer of responsibility for outstanding debts. Meantime a legacy of some $42,000 was ready to be paid over to the private corporation on May 25, 1964. Should it be allowed to go to the private corporation to pay debts, or should it go to the public corporation now in possession of the College of Medicine and Dentistry and responsible for its operation? Judge Herbert of the New Jersey superior court pointed out that the testamentary gift had been made with the charitable intent of supporting medical education:[7]

> Paying a legacy to a charitable corporation which can no longer carry on its charitable functions would defeat the terms of the trust implicitly impressed on the charitable gift. Payment to the Seton Hall College of Medicine and Dentistry, which will never again carry on the educational activities for which it was incorporated, would benefit the creditors of the college, but not the public. Such payment should not be made.

The court readily disposed of several arguments advanced to the contrary: (1) The testator was a Catholic, and his will named nine charitable legatees, all Catholic-affiliated. This would have been relevant if any choice had been available, but none exists, because there is now no Catholic medical college in the state. (2) Three of the other legatees were hospitals. They can not qualify because they do not carry on the functions of a medical college. (3) The "parent corporation" (Seton Hall University at South Orange) is not qualified because it now offers no medical education, either directly or through any affiliate.

---

[7] *Montclair National Bank and Trust Company* v. *Seton Hall College of Medicine and Dentistry*, 90 N.J. Super. 419, 217 A. 2d 897 (1966).

CHAPTER 14

EXEMPTION FROM
PROPERTY TAXES

IT IS QUITE GENERALLY AGREED that property owned by the state is exempt from taxation, and this, with only rare exceptions under peculiar circumstances, includes all the property of state institutions of higher education.

As to private colleges and universities, litigation continues to occur regarding the taxability of various properties owned by the institution but used only for purposes that are alleged to be only remotely ancillary to the educational purpose, or perhaps not used at all. There is no question but that the land, buildings, and equipment used directly for such educational purposes as classrooms, libraries, laboratories, faculty offices, and a great variety of closely related appurtenances are exempt under appropriate statutes in every state.

The same has also come to be true of residence halls or dormitories and dining halls for the exclusive accommodation of students. However, as a few recent cases disclose, there may be some question about the exemption of college-owned housing for faculty members, and college-owned properties used primarily as recreational facilities for faculty or students. The general tendency is toward regarding all such conveniences, within reason, as useful and essential

179

adjuncts to the accomplishment of the educational purpose of the institution, and therefore tax-exempt.

Property of State University Not in Use for Educational Purposes

An attempt to make certain parcels of real property owned by Indiana University, either directly or through the agency of an accessory nonprofit private corporation, subject to property taxation on the ground that they are not in immediate use for educational purposes but are held for varying periods pending ultimate educational use, seems to be under way.

In 1964 the county board of tax review voted to place eight such parcels on the county tax rolls. The university appealed to the state board of tax commissioners in January 1965, and that body ruled six of the parcels exempt, one partially exempt, and one taxable. In September the county assessor filed an appeal in the county superior court, which was dismissed. Appeal was taken to the Indiana supreme court, where it was held that the ruling of the state board of tax commissioners must stand, because under Indiana law a county or other local tax authority has no standing to contest the rulings of that body.

The case is reminiscent of *Wisconsin University Building Corporation v. Bareis*, 257 Wis. 497, 44 N.W. 2d 259 (1950), in which the supreme court of Wisconsin ruled that all properties held by this corporation in and around the city of Madison with a view to ultimate educational use by the University of Wisconsin are tax-exempt, because the real beneficial interest in them belongs to the state. That case is discussed at pages 180-181 in *The Colleges and the Courts, 1946-50*, published by the Columbia University Press in 1952.

Various Properties of Reputable Private College: Presidents' House; Guest House; Farm for Riding Horses Used in Physical Education

In 1965 Denison University came off victorious in a dispute with the Ohio Board of Tax Appeals, which had strangely insisted that even the President's House on the campus should be taxable.

Other parcels in question included Middleton House, a dwelling on an eight-acre plot about 1½ miles from the campus, used as a guest house and for occasional conferences and seminars. A caretaker and his family occupied a part of this house rent-free, and it produced no income for the university.

Lastly, a 127-acre farm across the street from the campus had on it the university's carpenter shop and lumber storage shed, a quonset hut housing the paint shop, and a dwelling house for the caretaker. The farm also contained a riding ring and an equitation trail for use in women's physical education, and a pole shelter for hay for the horses.

By a vote of 6 to 1, the Ohio supreme court held all tax-exempt, in an opinion by Judge Taft.[1] Judge Herbert dissented without opinion. In Ohio's perennially puzzling exemption statutes, Section 5709.07 of the Revised Code exempts "public colleges and academies and all buildings connected therewith, and all lands connected with public institutions of learning, not used with a view to profit."

The court cited and followed the half-century-old case of *Kenyon College* v. *Schnebly*, 81 Ohio St. 514, 91 N.E. 1138 (1909); and *overruled* its own divided decision of 1950 in *Wstern Reserve Academy* v. *Board of Tax Appeals*, 153 Ohio St. 133, 91 N.E. 2d 497 (1950). In that case Judge Taft had been one of the two dissenters from the opinion holding academy-owned faculty residences on the campus taxable. In discussion of the *Western Reserve* case at page 206 of *The Colleges and the Courts Since 1950*, it was said, "It may be hazarded with some confidence that the adverse decision in this case is not of widespread persuasive weight."

College-Owned Housing for Faculty Members

Concordia College in Moorhead, Minnesota, owned a dwelling-house several blocks from the campus and used it to provide temporary housing for new faculty members. The house had been acquired by bequest from a former professor of mathematics. It was not rented to the general public, and within nine years had been oc-

---

[1] *Denison University* v. *Board of Tax Appeals*, 2 Ohio St. 2d 17, 205 N.E. 2d 896 (1965).

cupied successively by five faculty members and their families. They
paid monthly rentals of around $75, and the house was not a "per-
quisite" or part of their compensation. The college owned three
houses used in this same manner. Believing that this operation had become indispensable to the successful management of its main educational enterprise, it brought suit to have the premises at 507 South
Tenth Street removed from the assessment rolls.

The trial court judgment was adverse; but on appeal was reversed and remanded by the Minnesota supreme court, which directed
that the property be removed from the tax-rolls.

In a thoughtful court-written syllabus it was said: [2]

> In determining whether ownership of faculty housing is rea-
> sonably necessary for the purpose of a private college, factors to
> be considered include:
> (1) expressed intent of the administration,
> (2) history of the acquisition and use of the facility,
> (3) necessity of such housing in obtaining instructors,
> (4) the use made of the realty,
> (5) the location,
> (6) the availability of other houses, and
> (7) the duties of the occupant.

Upon all these considerations the judgment favorable to the college was made. An old Minnesota precedent was favorable: In 1892
the supreme court had held that at Macalester College "residences
erected for the professors of the faculty on college land near but
not on the main campus were exempt from taxation."[3]

About two years later than this favorable Minnesota decision of
1963, and in the same year (1965) in which the Ohio court in the
Denison University case expressly overruled its own unfavorable
decision of 1950 in the *Western Reserve Academy* case, we find
the opposite position in an astringent opinion of the New Jersey
superior court, appellate division. The Pingry School, a private day
school for boys, organized as a nonprofit corporation and qualified
for tax exemption of its property "actually used for school purposes,"
was denied exemption of seven houses occupying about three acres
at the north end of its school grounds, and regularly occupied by mem-

---

[2] *Concordia College Corporation* v. *State*, 265 Minn. 136, 120 N.W. 2d
601 (1963).

[3] *Ramsey County* v. *Macalester College*, 51 Minn. 437, 53 N.W. 704, 18
L.R.A. 278 (1892).

bers of its faculty. Since 1958 the houses had been rented to teachers at moderate rates, and there was proof that the expenses of maintenace had exceeded the rental income.

When the headmaster was asked why the school maintained the houses as faculty residences, he was reported to have replied:

> It has the houses for two purposes. One is to be an additional attraction to get a good teacher that we particularly want, and Number Two, to keep those teachers that we think we particularly like.

It did not appear that any school use of the houses was alleged, such as conferences between teachers and students; and this perhaps made it easier for the court to sniff at the headmaster's response, and declare:

> To adopt that thesis as an underlying rationale in support of tax exemption would posit a rule that incidental benefits or inducements are tantamount to the statutory requirement of "actual use for" school purposes. Such a rule would engraft upon the statute an extended meaning not reasonably contemplated within a fair interpretation of the legislative intent.

The foregoing judgment of the appellate division was reversed unanimously by the seven-judge New Jersey supreme court, in an opinion written by Justice Schettino:

"Are they (the faculty houses) 'actually used' for school purposes? A review of the cases which have passed upon this and analogous issues leads us to the conclusion that they are. A finding as to exemption or not has been based on an investigation of a number of factors including the following: absence of a profit-making arrangement in the rental contract; desirability of providing available housing at or near the school and whether the provision of housing for its faculty is reasonably designed to further the educational purposes of the school."

After analysis of these matters the opinion concluded: "We are satisfied from a review of the record in the light of the construction to be placed on the statute that the faculty houses and the land upon which they are situated should be tax-exempt."[4] Accordingly it was so ordered.

---

[4] *Pingry Corporation* v. *Township of Hillside*, 46 N.J. 457, 217 A. 2d 868 (1966); reversing 86 N.J. Super. 437, 207 A. 2d 194 (1965).

Recreational Facility for Student Nurses

It was also in Minnesota that a private charitable hospital, operating a school for nurses, purchased a parcel of lakeshore property located 226 miles from the hospital grounds, for use as a recreational facility for the student nurses.

Here again the state supreme court decided in favor of the charitable institution on the issue of tax exemption. It was held that the lakeshore land and buildings were exempt, because the whole constituted a reasonably necessary and normal part of a school for the education of competent nurses.[5]

Unusual Situation in Which All Property of Private School Is Owned by State and Therefore Exempt, in Tennessee

In the city of Nashville a private vocational school known as the Watkins Institute dates from the 1880's. It owned a downtown building and also an outlying property in the city. The will of the donor in 1880 gave $100,000 and the real estate to the state of Tennessee as trustee for the institute and stipulated that the governor and senate should appoint three commissioners to have its superintendence and management, subject to inquiry by and under the protection of the state. By Chapter 49, Acts of 1881, the state accepted the trust.

The first floor of the downtown building and all of the outlying premises were always rented to tenants to produce income for the institute, and hence were never used directly for school purposes. Tennessee Code section 1085 (1) exempts from taxation all property owned by the state, as trustee or otherwise. This statute, said the court, is valid and not in violation of either the federal or state constitution. Thus there was no choice other than to hold all property of the institute to be tax-exempt, because it was owned by the state as trustee.[6]

This decision was scarcely more than an acceptance and follow-

---

[5] *State* v. *Fairfield Hospital Association,* 262 Minn. 184, 114 N.W. 2d 568 (1962).

[6] *City of Nashville* v. *State Board of Equalization,* (Tenn. App.), 363 S.W. 2d 520 (1962).

ing of the same judgment made by the supreme court of Tennessee in 1941, regarding the same issue and the same property.[7]

The case is a rare and atypical one, because nearly all private non-profit schools and colleges are incorporated as charitable corporations, and title to their property is held by the corporation; and with comparatively few exceptions such of their property as is not used directly for the educational purpose, but rented or invested to produce income, is taxable. The principal exceptions are a small number of older institutions whose original charters were granted as special acts of the legislature containing no reservation to the state of the right to amend or repeal without the consent of the trustees, and providing that *all* property of the institution should be forever tax-exempt.[8]

A Private School Is a "Public" School in Vermont

Millions of Americans have been mystified by the quirk of nomenclature whereby the ancient private schools in England, such as Eton and Harrow and others, are always referred to as "public schools." Something akin to the same inversion was utilized in a recent Vermont case to save a high-fee private preparatory school from taxation of its property, on account of a hiatus in the statutes relating to tax exemption. Generally such a school would be exempt under the statutes of almost any state, if it were a nonprofit corporation and had no history of making exorbitant gains from its operation.

One Vermont statute [VSA 32: section 3802 (4)] exempts "colleges, academies, or public schools." This was modified in 1941 by adding a section [3831 (a)] which provides that property acquired by a "college, university, or fraternity" after 1941 is taxable unless specifically exempted by the town or city. This is held not to apply to the Stowe Preparatory School, Inc. (newly incorporated in 1961) because it is not a "college"; and it is exempt under Section 3802 (4) because it

---

[7] *State ex rel. Beeler* v. *Nashville*, 178 Tenn. 344, 157 S.W. 2d 839 (1941).

[8] A recent "charter exemption" case is *State ex rel. Bannister* v. *William Jewell College*, 364 Mo. 199, 260 S.W. 2d 479 (1953), discussed at pages 199-200 in *The Colleges and the Courts Since 1950*. Cases of the same type involving the charters of several other private colleges and universities are discussed in Chapter IX (pages 48-52) in *The Colleges and the Courts, 1941-45*, and Chapter X (pages 44-47) in *The Colleges and the Courts, 1936-41*.

is held to be a "public school." Why the court chose not to consider it an "academy," exempted in the same section, is not apparent.

At any rate, the court was unequivocal in its orders: It enjoined the town of Stowe from collecting any taxes from the school. It also directed the town to remove the school property from the Grand List and refund about $1,400 a year in taxes paid under protest by the school for the years 1962 and 1963.[9] The small coeducational school had from 50 to 100 pupils who paid $2,200 a year for tuition and recreational facilities. Any income above cost of operation was used to retire debts.

---

[9] *Stowe Preparatory School, Inc.* v. *Town of Stowe*, 124 Vt. 392, 205 A. 2d 544 (1964).

CHAPTER 15

PROPERTY TAXATION OF
OTHER TYPES OF
EDUCATIONAL AGENCIES

THE CONCEPT OF EDUCATION in its broader senses has very wide and foggy horizons, extending far beyond the boundaries of universities, colleges, or academies in which the classroom face-to-face relationship of instructor and student predominates in the midst of indispensable accessory facilities such as libraries, laboratories, clinics, shops, dormitories, dining halls, and recreational facilities.

The courts are more or less continually faced with problems as to what other types of agencies, at least partly educational in their purposes and activities, are sufficiently so to justify their inclusion within the purview of the exemption statutes of the state. Among the types raising these questions are (1) professional associations, (2) organizations serving young people in various ways, such as YMCA's, YWCA's, Boy Scouts of America, Girl Scouts, Inc., and many others, and (3) miscellaneous nonprofit and allegedly charitable organizations for many and diverse purposes bearing some relation to education and the advancement of culture, direct or remote.

*In New Jersey Charitable Corporations Must Be
Domestic in Order to Be Exempt*

Broadcasting station WHYY, Inc., is a Pennsylvania corporation with its principal office in Philadelphia. Its purpose is to broadcast in Pennsylvania, New Jersey, and Delaware. It is licensed by the Federal Communications Commission to operate and telecast over Channel 12 as a noncommercial educational station, and registered in New Jersey as a foreign nonprofit corporation authorized to do business in New Jersey. It is financed by contributions from school systems and individuals, and accepts no commercial advertising. It has studios in Philadelphia and Wilmington, and its facilities in New Jersey consist of 50 acres at Glassboro, on which are a transmittal building and a 1,000-foot guy tower, "the heart of its broadcasting system."

The Glassboro property is taxable solely because the New Jersey exemption statute contains a section (NJSA Sec. 54:4-3.6) specifying that: "The following exemptions shall apply only where the association, corporation, or institution claiming the exemption owns the property in question and is *incorporated or organized under the laws of this state* and authorized to carry out the purposes on account of which the exemption is claimed."

Holding that these words must be interpreted literally, the superior court, appellate division, reiterates that exemption statutes must be construed strongly against the claimant, and that changes in the statutes are for the legislature, not the courts, to make.[1] On behalf of WHYY it was argued without avail that the section quoted is unreasonable and has no relation to the expressed objective of the legislation, which is to foster and encourage educational, charitable, and cultural endeavors.

County Medical Society Building Not Exempt in Georgia

The Fulton County Medical Society owned a building in Atlanta known as the "Academy of Medicine," and used it as the headquarters for its approximately 1,000 members and four paid employees. It housed offices, meeting facilities, and other usual appurtenances of a

---

[1] *WHYY, Inc.* v. *Borough of Glassboro*, (N.J. Super., A.D.), 219 A. 2d 893 (1966).

headquarters for an association of physicians and surgeons. An injunction against the collection of taxes on this property by the tax commissioner of Fulton County was obtained by summary judgment in a local court, but in 1964, this was reversed by the Georgia supreme court, in an opinion that was less than unanimous.[2]

The opinion for the majority of the court was written by Presiding Justice Head. It held that the medical society headquarters was not a "college, incorporated academy, or other seminary of learning" as mentioned in one exemption statute; and not within the meaning of another statute (GCA 92-201) which exempts "all institutions of purely public charity . . . all buildings erected for and used as a college, nonprofit hospital, incorporated academy or other seminary of learning. . . . *Provided*, the above-described property so exempted is not used for purposes of private or corporate profit or income."

Presiding Justice Head himself, however, also wrote an opinion dissenting in part, in which he was joined by Justice Quillian. They thought the fact that the building was used rent-free by such organizations as the Atlanta Milk Commission and the Traffic Safety Committee in the public interest, as well as the interchange of information among medical men that took place in the building, "could not help but benefit the public by the increased skill and knowledge thus engendered."

They also pointed out that the society did not operate for profits distributable to shareholders, and did not operate in competition with other businesses not enjoying tax exemption. They thought a broad interpretation of "purely public charity" would embrace the enterprise. This view was based in part on a Georgia precedent a quarter of a century old, in which land used for recreation and instruction of Boy Scouts was adjudged tax-exempt as a "purely public charity."[3]

State Medical Societies in Massachusetts and New Jersey

In 1960 the highest court in Massachusetts decided that real prop-

---

[2] *Camp* v. *Fulton County Medical Society*, 219 Ga. 602, 135 S.E. 2d 277 1964).

[3] *Tharpe, Tax Collector* v. *Central Georgia Council of Boy Scouts of America*, 185 Ga. 810, 196 S.E. 762, 116 A.L.R. 373 (1938).

erty owned and used by the Massachusetts Medical Society was not exempt from taxation. In the words of Justice Spalding, the indirect benefit to the public from having an enlightened medical profession was not sufficient to bring the medical society within the class traditionally recognized as charitable. The society operated primarily for the betterment of its members. Only a negligible percentage of its funds was used to aid needy medical students and needy doctors and their families. (Grants of $1,000 each annually were made to the medical schools of Harvard, Tufts, and Boston University for the benefit of needy medical students; and an annual award was also made to a graduating student of outstanding ability at each of these schools.)

The court cited with approval the Illinois decisions which came to similar conclusions regarding properties of the American Medical Association and the International College of Surgeons, which is an association with headquarters in Chicago.[4]

The Academy of Medicine of New Jersey is a private nonprofit organization of about 1,800 physicians and surgeons, owning and using two houses only a few doors apart as its headquarters. One of the houses contains the offices of the headquarters staff, some meeting rooms and seminar rooms, and a historical display room. The other is devoted chiefly to housing the largest medical library in the state.

The state division of tax appeals recently held both properties taxable; but on appeal to the superior court this decision was not wholly affirmed. As to the library house, the record was not entirely clear as to whether it was open and accessible to the public (if so, it might be exempt as a public library), or whether it was actually operated as a private library for the exclusive benefit of members of the academy. Therefore the decision as to it was remanded "for determination, upon such proofs as the parties desire to submit, as to whether the premises was on the taxing date actually and exclusively used as a public library."

As to the headquarters office house, the decision adverse to exemption was affirmed. Its use, thought the court, was not exclusively for

---

[4] *Massachusetts Medical Society* v. *Assessors of Boston*, 340 Mass. 327, 164 N.E. 2d 325 (1960); citing *American Medical Association* v. *Board of Review of Department of Labor*, 392 Ill. 614, 65 N.E. 2d 350 (1946), and *International College of Surgeons* v. *Brenza*, 8 Ill. 2d 141, 133 N.E. 2d 269, 61 A.L.R. 2d 1027 (1956), both of which are discussed at pages 228 and 229 in *The Colleges and the Courts Since 1950*.

the public, but largely for the private benefit of the members. This was true though the lectures, seminars, and exhibits held there were educational in nature. It was not a "college" within the meaning of the New Jersey statute because there was no regular instructional staff, no regularly enrolled students, and no scheduled classes.[5]

YWCA Low-Rental Home for Girl Students
Exempt in Nebraska

Across the street from the Central YWCA in Lincoln, Nebraska, is Annie L. Miller Hall, at 1429 N Street, an air-conditioned building containing 32 sleeping rooms (8 single and 24 double); a housemother's room, a small reception room, small living room, committee room, recreation room, kitchenette, and laundry room with facilities for washing and drying clothes. It is not open to the public, but has been owned and operated by the YWCA since 1946 as a home for young women aged 17 to 24 years whose personal incomes are not more than $250 per month, and who come to Lincoln, mostly from small towns in Nebraska, to attend business schools or similar training schools. The stay of any one lodger was limited to three years.

The rental rates were $18.50 to $32.50 per month. Some additional operating income came from the Community Chest and from individual gift accounts. Records of the past five years showed some operating loss, without counting any depreciation on the building.

Justice Messmore, speaking for the unanimous supreme court of Nebraska, held that Miller Hall is used for the charitable purposes of the YWCA (to provide moral surroundings, with religious overtones and proper supervision, for a limited time for young women as described), and is exempt from taxation. A lower court decision to that effect was affirmed.[6]

Nurses' Residence Owned by
Nonprofit Hospital

A Pennsylvania superior court holds that a large dwelling house

---

[5] *Town of Bloomfield* v. *Academy of Medicine of New Jersey*, 87 N.J. Super. 595, 210 A. 2d 420 (1965).

[6] *Y.W.C.A. of Lincoln* v. *City of Lincoln*, 177 Nebr. 136, 128 N.W. 2d 600 (1964).

adjacent to the grounds of a nonprofit hospital and used primarily as a home for registered nurses is properly tax-exempt as utilized solely for hospital purposes.[7]

The opinion was by Judge Montgomery, with Judge Watkins dissenting without recording his reasons. A certain resemblance between this case and those involving faculty housing owned by colleges and schools is observable.

Charitable Corporation Whose Sole Purpose Is to Benefit Nonprofit Hospital

The Vincent Club in Boston is an organization exclusively for the purpose of raising funds for the Vincent Memorial Hospital, which is the gynecological unit of the Massachusetts General Hospital, named for Mrs. J. R. Vincent, a well-known actress of the late nineteenth century. The club has operated continuously since 1892, and was incorporated in 1958. Its total contributions to the hospital over the years have exceeded $1 million. Currently it is giving about $50,000 a year, consisting of $10 each from the annual dues of its approximately 2,000 members, and about $30,000 as receipts from performances of its "annual review," as amateur theatrical show which is one of its principal activities.

The club owns and uses land and buildings at 71 and 73 Brimmer Street. No part of these premises is used or leased for any purpose other than the purposes of the club as above described. The property is tax-exempt, says a judgment of the supreme judicial court by Chief Justice Wilkins.[8] The court cited with approval one of its own decisions of 20 years earlier in a somewhat analogous case.[9]

Club for Youth, Known as Junior Achievement, Is Exempt in Minnesota

Junior Achievement of Greater Minneapolis, Inc., is a corpo-

---

[7] *Appeal of Shadyside Hospital,* (Pa. Super.), 218 A. 2d 355 (1966).

[8] *Board of Assessors of Boston* v. *Vincent Club,* (Mass.), 217 N.E. 2d 757 (1966).

[9] *Assessors of Boston* v. *World Wide Broadcasting Foundation of Massachusetts,* 317 Mass. 598, 59 N.E. 2d 188 (1945), discussed at page 60 in *The Colleges and the Courts, 1941-45.*

ration "to develop the understanding of young people as to the relationship and functions of the American free enterprise system by having the young people participate in projects" and learn of the various aspects of a business enterprise. Members are aged between 15 and 19, either males or females, from any public or private schools. The Minnesota supreme court holds that this organization is a "purely public charity" and therefore real estate owned and used by it is tax-exempt.

Justice Murphy, writing for the court, decided that Junior Achievement is not "an academy or seminary of learning," but: "It is nevertheless a school in that it provides a place where young people are educated and given an opportunity to acquire skills and experience not provided in public schools." Finally, "We conclude that the property is devoted to use as a 'purely public charity' and entitled to exemption under Minnesota Constitution, Article 9, Section 1, and Minnesota Statutes, Section 272.02."[10]

City Woman's Club in Lincoln, Nebraska

The Lincoln Woman's Club was incorporated in 1907 for purposes "educational, religious, charitable." (These are the words used in the Nebraska exemption statute.) The club sued to enjoin the collection of taxes on its headquarters building for the tax year 1962. During the early 'Sixties it had about 300 members, of whom 100 were life members who had paid $100 each, and 200 regular members each paying $6 a year. There were no paid officers.

Six departments were operated: (1) American Citizenship, (2) Bible, (3) Bridge, (4) Fine Arts, (5) Home, and (6) Kensington (making of garments for charitable distribution). The Fine Arts department provided some scholarships for art students, and most of the other five departments involved substantial amounts of serious study and teaching. Therefore the Nebraska supreme court readily concluded that the headquarters building was tax-exempt, except for the caretaker's apartment in the basement.

---

[10] *Junior Achievement of Greater Minneapolis, Inc.* v. *State,* 271 Minn. 385, 135 N.W. 2d 881 (1965).

One paragraph in Justice McCown's opinion for the court is of especial interest:[11]

> The City argues inferentially that since there is evidence that some activities are considered by some members to be "fun", such activities somehow cannot be religious, educational, or charitable. We cannot agree. There are many persons who enjoy education, many persons who find enjoyment in religion, and others who find fun in charity. The mental or emotional response of individuals to an activity certainly cannot be a judicial criterion in determining whether or not the activity is "religious", "educational", or "charitable".

Religious Educational Organizations and Activities in Various Forms

The supreme court of Montana in 1965 allowed a Methodist summer camp for children to recover real estate taxes paid under protest. The camp consisted of a 22-acre site with some 28 improvements, including 14 dormitory cottages, some faculty housing and employee accommodations, an auditorium-dining room building, a chapel and 4 classroom buildings, with storage, shop, and bathing facilities, garage, parking area, and boat dock, water-supply tank, and garbage-disposal. It operated principally for children, on a two-week rotating basis, accommodating about 150 at any one time.

Chief Justice James T. Harrison wrote the judgment holding that the property was "used exclusively for educational purposes" within the meaning of the exemption statutes.[12]

A Roman Catholic religious order, the Daughters of St. Paul, Inc., is a Massachusetts corporation with its Mother House in Boston. It operated a store in San Antonio, Texas, known as the St. Paul Catholic Book and Film Center, in a two-story-and-basement building owned by it, the first floor being occupied by the store, the basement used for storage, and the second floor a home for the four nuns who operated the business. The net income annually during the early 'Sixties was in the range of $15,000 to $20,000. Asking tax-exemption of the real property as "an institution of purely public charity," the order

---

[11] *Lincoln Woman's Club* v. *City of Lincoln*, 178 Neb. 357, 133 N.W. 2d 455 (1965).

[12] *Flathead Lake Methodist Camp* v. *Webb, County Treasurer*, (Mont.), 399 P. 2d 90 (1965).

met an adverse decision because a Texas statute [Article 7150 (7)] *defines* "an institution of purely public charity" as: (1) giving aid to members or others in sickness, distress, or death, (2)providing homes for helpless or dependent members, or (3) educating and maintaining the orphans of deceased members or others.

The property in question, the facts indicated, was not used for these purposes in any appreciable degree and therefore did not fit the specifications of the Texas statute to qualify it for exemption.[13]

The court cited its own contemporaneous decision in the *River Oaks Garden Club* case, next to be observed.

Garden Club Maintaining Historic Schoolhouse as Its Headquarters Not Exempt in Texas

By a narrowly divided vote, the Texas supreme court denied tax exemption to the Old Smith County Schoolhouse and grounds, owned and maintained as a historic landmark and headquarters by the River Oaks Garden Club, whose main activity was the education and enlightenment of its members and the public in the arts of growing and arranging flowers.

This was not, said the majority, "an institution of purely public charity" such as one clause of the state constitution permits to be exempted; nor was it a "school" such as is exempted under another clause.[14] This judgment affirmed a like decision by the court of civil appeals, which had reversed a favorable judgment of exemption in the trial court.

Chief Justice Calvert, for the majority, remarked that "It is but half a stride from the art of gardening to the art of interior decorating, and less than a half stride to the art of dramatics. Many others are but a stride away"—apparently meaning that instruction in these arts is neither charity nor schooling in the senses meant in the constitution—a conservative view.

A vigorous dissent was entered by Justice Norvell, in which Justices Greenhill, Griffin, and Smith joined him. They criticized

---

[13] *Daughters of St. Paul, Inc.* v. *City of San Antonio*, (Tex. Civ. App.), 387 S.W. 2d 709 (1965).

[14] *River Oaks Garden Club* v. *City of Houston*, (Tex), 370 S.W. 2d 851 (1963); reversing (Tex. Civ. App.). 360 S.W. 2d 855 (1962).

the majority's concept that "the only charity which is eligible for legislative exemption is one whose activities will *directly* lessen a financial burden which would otherwise be borne by the taxpayer." Recognizing the change and expansion that are inherent in the development of charity, Justice Norvell asked, "Where and when may we expect agreement as to educational work which the state or local government is under an obligation to finance?"

He and his dissenting colleagues maintained that the requirement for exemption is nothing more than that the garden club use the premises exclusively for the promotion of education and learning, without charge. "The fact that other organizations of the same purpose and use-pattern are allowed to assist in fulfilling that purpose under the control of the Garden Club, meets the letter and the theory of the statute and the constitution, as interpreted by our courts."

Occasional Fuel and Tire Tests on Automobile Speedway Do Not Make It Primarily a Scientific or Educational Agency

At Daytona Beach, Florida, there is a public authority known as the Daytona Beach Racing and Recreational Facilities District, which leased from the city a tract of land on which a 2½-mile motor vehicle race track was built and operated by the Daytona International Speedway Corporation, a private concern for profit. The lease from the district to the corporation stipulated that the district retained the right to use the property for "all public uses and purposes" when the facilities were not otherwise in use, for periods totaling not more than three months in each fiscal year.

The district, evidently hazarding a long-shot legal chance, sought exemption of the property from taxation as a scientific or educational institution because carefully measured tests of motor fuels and tires were occasionally made there with the consent or under the supervision of the private corporation. Article XVI, Section 16 of the Florida constitution requires "exclusive use" for exempt purposes. Here the showing was that the use for testing purposes was only partial and in small degree, and far from exclusive; and there was no evidence that it had any connection with any public purpose of the district, nor any proof that it was conducted without pecuniary profit to the private corporation. In these circumstances the Florida court of appeals could only hold that the property was not exempt from taxation.[15]

If the foregoing cases seem often to concern enterprises that are a far cry from universities or colleges, one must remember that the statutes touching tax exemptions often embrace many and varied categories of charitable institutions and agencies, and that only a small fraction or fragment of the field would be observed if we confined our vision only narrowly to cases actually involving formal institutions of higher learning.

The next following chapter continues in the area of state taxation but concerns itself with state taxes other than property taxes.

---

[15] *Daytona Beach Racing and Recreational Facilities District* v. *Paul*, (Fla. App.), 157 So. 2d 156 (1963).

CHAPTER 16

STATE TAXES OTHER THAN
PROPERTY TAXES

IN THIS CATEGORY are numerous kinds of state and local taxes, such as inheritance taxes, sales and use taxes, excise taxes on tickets of admission to athletic or theatrical exhibitions, and others. Some of the ways in which some of these revenue measures affect higher education in some states appear below.

State Inheritance Taxes: Exemption of Charitable
Legacies in Oregon May Be Affected by Residence
or Nonresidence of Probable Beneficiaries

The statutes and decisions of the various states are not uniform concerning the issue of exempting the testamentary transfer of legacies from residents of the state to charitable corporations outside the state (known to the law as "foreign corporations").[1] There are further questions as to what proportions of the activities of a domestic

---

[1] Some inklings of many of the older statutes and decisions are in Chapter XXIII, "Tax Exemption: Estate and Inheritance Taxes" in E. C. Elliott and M. M. Chambers, *The Colleges and the Courts*. New York: Carnegie Foundation for the Advancement of Teaching, 1936, 562 pp. (Out of print, but available in university and college libraries and state supreme court libraries.)

charitable corporation are carried on within and without the borders of the state, and whether or not any substantial percentage of the individual beneficiaries of the charity are likely to be nonresidents of the state, and whether or not this should affect the issue of exemption.

This last question appears in two recent Oregon decisions. The first of these concerned the estate of an almost incredible rarity—a public school teacher who became wealthy. The legendary principal of Jefferson High School in Portland, Hopkin Jenkins, who died in 1956 at the age of 83, leaving an estate of over $1 million, had drafted his will in 1948 and created a trust of more than $100,000 as the Jenkins Student Loan Fund "for the purpose of providing a fund of money for the advanced education of qualified boys and girls, beyond high school requirements."

The trial court declared this legacy exempt from the state inheritance tax, but the seven-judge Oregon supreme court, in an opinion by Justice Warner, reversed the judgment and held the transfer taxable because the carefully and skilfully drawn instrument said nothing about restricting the benefits to residents of the state.[2]

The court cited a New York decision of seven decades ago:

> It is the policy of society to encourage benevolence and charity. But it is not the proper function of a state to go outside its own limits, and devote its resources to support the cause of religion, education, or missions for the benefit of mankind at large. *In re Prime's Estate*, 136 N.Y. 347, 32 N.E. 1091, 18 L.R.A. 713 (1893).

And an astringent New Hampshire judgment of half a century ago, of the same tenor:

> The state itself is not a charitable institution, and does not authorize its representatives to spend the public money, by exemptions from taxation or otherwise, for purposes having little or no relation to the welfare of the inhabitants of the state. The purpose of such laws (exemption statutes) is the acquisition of some supposed public advantage. (Thus a bequest to a local auxiliary of the Women's Foreign Missionary Society, chiefly for "evangelization of heathen women," was held taxable.) *Carter v. Whitcomb*, 74 N.H. 482, 69 A. 779, 17 L.R.A.N.S. 733 (1908).

---

[2] *In re Jenkins' Estate: Unander* v. *United States National Bank*, 224 Ore. 144, 355 P. 2d 729 (1960).

It would seem that these old cases are only obliquely in point; and it is equally obvious that they represent a provincial concept of charity at the opposite pole from the views expressed by latter-day judges in New York and elsewhere. Witness, for example, the case of *People ex rel. Near East Foundation* v. *Boyland*, 201 Misc. 855, 106 N.Y.S. 2d 736 (1951), wherein a charitable enterprise most of whose beneficiaries were not residents of the state and whose activities were predominately outside the state, was held to be tax-exempt.[3] The exemption statute in Oregon, however [ORS 118.020 (1) (c)], exempts "devises, bequests, legacies, and gifts . . . if made to a person or persons or association of persons in trust for benevolent, charitable, religious, scientific or educational uses *within this state* (italics mine); and this wording might seem to be a firmer base for the 1960 decision in the *Jenkins* case than the excerpts from the old New York and New England opinions which the court quoted.

Under the same statute, however, the same court made a markedly different decision in a similar case in 1964, which, though said to be distinguishable, seems to be very close to a practical overruling of the *Jenkins* case.

Here Mildred Litster created the Litster Scholarship Trust, with awards to be made to "young men and young women who are in the graduating class or who have already graduated from Crater High School in Central Point, Oregon, or such other high school as may be the successor of Crater High School as the high school for the Gold Hill area, to enable them or to assist them in completing their first two years of college studies in a college or university."

Against the exemption of this transfer from the state inheritance tax it was pointed out that under the terms of the trust there was nothing to prevent awards being made to former graduates now living outside Oregon, and attending a college outside Oregon; and, impressed by this argument, and probably with one eye on the statute and the other on the *Jenkins* decision of only four years earlier, the trial court declared the transfer taxable.

This time Justice O'Connell spoke for the state supreme court, which reversed the judgment and held the transfer exempt from the

---

[3] Discussed at pages 226-227 in *The Colleges and the Courts Since 1950.*

inheritance tax.[4] Justice O'Connell noted that no one would be eligible for a scholarship award unless he had been an inhabitant of Oregon at some time, *i.e.*, while attending Crater High School; and he took a broad liberal view of the charitable purpose of the donor. He felt quite certain that the majority of the awards would be to Oregon residents. In any case, the awards would be an incentive toward improvement of the quality of Crater High School, and would thus tend substantially to benefit the state.

Mildred Litster's predominant purpose, he thought, was to benefit resident graduates of an Oregon high school; and it should be immaterial that a small number of nonresidents might benefit. This is diametrically different from the *rationale* of the *Jenkins* decision. It may not be too much to say the Oregon court within the space of four years moved from a literal blackletter interpretation of the statute to a more thoughtful and humane construction based on a more flexible definition of charity and a fuller recognition of charitable intent; from a tendency to rely on outdated precedents set by the courts in a distant section of the nation, toward study of the practicalities of the time and place.

Local Planned Parenthood Association in Ohio Is Held Charitable and Exempt from State Succession Taxes

In 1966 the Ohio supreme court decided that the Planned Parenthood Association of Columbus, Ohio, is an "institution for purposes only of public charity" within the meaning of Ohio's tax exemption statutes, and is not subject as a legatee to the state succession tax laws.[5]

Judge Schneider, writing the opinion for the court, found that the association is a nonprofit corporation organized and operating wholly within the state, for the primary purpose of providing any married or about-to-be married woman, regardless of her ability to pay, with medical information and knowledge concerning the physiology of con-

---

[4] *United States National Bank of Portland* v. *Belton*, 267 Ore. 368, 391 P. 2d 611 (1964).

[5] *Planned Parenthood Association of Columbus, Ohio* v. *Tax Commissioner, in re Estate of Weiler*, 5 Ohio St. 2d 117, 214 N.E. 2d 222 (1966).

ception and the means of contraception, and with necessary medical assistance for the utilization of the information.

State Sales and Use Tax in Illinois: "Retailers' Occupation Tax Act"

A cold war of long standing exists between large private retail vendors of college textbooks and nonprofit college bookstores operated by colleges and universities on their campuses.

In a recent year it was reported that the total volume of sales of textbooks and school supplies to college students in Illinois was $10,705,000, of which $4,791,000 was from college-owned stores, and $5,914,000 from private retail stores. Of the total of 214,000 students in Illinois, 74,000 or about 34 per cent, were attending colleges which did not operate bookstores. These figures might seem to indicate, in general, that where the college operates a bookstore, it handles slightly more than half of the local business.

Whether or not college-operated bookstores were exempt from the Illinois sales and use tax was the issue in a 1963 decision of the state supreme court. The Director of Revenue had ruled that sales of books in college bookstores were exempt. A private book vendor contested the validity of this ruling, and was met by a demurrer, which the lower court sustained. The supreme court of Illinois, however, reversed the judgment and held that college or university bookstores were not exempt.[6]

The matter hinges on the interpretation of certain clauses in the statutes, one of which purports to except from taxation "persons organized and operated exclusively for educational purposes, to the extent of their sales to students," and another of which excepts "sales of personalty not sold or offered for sale by persons organized for profit." The first of these clauses is obviously intended to exempt college-owned bookstores, and the second is apparently intended to destroy that exemption in large part, for the benefit of their privately owned competitors. This makes the voice of the statutes confusing and equivocal, not to say self-contradictory. The state supreme court, in an

---

[6] *Follett's Illinois Book and Supply Store, Inc.* v. *Isaacs*, 27 Ill. 2d 600, 190 N.E. 2d 324 (1963).

opinion by Justice Underwood, decided that in this state of affairs, sales of books by bookstores operated on campus by universities at prices substantially similar to those of competing retail stores, were not exempt.

The University of Illinois, the University of Chicago, and Northwestern University were concerned in the case as *amici curiae* (friends of the court). They testified that Justice Underwood's interpretation would effectively destroy the advantage that should be granted to nonprofit organizations organized primarily for the benefit of students. Seemingly the court conceded this, but took refuge in the assumed duty to give strict construction to tax exemption statutes. This, as is well known, is irreconcilable with another rule of construction, that such statutes are to be interpreted liberally in favor of nonprofit charitable agencies, and that organizations acting as agencies of the state are rarely taxed in any form.

State Tax on Football Admissions in South Carolina

Section 65-801, 1960 Cumulative Supplement to the South Carolina Code, stipulates:

> There shall be levied, assessed, collected, and paid upon all paid admissions to all places of amusement within this state a license tax of one cent for each ten cents or fractional part thereof paid for any such admission, but no tax shall be charged or collected on: . . . (4) Admissions charged by any eleemosynary or non-profit corporation or organization. . . .
>
> . . . .
>
> Such tax shall be paid by the person paying such admission price. . . .

Furman University, a private nonprofit corporation, collected and paid under protest $4,382 in taxes on its 1960 football tickets and sued to recover that sum on the ground that it was exempt under (4) in the preceding quotation. There was a judgment for the university in the court of common pleas, but this was reversed and remanded by the state supreme court, which held that the tax was not on the university, but on the purchasers of tickets. Therefore the university was not a "taxpayer" for purposes of this case, but merely a collection agent, and had no standing to sue for recovery.[7]

---

[7] *Furman University* v. *Livingston*, 244 S.C. 200, 136 S.E. 2d 254 (1964).

To pursue the reasoning, probably an individual ticket-purchasing taxpayer could sue, and probably recover; but he would recover only the few cents he himself had actually paid as a tax on the price of his tickets. The outcome of this case, with reference to the state tax on admissions to amusements, is the same as that determined by the United States Supreme Court in 1938 with reference to the federal tax of the same type.[8]

---

[8] *Allen* v. *Regents of University System of Georgia*, 304 U.S. 439, 58 S.Ct. 980, 82 L.Ed. 1448 (1938); discussed at pages 70-71 in *The Colleges and the Courts, 1936-40.*

CHAPTER 17

FEDERAL TAXATION

IT IS THE ESTABLISHED PUBLIC POLICY of the national government to encourage and materially assist the financing of colleges and universities by various provisions of the federal tax laws.

Exempted from federal income taxes on corporations are state and other public institutions of higher education, as well as all private universities and colleges that are registered with the Department of the Treasury as nonprofit charitable organizations. The only schools not exempt are those which are proprietary, or which fail to qualify as nonprofit and charitable. (One such case appears in this chapter.)

Federal income taxes applicable to individuals and to business corporations provide for deductions from gross income of sums given to charitable and educational organizatons; and in varying circumstances these gifts thus actually always cost the donor less than their full value, sometimes very much less, on account of tax savings; and it is often said that in rare circumstances such a charitable gift may cost the donor nothing. In this event, the net effect is that the donor is exercising an option of making his contribution to charitable objects of his choice, rather than to the government in the form of income taxes. Every charitable deduction provides this option to some extent. Under the federal estate and gift tax laws, deductions for gifts and bequests to charitable purposes are also provided for.

The federal Internal Revenue Code, as revised and amended from time to time by Congress, becomes immensely complicated. Together with numerous applicable treasury regulations and voluminous rulings of the Internal Revenue Service, plus the reports of many decisions of the United States tax court and higher federal courts in tax cases, it forms a body of law so complex and ever-changing that the task of a federal tax attorney is a very demanding full-time specialty.

In fact, industrious and insightful lawyers in the employ of business corporations, wealthy individuals, or charitable institutions are constantly alert to devise schemes of various kinds in the world of finance that will be in compliance with the letter of the tax laws but will bring tax advantages to their employers far greater than Congress intended. When such schemes succeed on a substantial scale, they are often followed by an amendment of the Internal Revenue Code designed to restore its operation to the real intent of Congress. This is known in popular parlance as "closing a loophole," and the story of this process constitutes a substantial part of the history of federal legislation on income and estate taxes.

There is nothing unlawful (in the absence of evidence to the contrary) in collaboration between a charitable institution and a wealthy prospective donor to devise a plan that will bring maximum tax advantages to both. However, the "still, small voice of conscience" may say that the aim of keeping barely within the letter of the law is far below a shining moral goal; and there is a shady area between honest estate planning and collusion to defraud the government. When such plans become the subject of litigation, the courts determine in each case whether they overstep the law, and it is always the prerogative of the Congress to amend the law if deemed necessary in the public interest.

Trusts for Education of One's Own Children Are Not Charitable, and Not Exempt from Federal Income Tax

In 1959, one Mr. Morrill established four 10-year trusts, one for the benefit of each of his four minor children, and named a corporate trustee of each. In each the income was to be accumulated until the child became 21 years of age, at which time the accumulated income, and thereafter any current income, was to be paid to the beneficiary. During the minority of the beneficiary, the trustee might at its discretion use the trust income "for the payment of room, tuition, books and travel to and from any private school, college, or other institution of learning at home or abroad." After 10 years the trusts were to terminate and the *corpus* of each revert to Mr. Morrill.

During the tax years 1959, 1960, and 1961 the children attended Vassar College, Connecticut College, Brown University, the Holderness School, and the Waynflete School. Mr. Morrill expressly assumed personal responsibility for all bills at Vassar and Connecticut. At the other three schools the trusts paid room and tuition fees, and Mr. Morrill personally paid all other bills. The United States district court had no difficulty in deciding that the income of the trusts was taxable to Mr. Morrill, on the theory that the education of his minor children is a father's own legal responsibility, and "trust income which is used to satisfy a legal obligation of the grantor is, in effect, distributed to him and is, therefore, taxable to him."[1]

The court quoted *Internal Revenue Code*, 1954, Section 677 a:

> The grantor shall be treated as the owner of any portion of a trust . . . whose income, without the approval or consent of any adverse party is, or, in the discretion of the grantor or a nonadverse party, or both, may be . . . (1) distributed to the grantor.

An earlier and somewhat similar case was that of three physicians and their wives at Ithaca, New York, who owned their offices, and conveyed this real estate to a trustee by an instrument providing that the income of the trust should be paid to the children of the grantors for the children's education. The physicians reserved the right to revoke the trust, and also retained effective means of control over the actions of the trustees. On their federal income tax returns they then deducted office-rentals paid by them to the trustee. The court thought this was a rather transparent transaction in which the tax-saving motive was evident, and held that the sums were not deductible. Through the flimsy film of the trust instrument, it appeared that they were in effect paying rentals to themselves for offices they still owned, for practical purposes; for in no event could the property pass to any remainderman other than the original owners.[2]

Internal Revenue Code Section 162 (a) (3) allows deduction of

---

[1] *Morrill v. United States,* (U.S.D.C., Me.), 228 F. Supp. 734 (1964).
[2] *Hall v. United States,* (U.S.D.C., N.Y.), 208 F. Supp. 584 (1962).

rentals only when paid for the use or possession of property "to which the taxpayer has not taken or is not taking title or *in which he has no equity*."

Payment to Be Applied Solely to Fees of One Named
Student Is Not Tax-Exempt Charitable Gift

In 1955 and 1956, a donor made gifts of approximately $550 each to Luther College in Decorah, Iowa, for "scholarships" and deducted these amounts from his gross income on his federal income tax returns. Prior correspondence between the donor and the college had established that these gifts would be applied solely for the benefit of one Robert F. Roble, a student known to the donor. Such a gift is not a charity in the eyes of the law, but only a private benevolence. Similarly, a gift for the sole benefit of the donor's descendants is not a charity, even though his descendants may be numerous. A charity must be for the benefit of an indefinite number of persons who will qualify as beneficiaries on some broader basis than that of being of the donor's blood. Accordingly the tax court denied the deduction, and was affirmed by the United States court of appeals in an opinion by Circuit Judge Castle, with Circuit Judges Knoch and Schnackenberg concurring.[3]

The same case involved another issue. The same donor had given five pieces of ancient Hellenistic-Syrian jewelry to the Oriental Institute of the University of Chicago, and deducted his appraisal of $42,500 value. The tax court reduced the value deductible to $15,000, and this judgment was also affirmed by the court of appeals, with Circuit Judge Knoch dissenting. The arguments about the appraisal are not germane to the issue of what constitutes a tax-exempt charitable gift, and need not be recited here.

When Trust Is By Its Own Terms Partly Private and
Partly Charitable, Tax Treatment of Long-Term
Capital Gains May Pose Difficult Questions

The Ellsworth M. Statler Trust was founded in 1920, its *corpus*

---

[3] *Tripp* v. *Commissioner of Internal Revenue*, (U.S.C.A., Ia.), 337 F. 2d 432 (1964).

consisting of large amounts of stock of the Hotels Statler Company placed in trust by the donor for the benefit of his descendants. The trustees were directed to make charitable gifts of not less than 15 per cent nor more than 30 per cent of the income each year, the charities to be chosen by majority vote of the trustees and Mr. Statler's children in joint session; but the trustees alone were to determine the exact percentage to go to charity each year. By 1954, the trustees were paying all the income remaining after the charitable set-aside to Statler's adult children; and upon the death of the last of these, the *corpus* was to go to other individuals, with no charity having any interest. In that year all the stock of the Hotels Statler Company (217,088 shares) was sold to the Hilton Hotels Corporation at about $50 per share, of which about $47 per share was long-term capital gain.

By a compromise agreed upon between the trust and the federal tax authorities in 1955, it was understood that $15.50 per share would be allocated to income; and of this, 15 per cent (less 2 per cent commissions) would be paid to charities, and the balance distributed to the private beneficiaries. The rest of the proceeds would be added to the *corpus* of the trust (and be subject to favorable tax treatment as capital gains). The result was that about $387,000 was paid to charities, amounting to $2.28 per share, and $31.56 per share was added to the *corpus*. The trust contended that only this last should be subject to the capital gains tax; but both the Commissioner of Internal Revenue and the tax court maintained that *both* the $2.28 per share and the $31.56, making a total of $33.84, should be taxed as capital gains. This judgment of the tax court was reversed by the United States court of appeals, holding that only the $31.56 per share was so taxable. The opinion was by Circuit Judge Friendly, with Circuit Judge Hays concurring, and with a dissenting opinion entered by District Judge Dooling.[4]

In support of the majority view, the court quoted from the opinion of Mr. Justice Owen J. Roberts in a 1934 decision of the United States Supreme Court:[5]

> The exemption of income devoted to charity and the reduction of the rate of tax on capital gains were liberalizations

---

[4] *Statler Trust* v. *Commissioner of Internal Revenue*, (U.S.C.A., N.Y.), 361, F. 2d 128 (1966); reversing 43 Tax Court 208 (1964).
[5] *Helvering* v. *Bliss*, 293 U.S. 144, 55 S.Ct. 17, 79 L.Ed 246 (1934).

of the law in the taxpayer's favor, were begotten from motives
of public policy, and are not to be narrowly construed.

Institution, To Be Tax-Exempt, Must Show That "No Part of Its Net Earnings Inured to Benefit of Any Individual" During Tax Years in Question

The Cleveland Chiropractic College in Kansas City, a charitable
corporation since 1922, found that it must pay the federal corporation
income tax on its net income for the years 1948 through 1951, because its president had so commingled its funds with his own private
and personal accounts that there was no effective knowledge or control of the college's income until 1952, some two years after an auditor
had been employed to disentangle its affairs.

There was evidence that during the years in question there had
been a substantial net income, due to the influx of "G.I." students
whose fees and maintenance were subsidized by the government;
but the accounts were promiscuously confused with the private affairs of its president, Dr. Carl S. Cleveland, Sr., and for the year 1951
it appeared that he had received some $28,000 ostensibly belong-
ing to the college, and had failed to report this sum as gross receipts
in his personal income tax return or in any other manner. In 1948 the
college had been granted tax-exempt status by the Internal Revenue
Service under Section 101 (6) of the *Internal Revenue Code* of 1939,
but this concession was retroactively revoked in November 1956.

The United States tax court sustained the decision that the college must pay the corporate net income tax for the years noted, plus
the 5 per cent penalty provided by law. The tax court did not hold
that the charter of the charitable corporation was a "sham," but only
that the corporation had failed to meet the burden of proof regarding
its entitlement to tax-exempt status. The judgment was affirmed by
the United States court of appeals.[6]

Charitable Trust May Forfeit Its Exemption If It Makes Loans to Its Creator Without Adequate Security

As a deterrent to certain practices of individuals who have been

---

[6] *Cleveland Chiropractic College* v. *Commissioner of Internal Revenue*,
(U.S.C.A., Mo.), 312 F. 2d 203 (1963).

known to create "family trusts" or "company trusts" as charitable organizations and then manipulate them in various ways for their own private advantage, Section 503 (a) 1 of the Internal Revenue Code provided for forfeiture of the exemption of the charitable organization "if it lends any part of its income or *corpus*, without receipt of adequate security and a reasonable rate of interest, . . . to the creator of such organization (if a trust)."

The William Clay, Jr., Foundation (charitable) was found to have made a loan of $10,000 to Management Trust Company, a commercial corporation controlled by the founder of the Clay Foundation. The facts developed as follows: Management Trust Company was Mr. Clay's corporation to hold and manage extensive real estate, chiefly farms. It had a net worth of "several hundred thousand dollars" and was in sound, solvent condition, but needed $10,000 cash in December 1954. Mr. Clay and his wife could easily have made the loan themselves, (and it would have been to their advantage to do so), but chose to have the foundation lend the money as a good investment. The foundation got a 4½% negotiable promissory note, and the loan was repaid in full in 1958, without ever having become delinquent and having been at all times secured by land worth many times its value.

The foundation's suit for refund of federal income taxes paid on account of the claim that this transaction forfeited its exemption was successful. District Judge Brewster said: "There are no facts in this case which intimate the existence of any of the well-known evils sought to be remedied by the statutes here involved.[7]

"Unreasonable" Accumulation by Charitable Foundation
May Cause Forfeiture of Tax-Exempt Status

Section 3814 of the *Internal Revenue Code* stipulates that, in the case of tax-exempt organizations as described in Section 101 (6),

> . . . if the amounts accumulated during the taxable year or any prior taxable year and not actually paid out by the end of the taxable year—
> (1) are unreasonable in amount of duration in order to carry out the charitable, educational, or other purpose or func-

---

[7] *William Clay, Jr. Foundation* v. *United States*, (U.S.D.C., Tex.), 233 F. Supp. 628 (1964).

tion constituting the basis for such organization's exemption under Section 101 (6); . . . exemption under Section 101 (6) shall be denied for the taxable year.

The well-known Danforth Foundation was founded in 1927 as a Missouri charitable corporation. The principal contributors were William Danforth, president of the Ralston Purina Company, and his wife. After 1936, said the federal district court, "The greater part of the assets was comprised of common stock of the company, which stock was voted by proxy held during 1951 and 1952 by Donald Danforth who succeeded his father as president of the company. William and Donald, and Dorothy Compton, daughter of the founders, were trustees of the foundation during the taxable years (1951 and 1952) involved in this case."

Up to 1951 the gifts of William Danforth and his wife to the foundation aggregated nearly $5 million. District Judge Regan continued: "Expenditures for programs designed by the end of 1951 could not be expected to exceed $300,000 in charitable grants, and under all programs designed by the end of 1952, expenditures could not be expected to exceed $500,000 in the immediate future. . . Meanwhile, subsequent annual income could reasonably be expected to exceed $1 million. The conclusion that the unexpended income of $1,104,990 in 1951 and $978,059 in 1952, making a total accumulation of $6,394,739 by the end of 1952, constitute unreasonable accumulations is inescapable." Thus the court held that the foundation had forfeited its tax-exempt status for the tax years 1951 and 1952 by reason of excessive accumulation and dismissed its action to recover income taxes assessed and paid for those years. This decision was affirmed by the United States court of appeals, and the Supreme Court of the United States declined to review the case.[8]

The decision was applicable only to the years 1951 and 1952. Subsequently the Danforth Foundation has employed a competent director and staff to plan and execute its charitable activities on a scale commensurate with its resources, so that it has not been vulnerable to the suspicion of "unreasonable accumulations," and its tax-exempt status has not thereby been endangered.

---

[8] *Danforth Foundation* v. *United States*, (U.S.D.C., Mo.), 222 F. Supp. 761 (1963); affirmed in (U.S.C.A., Mo.), 347 F. 2d 673 (1965); and *certiorai* denied in 382 U.S. 955.

The Hulman Foundation, Inc., in Terre Haute, Indiana, was incorporated in 1940 under the Indiana General Not-for-Profit Corporation Act, "to promote educational, literary, scientific, religious and charitable purposes." Its founder was Anton Hulman, Jr., financier and philanthropist, and he was its president and a member of its three-member board of directors. A 1941 letter ruling of the Internal Revenue Service granted it status as an exempt organization, not liable for income taxes, and with contributions and legacies to it deductible under the income and estate tax laws; but a letter ruling in 1956 revoked this exemption for the tax years 1951-54, on account of alleged unreasonable accumulation during those years.

Said this letter, "A recapitulation of your operations for the years 1951-54 reflects income receipts, exclusive of gains on sale of securities, totaling $887,292 as compared with donations of $110,194 for charitable purposes." The net worth of the corporation had grown from $82,000 in 1941 to $3,866,000 in 1953. During the decade 1940-50 the ratio of donations to income was about 45 per cent; but for 1951-53 it had been less than 11 per cent. The list of donees during the period 1940-54 included the city of Terre Haute, the state of Indiana, Rose Polytechnic Institute (a private school of engineering), Indiana State College (now Indiana State University), Purdue University, the American Red Cross, and several hospitals, churches, community funds, social agencies, charitable and civil organizations, mostly but not all in Terre Haute.

It seems that during the later years of this period the attention of the foundation began to be concentrated on the provision of a "civic auditorium, field house, athletic field, and coliseum" for the benefit of the inhabitants of the city and county and the surrounding area; and this may account for its engaging in various borrowings and investments intended to increase its earning-capacity and financial position during 1951-54. In 1956 the foundation created by trust indenture a perpetual charitable trust named the Hulman Public Building Trust, devoted to the financing, erection, and maintenance of the public building project.

After the foundation had informed the Internal Revenue Service of its policy of contributing its accumulated income and any tax refunds it might receive to the building trust, in 1960 a third letter ruling restored its status as an exempt organization; and it sued for a refund of income taxes paid for the years 1951-54. A favorable judgment of the United States district court allowed it to recover some $120,000.

District Judge Holder concluded that it was entitled to exemption for the years 1951-54 because its earnings did not inure to the benefit of any private individual, its accumulations were not unreasonable, the accumulated income was not used to any substantial degree for purposes other than those on which exemption was based, or invested in a manner to jeopardize the carrying out of the corporation's exempt purposes, and its objective of financing a civic building was reasonable.[9]

The *Hulman Foundation* case is reminiscent of the *Samuel Friedland Foundation* decision of 1956, in which the accumulative activities of that foundation over a few years were adjudged not to have deprived it of its character as an exempt organization. There the concrete object was to accumulate funds to provide a medical research building at Brandeis University.[10]

"Unrelated Business Income" of Corporation to Promote Social Welfare Is Not Exempt from Corporation Income Tax

Section 501 (c) (4) of the *Internal Revenue Code* of 1954 provided for the exemption of "civic leagues or organizations not for profit but operated exclusively for the promotion of social welfare . . ."

The People's Educational Camp Society, Inc., was a nonstock, nonprofit membership corporation organized in New York in 1920 by the Rand School of Social Science, which in turn was operated by the American Socialist Society. The purpose of the new 1920 corporation was to take title to a resort area of 2,196 acres in the Pocono Mountains of Pennsylvania, named Camp Tamiment. The corporation was not to exceed 35 members, elected by its board of directors and approved by the other members.

It immediately took over and operated Camp Tamiment, and for

---

[9] *Hulman Foundation, Inc.* v. *United States,* (U.S.D.C., Ind.), 217 F. Supp. 423 (1962).

[10] *Samuel Friedland Foundation* v. *United States,* (U.S.D.C., N.J.), 144 F. Supp. 74 (1956). Discussed at pages 246-247 in *The Colleges and the Courts Since 1950.*

the next 20 years the operation was generally self-sustaining and steadily profitable, so that by 1941 the value of fixed assets was nearly $400,000 and annual gross income was about $282,000. By 1951 assets were $1,125,000 and gross annual income $840,000. By 1956 assets were $2,302,000 and gross income $943,000. Funds held as "surplus" or "reserves" were $311,000 in 1941, and went up to $1,573,000 in 1951 and $2,226,000 in 1956.

By 1956 both the Rand School and the American Socialist Society had ceased to exist; but the People's Educational Camp Society, Inc., in addition to operating Camp Tamiment on the scale previously sketched, had acquired the New York City property which housed its own offices and the library of the Rand School. It continued to operate the library as a public institution. Camp Tamiment was a large and flourishing Poconos resort open to the general public at $12 to $19 per day per person, and operating on a profitable basis.

In these circumstances the Internal Revenue Service undertook to collect a sum in excess of $25,000 as income tax due from the corporation for the tax year 1956, and the corporation resisted on the ground that it was an exempt organization. The United States tax court denied the exemption, and this judgment was affirmed by the court of appeals in an opinion by Circuit Judge Waterman in which Circuit Judge Smith joined and from which Circuit Judge Hays dissented.

Deciding that the commercial operation of Camp Tamiment was more than 90 per cent of the total activities of the corporation, the two majority judges held that the presence of a single non-exempt purpose, if substantial in nature, will destroy the exemption, regardless of the number or importance of truly exempt purposes.[11]

Purchase of Industrial Plant by Charitable Corporation May Be Under Conditions Giving Seller Large Tax Advantages: Clay Brown Case of 1965

In earlier years several cases have been observed, involving the acquisition of business enterprises by charitable corporations under various plans and in various circumstances, such that the transaction

---

[11] *People's Educational Camp Society, Inc.* v. *Commissioner of Internal Revenue,* (U.S.C.A., N.Y.), 331 F. 2d 923 (1964); affirming 39 Tax Court 756 (1963).

was expected to inure to the great benefit of a nonprofit institution of higher education; and the tax consequences, under federal and state tax laws, have been noted, including some amendments apparently occasioned thereby.[12]

Seemingly a new type of loophole was discovered in the much-talked-of *Clay Brown* case, which was decided favorably to the taxpayer by a United States court of appeals in 1963 and made its way to the United States Supreme Court in 1965, where the judgment was affirmed. Both tribunals took occasion to remark in their opinions that if the result was deemed not to be in accord with the intent of Congress, the Congress was free to amend the statutes accordingly. It was reported in August 1966 that bills had indeed been introduced in the House of Representatives, intended to make such results impossible in the future, and sponsored by members of the Committee on Ways and Means.

Clay Brown was president of Clay Brown and Company, a family corporation owning and operating a sawmill and lumber business near Fortuna, California. The firm had prospered, and in 1952 Mr. Brown and the other stockholders agreed to sell all its stock to the California Institute for Cancer Research for $1,300,000. The business would be operated by a new corporation formed for that purpose by the attorneys for the sellers with Mr. Brown as manager and having the right to name his own successor. The new company would pay to the institute 80 per cent of its annual pretax profits, and each year 90 per cent of this amount would be applied as a reduction of the purchase price owed to the former stockholders by the institute.

---

[12] *Century Electric Company, Petitioner,* Docket No. 13115 in United States Tax Court, decided October 31, 1950. (Claimed deductible loss in sale and "lease-back" of industrial plant, the purchaser being William Jewell College), discussed at pages 122-123 in *The Colleges and the Courts, 1946-50.*

State ex rel. Bannister v. *Trustees of William Jewell College,* 364 Mo. 199, 260 S.W. 2d 479 (1953). (Industrial plant owned by college held exempt from state and local property taxes by virtue of broad charter provision for exemption of all property of the college), discussed at pages 199-200 in *The Colleges and the Courts Since 1950.*

C. F. Mueller Company v. *Commissioner of Internal Revenue,* (U.S.C.C.A.), 190 F. 2d 120 (1951), and *Knapp Brothers Shoe Corporation* v. *United States,* 135 U.S. Court of Claims 797, 142 F. Supp. 899 (1956). (Purchase of businesses by newly-created corporations under whose charters all profits would accrue to New York University), discussed at pages 242-244 in *The Colleges and the Courts Since 1950.*

The stockholders received non-interest-bearing promissory notes from the institute for the appropriate sums.

The purchase agreement was that the institute would part with no money of its own. It was to make a down payment of $5,000 derived from the assets of the business, and the remainder of the purchase price within 10 years, wholly derived from the earnings of the company, as here indicated. The institute was under no obligation to pay unless the earnings of the company were sufficient to provide the necessary funds. In case of default, ownership would revert to the sellers.

Default and reversion occurred in 1955, whereupon the sellers consented that the institute should sell the property and retain 10 per cent of the proceeds, and turn over the remainder to the original stockholders. This was done, and the total of payments from all sources then aggregated slightly over $936,000. On their income tax returns Mr. Brown and the other stockholders reported their respective shares of this sum as a gain from the sale of capital assets (capital gains being taxed at lower rates than ordinary income). The Internal Revenue Service insisted that these sums must be reported as ordinary income and taxed as such. The United States tax court took an opposite view, and held that the transaction was a *bona fide* sale, so that the sellers could treat the proceeds as long-term capital gains. This judgment was affirmed by the United States court of appeals; and, sensing the importance of the case, the United States Supreme Court consented to review it, and affirmed it by a divided vote of the Justices.[13]

The opinion for the majority of the high tribunal was written by Mr. Justice Byron White. It is a studious 5,000-word discourse tracing the history of related cases, concluding that "the Commissioner's position here is a clear case of overkill if aimed at preventing the involvement of tax-exempt entities in the purchase and operation of business enterprises. There are more precise approaches to this problem as well as to the question of the possibly excessive price paid by the charity or foundation. And if the Commissioner's approach is intended as a limitation upon the tax treatment of sales generally, it

---

[13] *Commissioner of Internal Revenue* v. *Brown*, 380 U.S. 563, 85 S.Ct. 1162, 14 L.Ed. 2d 75 (1965) after granting *certiorari* in 377 U.S. 962, 84 S.Ct. 1647, 12 L.Ed. 2d 734 (1964); affirming (U.S.C.A.), 325 F. 2d 313 (1963).

represents a considerable invasion of current capital gains policy, a matter which we think is the business of Congress, not ours."

Mr. Justice Harlan wrote a brief separate concurring opinion. Some of his introductory words are helpful toward a clear understanding of the facts:

> Were it not for the tax laws, the . . . transaction with the Institute would make no sense, except as one arising from a charitable impulse. However, the tax laws exist as an economic reality in the businessman's world, much like the existence of a competitor. Businessmen plan their affairs around both, and a tax dollar is just as real as one derived from any other source. The Code gives the Institute a tax exemption which makes it capable of taking a greater after-tax return from a business than could a nontax-exempt individual or corporation. (The sellers) traded a residual interest in their business for a faster payout apparently made possible by the Institute's exemption. (The sellers) gave something up; they received something substantially different in return. If words are to have meaning, there was a "sale or exchange."
>
> Obviously the Institute traded on its tax exemption. The Government would deny that there was an exchange, essentially on the theory that the Institute did not put anything at risk; since its exemption is unlimited, like the magic purse that always contains another penny, the Institute gave up nothing by trading on it.
>
> . . . .
>
> The illumination which has been provided in the present case convinces me that the position taken by the Government is unsound and does not warrant reversal of the judgment below. Therefore I concur in the judgment to affirm.

Four other justices concurred without opinion, making the majority of six. Mr. Justice Arthur J. Goldberg wrote a 3,500-word dissent in which he was joined by Chief Justice Earl Warren and Mr. Justice Hugo Black. Some of the words of the dissenting opinion add further to the clarity of the picture:

> The business thus continued under a new name with no essential change in control of its operations.
>
> . . . .
>
> In essence (the sellers) conveyed their interest in the business to the Institute in return for 72 per cent of the profits of the business and the right to recover the business assets if payments fell behind schedule.
>
> At first glance it might appear odd that the sellers would enter into this transaction, for prior to the sale they had a right to 100 per cent of the corporation's income, but after

the sale they had a right to only 72 per cent of that income
and would lose the business after ten years to boot. This transaction, however, afforded the sellers several advantages.

Going on to show that the sellers gained greatly by having
their share of the profits taxed as capital gain rather than as ordinary
income, Mr. Justice Goldberg said:

> Without the sale they would receive only 48 per cent of
> the business earnings, the rest going to the Government in cor-
> porate taxes, and this 48 per cent would be subject to personal
> taxation at ordinary rates. In effect the Institute sold . . . the
> use of its tax exemption, enabling (the buyers) to collect
> $1,300,000 from the business more quickly than they otherwise
> could and to pay taxes on this amount at capital gains rates.
>
> . . . .
>
> In any realistic sense the Government's grant of tax exemption
> was used by the Institute as part of an arrangement that allowed
> it to buy a business that in fact cost it nothing. I cannot be-
> lieve that Congress intended such a result.

Continuing, he said:

> The Court today legitimates this bootstrap transaction and
> permits (the sellers) the tax advantage which the parties sought.
> The fact that respondent Brown, as a result of the Court's hold-
> ing, escapes payment of about $60,000 in taxes may not seem
> intrinsically important—although every failure to pay the proper
> amount of taxes under a progressive income tax system impairs
> the integrity of that system. But this case in fact has very broad
> implications. . . . The outcome of this case will determine
> whether this bootstrap scheme for the conversion of ordinary
> income into capital gain, which has already been employed on a
> number of occasions, will become even more widespread. It is
> quite clear that the Court's decision approving this tax device
> will give additional momentum to its speedy proliferation. . . .
> I believe that the Court's holding not only deviates from the
> intent of Congress but also departs from this Court's prior de-
> cisions.

In his concluding paragraph, he employed vigorous expression:

> The tax avoidance routes opened by the Court's opinion will
> surely be used to advantage by the owners of closed corporations
> and other income-producing assets in order to evade ordinary
> income taxes and pay at capital gains rates, with a resultant
> large-scale ownership of private businesses by tax-exempt organi-
> zations . . .
>
> . . . .
>
> I would hold . . . in order to prevent serious erosion of the
> ordinary income tax provisions of the Code, that the bootstrap

transaction revealed by the facts here considered is not a "sale" within the meaning of the capital gains provisions of the Codes, but that it obviously is an "artful device," which this Court ought not to legitimate. The Court justifies the untoward result of this case as permitted tax avoidance; I believe it to be a plain and simple case of unwarranted tax evasion.

Federal Estate Tax Cases

Various circumstances surrounding the transfer of property to charitable legatees frequently raise perplexing questions as to the amount properly deductible from the gross estate under the federal estate tax statute. Some cases of this kind have been discussed at pages 251-253 in *The Colleges and the Courts Since 1950;* pages 117-121 in *Same, 1946-50;* and pages 73-83 in *Same, 1941-46.*

Estate Tax Is Determined at Time of Death of Testator. When a large residuary estate was bequeathed to a natural person who un-expectedly died before the bequest took effect as to him and within the time for filing the estate tax return, whereupon the residuary estate passed to six named contingent beneficiaries, all organized and oper-ated exclusively as charities, an effort was made to recover some $241,000 paid as estate taxes, on the ground that the residuary estate had actually gone wholly to charity. There was no recovery. The United States court of appeals said: "The tenor of the opinions . . . is that the estate tax is determined at the time of death (of the testator) and the charitable bequests must be definite in ascertainment and not subject to some contingency, the happening of which is uncertain."[14]

No Deduction of Deferred Charitable Gift Where Trustee of Lifetime Trust for Donor's Widow Has Unlimited Power to Invade Principal. A Massachusetts decedent in 1956 created two trusts, his widow to be the sole beneficiary of the *income* of both until her death. Then one-fourth of the principal of one trust would go to the president and Fellows of Harvard College. The trustees of both trusts for the widow were, however, authorized to pay her such sums from the *principal* as they "in their uncontrolled discretion may deem nec-

---

[14] *City National Bank and Trust Company of Columbus* v. *United States,* (U.S.C.A., Ohio), 312 F. 2d 119 (1963); affirming (U.S.D.C.), 203 F. Supp. 398 (1962).

essary or advisable for her comfortable support and maintenance and for any other reasonable requirement."

The last five words quoted, said the court, rendered it impossible to ascertain the amount of the charitable gift. Hence it could not be deducted, and the requested refund of some $9,000 paid as estate tax was refused.[15]

> Whether the power of invasion is subject to a fixed standard depends upon the terms of the power and the construction placed thereon by the law of the state which would have jurisdiction to construe the will.

Massachusetts had never construed the words "other reasonable requirement" in this context as denoting a fixed standard, and therefore the federal courts declined to do so. The court of appeals stated the broad general rule:

> Where a trust is created for both a charitable and a private purpose, a deduction may be taken for the charitable interest only insofar as such interest is presently certain and ascertainable in amount.

Holding that "the test is the extent of the power to invade, not the likelihood of invasion," the court thought it immaterial that the widow in this case had substantial property of her own, and had never asked to invade the principal of either of the two trusts; and the income of the two trusts was much more than the customary living expenses of both the widow and her spouse before his death.

Some Federal Courts Allow Deduction Where "The Possibility of Invasion Is So Remote as to Be Negligible." The circumstances were different in the case of Raymond D. Havens, a professor of English at Johns Hopkins University who died in 1954. He was survived by his sister, aged 65 and in an advanced stage of senility in a nursing home. She had a personal income of more than $10,000 a year, and some $135,000 of principal assets. Professor Havens bequeathed his residual estate of $315,000 to her for life, then to the Johns Hopkins University for the endowment of the library in the humanities. His will authorized the trustee bank to expend, in its discretion, such part of the *net income* as might be necessary for the maintenance and comfort of his sister.

---

[15] *State Street Bank and Trust Company v. United States*, (U.S.C.A., Mass.), 313 F. 2d 29 (1963); affirming 207 F. Supp. 955 (1962).

His executor claimed a deduction of the entire residuary estate for purposes of the federal estate tax, arguing that it was a practical certainty that the whole amount would go to Johns Hopkins University, the charitable remainderman. The district director of internal revenue insisted that the amount of the deduction must be reduced by the actuarially computed value of the sister's life estate, which was $111,000. The United States district court held for the executor, saying: "The possibility that *any of the income* from the trust under the will of Dr. Havens will be used for the benefit of his sister is so remote as to be negligible; it is highly probable that the Johns Hopkins University will ultimately receive the entire trust property, *income as well as principal*. There is no 'uncertainty appreciably greater than the general uncertainty that attends human affairs.' "[16]

This view is in the tradition of the landmark case of *Ithaca Trust Company v. United States*, 279 U.S. 151, 49 S.Ct. 291, 73 L.Ed. 647 (1929).

---

[16] *Mercantile–Safe Deposit and Trust Company* v. *United States*, (U.S.D.C., Md.), 172 F. Supp. 72 (1959).

PART FOUR

SUPPORT FROM PRIVATE SOURCES
PROPERTY; OTHER MATTERS

Income from Private Sources: Contracts of Subscription

Income from Private Sources: Charitable Trusts for
Higher Education

Financing Capital Improvements

Institutional Real Property

Limitations on Land-Use: Zoning; Urban Renewal

The Tort Responsibility of Public Institutions

The Tort Responsibility of Private Colleges and
Universities

Accessory Education Corporations and Associations

CHAPTER 18

INCOME FROM PRIVATE
SOURCES: CONTRACTS OF
SUBSCRIPTION

ALMOST ALL COLLEGES AND UNIVERSITIES receive promises of gifts payable at some future time or times, or upon or after the occurrence of some specified event. Sometimes the specified event is the death of the donor; but a promise or contract payable after death is legally distinct from a bequest by will, and the two are subject to interpretation under different statutes and different bodies of precedents.

A promise or contract to make a gift is commonly called a "subscription." The etymology of the word calls up a picture of a written statement with the signature of the maker appended below; but, like contracts in general, the statement may be merely oral. However, there is a widespread custom among charitable organizations of circulating "pledge cards" on which the donor can stipulate the amount or amounts he intends to contribute, and affix his signature.

The central issue in the litigation of subscriptions is the question of whether the statement, either written or oral, is a mere "naked promise" (unsupported by "consideration," which is defined as a reciprocal promise or act by the promisee which is a detriment to the promisee or a benefit to the promisor), not enforceable in court, or whether a "consideration" is present, making the transaction a contract binding upon its maker during his life and upon his estate after his death.

The well-known theories on which the courts have rationalized the inception and validity of subscription contracts are three: (1) the doctrine of *promissory estoppel*, under which "consideration" is imported to support the contract as soon as the donee performs some act in reliance on the promise; (2) the doctrine of *mutuality of consideration*, in which the promise of each subscriber among others is conceived as constituting the "consideration" for each of the others; and (3) the doctrine of *public benefit* or *public policy*, under which the mere fact that the enterprise proposed to be financially supported is a useful and worthy one that will conduce to the public welfare is seen as a sufficient "consideration" for the promise or promises.

The first of these theories was principally relied on by a New York surrogate, though he was not entirely uninfluenced by the third, in holding that oral promises to pay $500 to the United Jewish Appeal of Greater New York were good against the estate of the promisor after his death. Said Surrogate Samuel Di Falco:

> The agreed facts submitted in the case at bar establish that the respondent charity entered into contracts and incurred liability in reliance upon the pledges made by this decedent and others.

It appeared that during three recent years the United Jewish Appeal had borrowed a total of some $60 million from seven banks on the strength of its outstanding pledges, to support numerous charitable enterprises efficaciously. Indisputably great reliance was placed on the subscription promises.[1]

The surrogate's gesture of deference to the doctrine of public benefit was in the following words: "A review of the authorities would indicate that the trend of judicial decision during the last century has been towards the enforcement of charitable pledges almost as a matter of public policy . . ."

He then continued with a quotation from the renowned Judge Benjamin N. Cardozo in a 1927 case decided by the New York court

---

[1] *In re Estate of Louis Lipsky*, (Surrogate's Court, New York County), 45 Misc. 2d 320, 256 N.Y.S. 2d 429 (1965).

of appeals, concerning a subscription to Allegheny College in Pennsylvania:[2]

> In discussing the trend and the gradual expansion of the strictures of the "moulds of consideration" as applied to charitable subscriptions, Judge Cardozo stated:
> "Very likely, considerations of public policy have shaped, more or less subconsciously, the rulings thus made. Judges have been affected by the thought that defenses of that character (against the enforcement of subscription promises) are breaches of faith towards the public, and especially towards those engaged in the same enterprise, and an unwarrantable disappointment of the reasonable expectations of those interested."

Relations between Dillard University in New Orleans and a local union of the International Longshoremen's Association seem to have been plagued by confusion of identities on both sides. In 1962 the university was met with a judgment of nonsuit when it sought to enforce a subscription pledge of $10,000 against the union, because the name of the university itself did not appear on the pledge card.[3]

In 1964, in a second action on this pledge, which was to the "Flint-Goodridge Hospital Expansion Fund" (the hospital being owned by the university), there was evidence that the president of the union local had in fact signed the pledge card in the name of the union without authorization, and that the local was actually unaware of the matter and could not have had any intent to be bound by the signature. Its president testified he had signed the card as a "propaganda gimmick" to encourage other contributions, but without authority from his local. Thus the university's suit to recover the unpaid balance of $8,400 was defeated. It appeared that the president of the union local had, however, raised "several thousand dollars" for the fund by his own efforts in soliciting, but kept no record thereof; and had given $150 of his own money, not credited to the union pledge.[4]

---

[2] *Allegheny College* v. *National Chautauqua County Bank*, 246 N.Y. 369, 159 N.E. 173, 57 A.L.R. 980 (1927). Digested at page 357 in *The Colleges and the Courts* (1936).

[3] *Dillard University* v. *Local Union 1419, International Longshoremen's Association*, (La. App.), 144 So. 2d 710 (1962).

[4] *Dillard University* v. *Local Union 1419, International Longshoremen's Association*, (La. App.), 169 So. 2d 221 (1964); *certiorari* denied by the supreme court of Louisiana, 247 La. 342, 170 So. 2d 864 (1965), with Justice Sanders and Justice Summers dissenting.

The Louisiana supreme court declined to review this case, but in the entry refusing a writ of *certiorari* two of the justices—Sanders and Summers—noted their dissent and expressed the view that the writ should have been granted, accepting the case for review.

CHAPTER 19

INCOME FROM PRIVATE SOURCES: CHARITABLE TRUSTS FOR HIGHER EDUCATION

Without actually repeating the classic definition of charity in a legal sense, it is possible to observe some contemporary decisions which serve as brush strokes indicating some of its boundary lines. All the cases in this chapter fall into two general classes: (1) those concerned with the inception of charitable trusts, and (2) those dealing with the operation and execution of such trusts for higher education. Nearly all involve the interpretation of wills, for many such trusts are of testamentary origin.

The Charitable Trust and the Charitable Corporation

At the outset it may be well to quote from a California appellate court a statement of our favorite thesis that *all* property and funds of a nonprofit charitable corporation are held under at least some species of charitable trust obligation, though not all the assets may be impressed with that obligation in the same degree. (For example, not all types of assets are beyond the reach of creditors; but permanent endowment is so immune.) The statement is typical of several California decisions and of others in other states:[1]

> A devise to a society organized for a charitable purpose without a declaration of the use to which the gift is to be put is given in trust to carry out the objects for which the organization was created.

In the case that evoked the foregoing statement a California testatrix had made bequests to nine charitable organizations, including the American Cancer Society, the University of California (for research in osteoarthritis), Alcoholics Anonymous, and six others. Alcoholics Anonymous declined to accept the gift, and this raised the issue: Did the bequest create a charitable trust, so that the *corpus* must go to another suitable charitable donee selected by the court in accord with the doctrine of *cy pres* (under which, when a trust becomes impossible of execution in strict conformity with its terms, the court may modify the terms in order to preserve the trust and effectuate the charitable intent of the donor *as nearly as possible*)?

The answer was affirmative, even though the will provided for direct distribution to the named charitable legatees, "free from any trust." Evidently such a condition is impossible and a nullity in the view of the California judges, who quoted and followed earlier California precedents.[2]

Charitable Purpose and Political Purpose Can Coexist, If Charity Has Primacy and Predominance

Would a bequest to trustees to help further the adoption of the Equal Rights Amendment to the United States Constitution, and to employ funds to contribute to the Maryland Branch of the National Woman's Party, and to aid women in distress as a result of any inequalities in the laws, create a charitable trust? Or would it fall short because the purposes include efforts to change existing law?

---

[1] *Matter of Estate of Katherine Faulkner v. Wells-Fargo Bank and Union Trust Company*, 128 Cal. App. 2d 575, 275 P. 2d 818 (1954).

[2] Including *Los Angeles County Pioneer Society*, 40 Cal. 2d 852, 257 P. 2d 1 (1953), discussed at pages 282-283 in *The Colleges and the Courts Since 1950;* and *In re Estate of Clippinger*, 75 Cal. App. 2d 426, 171 P. 2d 567 (1946).

Maryland's highest court says: "Trusts to eliminate discrimination and to provide relief for persons discriminated against are generally upheld as charitable," although there are a few early Massachusetts decisions to the contrary; and[3]

> If a trust is essentially charitable in nature, it is still charitable even though one of its purposes is to endeavor to effectuate a change of existing law.

Thus the bequests named were regarded as exclusively for charitable purposes, so as to be exempt from inheritance taxes.

Governmental Unit May Accept and Operate Charitable Trust

Although this theory has been sound for more than a century, yet as recently as 1966 the right of the city of Oxford in Mississippi to accept and administer a charitable trust was questioned. A local and private law of the Mississippi legislature of 1938 (Chapter 592) authorized the city of Oxford to acquire and hold property "for an art museum," and to operate the museum, under the will of Mary C. Buie. Her sister, Miss Kate A. Skipwith, had already given the city a plot of land for the purpose in 1937, in order to circumvent the *mortmain* clause of the Mississippi constitution (which prohibited charitable devises of real property, and was not repealed until 1941).[4] She also had a small museum building erected on the land, and the city has operated it since 1939 as the Mary C. Buie Museum. It contains original letters from George Washington, John Hancock, and other heroes of the Revolutionary period, as well as art objects and other items of historical and esthetic value. It is within two blocks of the campus of the University of Mississippi. Miss Skipwith's will bequeathed additional funds to the city for the purpose of building an addition to the museum and of assisting the city in operating it. It was contested unsuccessfully by her surviving next-of-kin.[5]

---

[3] *Register of Wills for Baltimore City* v. *Cook*, 241 Md. 264, 216 A. 2d 542 (1966).

[4] The impact of the *mortmain* clause is illustrated in part in *Mississippi College* v. *May*, 235 Miss. 200, 108 So. 2d 703 (1959), discussed at pages 269-271 in *The Colleges and the Courts Since 1950.*

[5] *Alden* v. *Lewis*, (Miss.), 182 So. 2d 600 (1966).

If Legatee Refuses or Fails to Undertake to Devote
Entire Charitable Bequest to Charitable
Purposes, He Is Disqualified

A Milwaukee lodge of the Benevolent and Protective Order of Elks was named as remainderman in the will of a Wisconsin decedent, to take only for charitable purposes, unspecified. The testator's executor asked the court to require the lodge to designate the charitable uses to be made of the trust income which it was to receive. When the lodge declined to designate such purposes, the trial court held that the lodge was disqualified to administer the trust, and appointed other trustees to do so. This decree was affirmed by the Wisconsin supreme court, saying that the will created a charitable trust, even though the word "trust" did not appear in the instrument; and if there appears to be any possibility that the intended trustee may use any part of the bequest for private noncharitable purposes, he will be removed and a new trustee will be appointed by the court.[6]

Inception of Testamentary Charitable Trust
Is on Day of Donor's Death

The will of a deceased physician in Arizona bequeathed the residue of his estate to a charitable corporation dedicated "primarily to medical research or related scientific subjects," either to be founded by the donor during his life or by the will of his widow; or, if neither, then the testator's executors were directed to organize such a corporation to receive the residuary bequest. The widow contested the will—arguing that it was too indefinite to create a valid trust, that no charitable legatee competent to take was in existence, and that the donor should be adjudged to have died intestate as to the residue. Favorable judgment for the widow in the trial court was reversed by the supreme court of Arizona, on the principle that no trust shall fail for want of a trustee.

The donor's charitable intent was clear. The direction that his executors should obtain a charter made them trustees of the fund until the formal organization of the corporation or foundation. "The

_____

[6] *In re Estate of Conrad Raulf*, 28 Wis. 2d 514, 137 N.W. 2d 416 (1965).

equitable interest immediately passes to the portion of the community to be benefited and remains there indefinitely."[7]

No Charitable Trust Will Be Allowed to Fail for Want of a Trustee

A Georgia testatrix bequeathed the residue of her estate to her personal attorney "to be distributed by him to or among child welfare organizations such as the Pine Mountain Children's Home or Hillside Cottages, Inc., after he has thoroughly investigated the comparative needs of such worthy organizations. His judgment shall be final in this matter."

The attorney died in 1960, before the death of the testatrix in 1963. Her executors therefore asked the court for instruction as to whether to distribute the residue as her attorney had been directed to do, or to let it go under the law of descent and distribution to her heirs-at-law. The heirs contended that the trust died with the death of the attorney.

The trial court appointed a trustee to replace the deceased attorney and make distribution in accord with the will, and directed the executors to pay the residue to the trustee for that purpose. This decree was affirmed by the state supreme court in an opinion by Justice Candler, who quoted *Georgia Code* Section 108-32: "A charity once inaugurated is always subject to the supervision and direction of a court of equity, to render effectual its purpose and object." And he continued: "If a gift is made for a charitable purpose, it is immaterial that the trustee is uncertain or incapable of taking, or that the objects of the charity are uncertain and indefinite. It will, nevertheless, be sustained."[8]

When Instrument Is Unclear

A Missouri testatrix created a trust, to begin upon the death of her husband, to consist of five equal parts for the benefit of a named charitable institution and four named individuals, to continue thus for

---

[7] *Estate of J. N. Harber*, 99 Ariz. 323, 409 P. 2d 31 (1965).
[8] *Simpson v. Anderson*, 220 Ga. 155, 137 S.E. 2d 638 (1964).

a period of 10 years. If all four individual beneficiaries died within that period, the trust was to terminate and the *corpus* to be distributed 90 per cent to Washington University and 10 per cent to the Webster Groves Presbyterian Church. There was no direction as to what was to be done if any of the four individual natural persons survived the 10-year period. These four were all females, aged respectively 53, 55, 59, and 6. The probability was high that some, and possibly all of them, would survive more than 10 years. A majority of the state supreme court affirmed a trial court decision that the fund must go to the university and the church at the end of 10 years, regardless of the survival of the natural persons.

Three of the justices dissented. It seemed unlikely that the testatrix would have wanted to support three of the individual beneficiaries for 10 years and then leave them without support in old age, and equally unlikely that she would want to support the child up to age 16 and then leave her without funds when she would most need them for support and education; but the will expressed no intent that the trust should continue or the *corpus* should go to the survivors of the 10-year period. Hence the dissenters' view was that she died intestate as to that point, because a court will not write a will for a decedent.[9]

Operation and Execution of Charitable Trusts

Three cases provide some inklings of the extent to which the courts approve minor deviations from the original intent of the donor when they are adjudged necessary on account of the passage of time and changed conditions, in the interest of continuing the vitality of the trust and effectuating the general charitable motive.

Arnold Arboretum Has Had Its Day in Court. More than 20 years ago the Harvard Corporation, as trustee of the Arnold Arboretum (which consisted of large botanical gardens, a large herbarium, and an extensive botanical library at Jamaica Plain in the Boston area, plus an endowment of several millions of dollars dating from the first gift in 1872), began to consider and plan moving the major part of the books and specimens to the Harvard Herbarium in Cambridge, in what was believed to be the best interests of science teaching and research.

Some influential friends of the arboretum have resisted this pol-

---

[9] *Mercantile Trust Company* v. *Sowell*, (Mo.), 359 S.W. 2d 719 (1962).

icy for many years, asserting that it amounts to a breach of trust and breaks down the arboretum as an integrated scientific institution. In 1955 the Massachusetts supreme judicial court refused to direct the attorney general to bring suit on the relation of these objectors, after he had refused to do so at their request.[10] A decade later a different attorney general brought such a suit, which terminated in 1966 with a divided opinion of the supreme judicial court which found no breach of trust and sustained the position of the Harvard Corporation.[11]

Justice Whittemore wrote a 7,000-word opinion for the majority. Justices Spiegel and Kirk joined in a 3,000-word dissent, believing that there was a breach of trust and that the books and specimens should be ordered returned to Jamaica Plain. The Chief Justice and Justice Reardon took no part, because each either was or had been a member of the Harvard Corporation.

Endowment Funds: Trust Instrument May Place Limitations on Their Investment. The will of Jefferson D. Robinson, who died in 1929, bequeathing a trust fund for the use of the Toledo Hospital, recites: "I hereby direct that all investments of capital by me directed to be made shall be in interest-bearing securities issued by the United States of America or by any governmental subdivision of the state of Ohio."

An Ohio statute of 1953 (General Code of Ohio, Section 2109.973) authorizes fiduciaries to invest "up to 35 per cent in investments, including common stocks, in which a prudent man would invest"; but this authorization is expressly limited by a prefatory clause: "Except as otherwise provided by law or by the instrument creating the trust." Thus when the trustee and the beneficiaries joined in a petition that the trustee be allowed to follow the statute in disregard of the will, the request was denied by the Ohio supreme court. Nor could the broadening of the investment policy be done under the theory of *cy pres,* the court declared. It also remarked that the Ohio statute is much less liberal than the British Trustee Act of 1925 (15 Geo. V, 551, Ch. 19, Sec. 52), and similar statutes in some American states.[12]

---

[10] *Ames* v. *Attorney General,* 332 Mass. 246, 124 N.E. 2d 511 (1955), discussed at pages 288 and 289 in *The Colleges and the Courts Since 1950.*

[11] *Attorney General* v. *President and Fellows of Harvard College,* (Mass.), 213 N.E. 2d 840 (1966).

[12] *Toledo Trust Company* v. *Toledo Hospital et al.,* 174 Ohio St. 124, 187 N.E. 2d 36 (1962); affirming (Ohio App.), 192 N.E. 2d 674 (1962).

Is Rice University Authorized to (1) Charge Tuition Fees, and (2) Admit Negro Students? The indenture of William Marsh Rice, founding and endowing Rice Institute in Houston (now Rice University), in 1891, contemplated that the institution should be tuition-free and open to white students only. The trustees, having concluded that both of these practices were no longer desirable, asked for instructions permitting them to deviate from both, in the best interests of the institution and to best effectuate the donor's general charitable intent. In the trial court some representatives of the alumni and of donors were allowed to intervene in the case, and one group of them, headed by one Coffee, opposed the petition of the university. The decree was in favor of the university. The interveners appealed, and the court of civil appeals dismissed this appeal, holding that the interveners had no such financial stake in the university as would give them standing to sue in an effort to control its management. In the trial court the attorney general had been the defendant, as required by statute (Article 4412a) and he had not appealed; and in the view of the court of civil appeals, he was the only real defendant and the only possessor of the right to appeal.

When the case reached the Texas supreme court in 1966, that tribunal reversed the court of civil appeals and remanded the case for consideration on the merits. The decision was by a vote of 4 to 3 of the justices. The majority, in an opinion by Justice Greenhill, held that it was error for the court of civil appeals to dismiss the appeal solely on the ground that the interveners had no standing to appeal. "The place to have challenged their interest and their right to intervene was in the trial court."[13] Justices Smith, Norvell, and Hamilton dissented, insisting: "The opinion of the court of civil appeals is correct and well supported by authority."

Since the division in the supreme court and the resulting reversal and remanding arose solely out of a procedural issue, it seems probable that the original decree in favor of the university will ultimately be sustained.

---

[13] *Coffee* v. *William Marsh Rice University*, (Tex.), 403 S.W. 2d 340 (1966), reversing (Tex. Civ. App.), 387 S.W. 2d 132 (1965).

Heirs of Donor of Charitable Trust Have No Interest Unless As Provided by Reversionary Clause in Instrument

The principle asserted by the Texas court of civil appeals in the foregoing Rice University case is well supported, at least in part, by an Iowa decision which says:[14]

> Where the donor has effectually passed out of himself all interest in the fund devoted to a charity, neither he, nor those claiming under him, have any standing in a court of equity as to its disposition and control.

The Kletzing-McLaughlin Memorial Foundation College, an Iowa charitable corporation, operated a college from 1936 to 1951, when its assets were turned over to the Chicago Evangelistic Institute, an Illinois corporation. The widow and five children of the deceased original donor sued, asking equitable and declaratory relief against the college corporation for failure to function according to its charter and ceasing to operate the college.

Mr. Kletzing and his spouse had conveyed land to the college in 1936 for its campus. The only restriction in the deed was that the property should not be encumbered by mortgage or other lien, and in the event this restriction was violated, the land would revert to the donors or their heirs. No violation occurred or was alleged. Justice Garfield of the Iowa supreme court, affirming the dismissal of this case, said: "The settlor of a trust or his heirs cannot sue to enforce the trust unless there is some reservation or condition which amounts to a property interest therein."

---

[14] *Amundson* v. *Kletzing-McLaughlin Memorial Foundation College*, 247 Iowa 91, 73 N.W. 2d 114 (1955).

CHAPTER 20

FINANCING CAPITAL
IMPROVEMENTS

FINANCING the acquisition of sites, buildings, and equipment for colleges and universities may be accomplished by (1) acceptance of gifts from private sources or grants from governmental agencies, (2) legislative appropriations for capital outlay ("pay-as-you-go"), (3) various forms of borrowing, or (4) some combination of these.

Borrowing by the issuance of bonds, for example, may mean "general obligation bonds" of the state itself, which are regarded by investors as most secure, and therefore are salable with relatively low rates of interest; or bonds issued by some statewide "building authority" as in Illinois, New York, Georgia, and a few other states; or the so-called "revenue bonds" issued on the responsibility of a single institution or of a governing board governing more than one institution. Bonds of this latter type may pledge the entire resources of the institution, or they may pledge only the income to be derived from the operation of the facilities financed (room rents from dormitories, board charges from dining halls, and the like) in which event the facilities are called "self-liquidating"; or they may pledge all student tuition fees or a specified percentage thereof.

This latter expedient is sometimes resorted to in the case of *academic* structures (classroom buildings, libraries, laboratories, faculty offices) which are not normally income-producing and therefore can not be "self-liquidating." The pledging of student tuition fees at public institutions for financing capital outlays is not to be commended, if only because such bonds are usually salable only when bearing a rate of interest substantially higher than the rates on "general obligation" bonds; and a difference of a few decimal points, applied to an issue of several millions of dollars and extending over a period of 20 to 50 years may well mean ultimately the loss of a million or more dollars of public money.

Many of the states have archaic provisions in their constitutions which place a rigid limitation of only a few hundred thousand dollars on the total of state indebtedness which may be outstanding at any one time. In a few instances these provisions have been repealed or amended to raise the limitation, but in other instances attempts to amend them have failed. In that event, it may be possible to create a statewide "building authority" whose bonds are declared not to be obligations of the state.

It was the existence of the constitutional limitations which forced the invention of the "self-liquidating" scheme for financing dormitories, dining halls, and other income-producing student service buildings in the 1920's; and the plan has been developed, refined in various forms, and widely used for that purpose ever since, so that in general relatively little tax money has gone into the construction of these income-producing *nonacademic* buildings over the past 40 years.[1]

In some states, however, the consensus is that it is not good public policy to set the student charges for board and room sufficiently high to cover in full the amortization of the cost of the dormitories and dining halls; and accordingly the legislatures make appropriations to cover at least some fraction of the total. The current policy of the state of Georgia is that the legislature provides half the total cost of such buildings, leaving the other half to be "self-liquidated." This, of course, enables the charges to students for board and room to be set at levels substantially lower than otherwise.

---

[1] Some of the early history of this movement is recited at pages 474-491 in *The Colleges and the Courts* (1936) in Chapter XXX, "Financing Buildings at State Institutions Without Appropriations for Capital Outlay."

*Curators of the University of Missouri Have Power
and Duty to Finance Self-Liquidating
Facilities on Their Own Initiative*

In a majority of the states the habit of the legislatures of keeping a close watch on the state universities and colleges has led to the custom of regarding the institutional governing boards as without power to undertake any building projects, even those which do not involve the use of any state tax funds, except under explicit statutory authorization by the legislature. This is not true of the governing boards of the great constitutionally independent universities such as the regents of the University of Minnesota and a few others.[2] It is also not true of the board of curators of the University of Missouri, which, though mentioned in the state constitution, is expressly made subject to the commands of the legislature in some matters. The Missouri legislature, in contrast with those of some other states, has wisely followed the policy of giving the curators broad statutory authority to operate the university and has generally abstained from interfering. Approving the continuance of this policy, a 1966 decision of the state supreme court confirmed the right of the curators to proceed with an issue of "revenue bonds" to finance the construction of a parking facility at the Columbia campus.

In June 1965 the curators approved plans for the $400,000 bond issue to finance a parking facility for 2,649 motor vehicles and adopted a resolution explaining the necessity and declaring the intent that the only feasible financing was by bonds which would not be general obligations of the state of Missouri or of the curators, but would be payable only out of income produced by the operation of the parking facility. To assure prospective bond-buyers that the transaction was lawful, the curators persuaded the attorney general to ask the supreme court for a writ of *mandamus* to compel their president (of the board of curators) to execute the bonds.

The writ was granted by the unanimous court (Justice Finch not

---

[2] See *Fanning* v. *Regents of the University of Minnesota,* 183 Minn. 222, 236 N.W. 217 (1931), discussed at pages 488-489 in *The Colleges and the Courts* (1936); see also pages 134-145 (Chapter IX, "State Institutions: Constitutionally Independent Corporations").

participating) in an opinion by Chief Justice Storckman, in which he said:[3]

> The Curators are more than a mere regulatory agency. It is the clear intent of the Constitution and statutes to confer on them the authority to select sites on which to carry out the functions of the University and to acquire real estate for such purposes by purchase or condemnation. It is also clear that the Curators are authorized to construct improvements on the real estate constituting the site of a University function. In fact such authority is spelled out as a *duty* of the Curators by the statute.

In the course of the opinion relevant parts of the state constitution and statutes were quoted. Article 9 of the constitution of 1945, Sections (a) and (b):

> The government of the state university shall be vested in a board of curators consisting of nine members appointed by the governor . . .

and

> The general assembly shall adequately maintain the state university and such other educational institutions as it may deem necessary.

Implementation of these words is provided for in Section 172.260, *Missouri Statutes*:

> It shall be the duty of the curators to provide for the protection and improvement of the site of the university. . . as selected and established by law; to erect and continue thereon all edifices designed for the use and accommodation of the officers and students of the university, and to furnish and adapt the same to the uses of the several departments of instruction.

Reliance was also placed on a decision of the same court 20 years earlier, holding that the curators had power, without asking for authorization by the legislature, to issue "revenue bonds" in the amount of $2,732,000 to finance necessary self-liquidating dormitories.[4]

---

[3] *State ex rel. Curators of University of Missouri* v. *Neill*, (Mo.), 397 S.W. 2d 666 (1966).

[4] *State ex rel. Curators* v. *McReynolds*, 354 Mo. 1199, 193 S.W. 2d 611 (1946); discussed at pages 168-169 in *The Colleges and the Courts, 1946-50*.

Arrangement for Cooperation of State College and Local Public School District in Construction of High School Building

A New Mexico statute of 1937 authorized the Western New Mexico State Normal School (now Western New Mexico University) and the Silver City Public School District jointly to erect and operate a high school building, to be attended free of charge by pupils of the district and also to be used for practice teaching by the normal school. The act expressly stipulated that if and when the building ceased to be operated as a high school, its title should be transferred to the school district. The state institution discontinued the high school in 1960, because for that year the state appropriated no funds for its operation.

Hoping to retain title to the building, however, the state college refused to transfer it to the school district, and resisted on the ground that the germane portion of the act of 1937 was invalid because not stated in the title of the act. This transparently technical objection was given no countenance by the trial court. A writ of *mandamus* was issued to compel the transfer, and this judgment was affirmed by the state supreme court.[5]

Twenty-seven years earlier the same court had interpreted the same statute of 1937, and had denied an injunction sought by a taxpayer in the school district who objected to the use of district tax funds for the construction of the building.[6] Thus both the inception and the termination of the cooperative arrangement seem to have been attended by acrimonious litigation.

Federal Grants Under Higher Education Facilities Act of 1963

The trustees of the Paducah Junior College in Kentucky, having determined to move the college from its inadequate downtown site, and having acquired a suitable site in a suburban location, executed a

---

[5] *Silver City Consolidated School District No. 1* v. *Regents of New Mexico Western College*, 75 N.M. 106, 401 P. 2d 95 (1965).

[6] *White* v. *Board of Education of Silver City*, 42 N.M. 94, 75 P. 2d 712 (1938); discussed at pages 105-106 in *The Colleges and the Courts, 1936-40.*

contract October 10, 1963, with the Feast Construction Company for general construction of the new academic plant; and the contractor began work October 16 in order to take advantage of prevailing good weather. The trustees issued $1,350,000 of Junior College Revenue Bonds dated November 1, 1963, and completed the sale of these bonds December 20, 1963.

An application for a grant of $582,227 was made to the United States Commissioner of Education under the Facilities Act of 1963. It developed that the commissioner rejected this application on account of the following section of the Act [20 U.S.C.A. Section 751 (c)]:

> The term "development cost", with respect to an academic facility means the amount found by the Commissioner to be the cost, to the applicant for a grant or loan under this chapter, of the construction involved and the cost of necessary acquisition of the land on which the facility is located and of necessary site improvements to permit its use for such facility, but *excluding any cost incurred before, or under a contract entered into before, December* 16, 1963.

In these circumstances the United States district court could only conclude that "The Commissioner's finding that the funds sought in plaintiff's application for a grant covered development costs incurred under a contract entered into prior to the enactment of the Act on December 16, 1963, was correct and his denial of the grant was proper."[7]

Senior District Judge Roy M. Shelbourne went further and declared that the district court had no jurisdiction in the case, because, so far as the portion of the act pertaining to grants is concerned, the right to seek judicial review is confined to a state dissatisfied with the commissioner's final action regarding approval of a state plan.

State Board of Education Bond Issue in Florida in 1963

Florida enacted a statewide gross receipts tax (Chapter 203, Florida Statutes Annotated). A constitutional amendment adopted by ref-

---

[7] *Paducah Junior College* v. *Secretary of Health, Education, and Welfare,* (U.S.D.C., Ky.), 255 F. Supp. 147 (1966).

erendum November 5, 1963 (Florida Constitution, Article XII, Section 19), created a trust fund from the proceeds of this tax and authorized bond issues against this fund by the state board of education, to be limited to $75 million for the biennium 1963-65 (not exceeding $45 million for state universities and not exceeding $30 million for local public junior colleges) for capital improvements. The bondholders have recourse only to the fund specified, and the power of the state board of education to issue the bonds is to be exercised "only to obtain funds for capital outlay projects theretofore authorized by the legislature."

The legislature of 1963 proceeded to authorize a total of $87,877,000 for these purposes, including $51,897,000 for the universities and $35,980,000 for the junior colleges. These sums exceeded the amount of the bond issues authorized for the biennium 1963-65; but the constitution limits only the amount of bonds issued and does not inhibit the total of expenditures authorized. Thus a bond issue of $75 million during biennium 1963-65 was valid.[8]

Refinancing of Self-Liquidating Nonacademic Buildings in Alabama

In 1965, Troy State College in Troy, Alabama, needed to finance a new dormitory for 538 men and improve the existing Shackelford Hall to house an additional 210 women. The revenues from the new dormitory and the renovated Shackelford Hall would not, standing alone, be sufficient to provide adequate security to enable the state board of education to sell bonds in the amount of $1,460,000 required for the purpose. It was necessary to pledge, also, revenues from existing facilities. These included a dining hall and seven dormitory buildings. The income from all but three of these was already pledged to the payment of outstanding bonds of the board of education, issued in 1957, 1959, 1961, and 1962. They bore interest at rates ranging from 2⅞ per cent to 3½ per cent. The federal government was holder of them all. The government committed itself to accept in exchange new bonds which would be secured by the income from all the self-liquidating facilities at Troy State College, and to buy in addition, at par, the $1,460,000 in new bonds to finance the needed

---

[8] *State* v. *State Board of Education* (Fla.), 165 So. 2d 161 (1964).

new facilities, to bear interest at the rate of 3 per cent, on condition that the bonds be offered for public sale and no would-be purchaser offered a more favorable bid.

Section 37, Title 52, Code of Alabama 1940, as amended by Act No. 23, Acts 1957, page 893, expressly authorizes refunding of bonds under specified conditions. Amendment CLX to the constitution of 1901, adopted in December 1961, declares that revenue bonds at any time issued do not create debts of the state, but does not mention bonds issued for the purpose of refunding. The state supreme court holds that refunding is a detail below the level of generality appropriate for the language of the constitution, and therefore absence of specific mention of it is of no consequence—it is included anyway. It is also immaterial that some of the bonds to be refinanced were issued before the adoption of Amendment CLX, and some later—the phrase "at any time issued" in the amendment covers everything. Hence the issue of the whole new series of bonds, consisting of $1,876,000 for refunding old bonds and $1,460,000 in new bonds to finance new facilities, is in conformity with the constitution and statutes.[9]

The question of whether pledging the income from pre-existing income-producing buildings to the payment of bonds to finance additional new facilities creates a debt against the state has been litigated in some other states, and sometimes decided adversely.[10] In fact, the supreme court of Alabama had decided it adversely in 1957 in *Opinion of the Justices*, 266 Ala. 78, 93 So. 2d 923, advising that the state board of education could not finance a new dormitory at the state Agricultural and Mechanical Institute for Negroes by pledging rentals from the new building and also rental income from a pre-existing older dormitory building on the same campus. The reasoning was that pledging income from the older building would be pledging funds which already belonged to the state, and would violate Section 213 of the constitution. No doubt this advisory opinion was of some influence toward the adoption of Amendment CLX about four years later, in 1961.

---

[9] *Pincard* v. *State Board of Education*, (Ala.), 189 So. 2d 153 (1966).
[10] Examples are *Wells* v. *Stuck et al.*, (Ark.), 215 S.W. 2d 697 (1948), discussed at page 174 in *The Colleges and the Courts, 1946-50*; *Boe* v. *Foss*, 76 S.D. 295, 77 N.W. 2d 1 (1956), discussed at page 308 in *The Colleges and the Courts Since 1950*.

CHAPTER 21

INSTITUTIONAL REAL PROPERTY

AMONG THE ISSUES touched here are (1) statutory authority to select two-year public college sites in New York and California; (2) the exercise of eminent domain by and against colleges and universities in various circumstances; and (3) contracts for the construction of buildings, involving builders, architectural services, and various transactions with and among subcontractors, suppliers, materialmen, and sureties. The financing of capital improvements has been touched upon in Chapter 20.

Selection of Community College Sites

New York statutes provide that a county can be the "sponsor" of a local two-year public college (Education Law, Sections 6301 and 6302) but do not define with precision the line between the powers of the college board of trustees and those of the county board of supervisors in the final selection of a site for the college.

The Board of Trustees of Sullivan County Community College, influenced in part by the promise of a wealthy citizen that if a certain site in the Town of Fallsburgh were selected he would give the college half a million dollars, accepted deeds to the site as a gift; but the Sullivan County Board of Supervisors rejected the site by a vote of 8 to 7, and the issue went to court. No statute or decision had unmistakably settled this question, but Justice Isadore Bookstein readily decided that the power of final decision rests in the county board of supervisors. He held that the Community College board of trustees had authority to accept the gift of a tract of land without the consent of the county board, but that the college board's recommendation of a site can be no more than advisory, and may be rejected by the county board.[1]

A more generous view of the powers of a junior college board of trustees was evidenced in a California appellate court case in which the owner of "Rainbow Ranch" in San Diego County asked for injunctive and declaratory relief to compel the Board of Trustees of the Oceanside Carlsbad Junior College District to select "Rainbow Ranch" as the college site.

Only a few days before the bond election of 1961 the board had announced its rejection of this site in favor of another known as the Sonya Henie property, because the board believed a majority of the electorate favored the Henie site. The electorate approved the bond issue, without which no site could have been purchased. The board's action was within its powers, thought the court, The wisdom, expediency, or reasonableness of the board's acts may not be challenged. A court will intervene only if it is alleged that the board failed to follow procedures mandated in the statutes, or acted fraudulently, arbitrarily, or capriciously.

In this instance records put in evidence showed that the board had in fact complied with all statutory mandates, including the obtaining of favorable reports from the state department of education and the local planning commission regarding the Henie site; and no fraud or caprice was alleged or proved.[2]

It was within the board's proper sphere of discretion to announce its choice suddenly only a few days before the election, without having made any lengthy and elaborate investigation of the favored site, such as it had previously made of "Rainbow Ranch" and other proposed sites.

---

[1] *Meyer* v. *Wiess*, 47 Misc. 2d 1056, 263 N.Y.S. 2d 813 (1965); affirmed, 25 A.D. 2d 174, 268 N.Y.S. 2d 226 (1966).

[2] *Arthur* v. *Oceanside Carlsbad Junior College District*, 216 Cal. App. 2d 656, 31 Cal. Rptr. 177 (1963).

Exercise of Eminent Domain

There is no dispute that higher education is a public purpose, within the meaning of the legal principle which is said to make inherent in every state legislature the power to take private property by condemnation for a public purpose, and compensate the private owner justly. Many decisions in many states have sustained the extension of this power to local governmental subdivisions and to public schools and colleges.

Kansas State Board of Regents Can Acquire Land by Condemnation but Not by Purchase. A curious example of a state-wide board governing several state universities and colleges, but without authority to buy land by negotiation with the owners, is furnished by Kansas.

Recently the Kansas State University at Manhattan needed to obtain a tract of land suitable for use for a "Summer Shielding Development Program" which is a project of its Shielding Institute sponsored by the Department of Nuclear Engineering. Control of suitable land was a prerequisite to the making of a federal grant to support the research in part.

The Kansas State University Endowment Association (a private nonprofit corporation accessory to the university) leased 175 acres adjacent to the Fort Riley military reservation for five years, 1962-1967, and took an option to purchase 290 acres, including the leased land, with the option to expire May 1, 1964.

The university was awarded the federal grant and entered into the use of the land under a sublease from the endowment association. Then on June 5, 1963, the state board of regents filed a petition for condemnation of the land covered by the lease.

Three months later the landowners filed a motion to dismiss the condemnation proceedings, alleging that the endowment association was no more than an agent of the state board of regents, and that the existence of the uncompleted lease estopped the regents from taking the land by condemnation.

In complicated litigation in the lower courts the right of the regents to take the land by condemnation was upheld, and these judgments were affirmed by the supreme court of Kansas.[3]

---

[3] *Murray* v. *State Board of Regents,* 194 Kan. 686, 401 P. 2d 898 (1965).

The opinion, written by Commissioner Hatcher and approved by the whole court, said:

> The legislature has not seen fit to authorize the State Board of Regents to acquire land by negotiation and purchase . . . nor to negotiate options to purchase, and it had no authority to do so. No doubt the Endowment Association entered into the lease and option agreement for the purpose of assisting Kansas State University in obtaining government grants for the purpose of conducting nuclear research programs, but its assistance could not go beyond the power of the University and the State Board of Regents to act.
>
> The Endowment Association could not by agreement, or under the claim of agency, extend the power of the State Board of Regents beyond that granted by the legislature.

California Gives Power of Eminent Domain to Private Universities and Colleges, but Not to Private Schools Below College Level. The spectacle of a small private Jewish elementary school bringing a condemnation proceeding against the University of Southern California is somehow faintly reminiscent of David and Goliath. The Yeshiva Torath Emeth Academy was leasing some property from the university, and determined to acquire ownership of this property by the exercise of eminent domain. The action was met with a general demurrer (plea of no cause of action) in the trial court, which was there sustained, and this determination was affirmed in the court of appeal, by Justices Shinn, Ford, and Files.

The court noted that Section 1238 of the Code of Civil Procedure authorizes eminent domain for the use of "Any educational institution of collegiate grade within the State of California, not conducted for profit," but does not contain any indication of any intent to include private schools below college level. Said the opinion by Presiding Justice Shinn: "The plaintiff (Yeshiva Torath Emeth) is attempting to exercise a right it does not possess." And "The right to condemn property has not been extended to private elementary schools."[4]

In New York, Public School District Can Not Condemn Land Belonging to Private College. Pace College in New York City owned 50 acres of unimproved land in Westchester County, north of the city. At a time when the tract was temporarily vacant and unused, but in-

---

[4] *Yeshiva Torath Emeth Academy* v. *University of Southern California,* 208 Cal. App. 2d 618, 25 Cal. Rptr. 422 (1962).

tended for use as the site of a Westchester branch of Pace College, a local public school district started condemnation proceedings to acquire it by eminent domain for public school purposes. Under New York law property owned and intended for educational use by a private college is regarded as "devoted to a public purpose"; and, in the words of the court, "If the subject parcel is already devoted to a public use, it may not be condemned in the absence of specific statutory authority therefor, and unless the plaintiff is the sovereign state of New York." Public school districts have the power of eminent domain, but their corporate identity is not merged with that of the state though they are agencies of the state. Thus the condemnation proceeding was dismissed, and summary judgment awarded to Pace College.[5]

In support of the "public use" theory for private college property, the court cited the 1934 California decision in which the University of Southern California, a private institution, was permitted to seize by eminent domain certain small plots necessary to make its library accessible and its approaches esthetically improved.[6]

Contracts for Construction of Buildings

Often mandatory provisions of the state statutes apply to the procedure in letting contracts for buildings and equipment, especially when the institution belongs to a state or a local civil subdivision. Certain details as to the advertising for bids, the preparation of specifications, and the awarding of a contract to the "lowest responsible bidder" are usually prescribed, though sometimes only directed in words which the courts will not construe as completely mandatory. It is also true that provisions of this kind in the general statutes of the state, intended to apply to all departments, agencies, institutions, and instrumentalities of the state, may be interpreted as not applicable to a new and peculiar type of public corporation created by some states and usually known as a "State Building Authority" or state-wide "College Dormitory Authority" or some similar name, as will soon be observed.

---

[5] *Board of Education of Union Free School District No. 2 of Towns of Ossining et al.* v. *Pace College*, 50 Misc. 2d 806, 271 N.Y.S. 2d 773 (1966).

[6] *University of Southern California* v. *Robbins*, 1 Cal. App. 2d 523, 37 P. 2d 163 (1934); *certiorari* denied, 295 U.S. 738, 55 S.Ct. 650, 79 L.Ed. 1685 (1934).

Beyond the inception of the building contract, there arise questions as to its execution, the responsibility of the prime contractor and his surety in case of default, the respective rights of subcontractors, suppliers, materialmen, and others involved in the construction as against the prime contractor, the institution, and the sureties that furnished the contractor's bond.

Contracts with architects as well as with builders are also in the picture, and one of the recent cases confronted the court with the delicate task of determining precisely what is embraced within architectural services, as distinguished from engineering services, in a state which licenses and regulates both of those professions and prohibits persons unlicensed as architects from practicing that profession.

New York State Dormitory Authority Has Wide Latitude in Letting Contracts. The dormitory authority in New York is a species known as a "public benefit corporation," almost *sui generis*, and generally held to be not subject to the various statutory restraints imposed on other more common types of public corporations.[7]

For example, it is not required to award a contract to the lowest responsible bidder; and it seems that it may vote to award a contract and soon thereafter rescind that action without being liable for breach of contract.

The minutes of the dormitory authority for April 12, 1965, show the following:

"It was moved, duly seconded, and VOTED to award the general construction contract for the Life Science Building at C. W. Post College of Long Island University to Schumacher and Forelle, Inc., Great Neck, L.I., in the amount of $1,571,000, as bid on March 31, 1965."

Four weeks later, on May 10, it adopted another resolution rescinding the above (apparently at the suggestion of C. W. Post College) and rejecting all bids and authorizing the solicitation of new bids.

Schumacher and Forelle brought an action asking the court to direct the dormitory authority to award the contract in accord with its resolution of April 12. The action in the trial court was unsuccessful. Justice Harold E. Koreman dismissed the case, saying: "The Public Authorities Law does not require the Dormitory Authority to adver-

---

[7] See *Braun* v. *State of New York*, 203 Misc. 563, 117 N.Y.S. 2d 601 (1952), digested at page 364 in *The Colleges and the Courts Since 1950*.

tise for bids and does not require the Authority to do any particular thing in relation to the awarding of a contract. . . . Nor is the Authority required to award a contract to the lowest bidder."

He concluded that in this case there "is no duty imposed by law to award the contract." Hence, he thought, "It is not necessary to determine whether the Authority effectively accepted petitioner's offer as a result of its April 12 resolution."[8]

In Maryland, Successful Bidder Who Made Major Mistake in His Base Proposal Is Entitled to Have His Bid Cancelled. Mount St. Mary's College at Emmitsburg, Maryland (a private Roman Catholic institution, not to be confused with St. Mary's College of Maryland at St. Mary's City, a state institution), invited bids for the construction of a student union building and a dormitory. These jobs turned out to cost respectively about $735,000 and $660,000, for a total of slightly less that $1,400,000. These figures are useful as an aid in grasping the lowest bidder's error in his proposal. He inadvertently omitted $84,000 for kitchen and snack-bar equipment in the union building, and $85,000 for built-in furniture in the dormitory.

The error was not the result of sheer stupidity or inattention. The court used words to the effect that the form provided by the college for the proposal "though not ambiguous, was confusing," so that the contractor had submitted a proposal on which, if held to it, he stood to lose perhaps $150,000 to $200,000; and he had soon discovered his error.

The United States district court decided that, in substance, the mistake was of such grave consequence as to make the enforcement of the contract unconscionable, that it was not the result of any violation of a positive legal duty or of culpable negligence, and that the other party was in *status quo* and suffered no prejudice other than the loss of his bargain. (The college awarded the contract to the next lowest bidder.) Hence the original successful bidder (who had submitted the erroneous bid) was entitled under Maryland law to have his bid cancelled and his bid bond returned. This judgment was affirmed by the United States court of appeals.[9]

---

[8] *Schumacher and Forelle, Inc.* v. *Johnson*, 47 Misc. 2d 65, 261 N.Y.S. 2d 943 (1965).

[9] *Mount St. Mary's College* v. *Aetna Casualty and Surety Company*, (U.S.C.A., Md.), 344 F. 2d 331 (1965); affirming 233 F. Supp. 787 (1964).

Materialman Is Entitled to His Money. Two cases illustrate the tendency of the courts to guard the interests of materialmen as against those of defaulting prime contractors, subcontractors, or sureties for the performance of building contracts.

The Florida Electrical Supply Company, Inc., having furnished materials to Dunn, the electrical subcontractor on a Florida State University building for which Winchester was the prime contractor, sued the prime contractor, the subcontractor, and the surety to recover the unpaid price of the materials. Judgment in favor of the supplier in the trial court was affirmed in the court of appeal. He was not limited in his recovery to a sum mentioned in an affidavit furnished by the subcontractor to the prime contractor; and he was not estopped by an amount fixed in a notice he had been required to furnish by statute, where there was no showing of reliance on this or change in position of the parties sued on account of it.

Said the court: "No hardship is imposed on either the contractor or his surety. They know before the contract and bond are executed that any person supplying labor or material in the prosecution of the work is intended to be protected by the bond. If any part of the work is sublet or the contractor assigns his contract, it is an easy matter for him to take security from the subcontractor that all obligations for labor and material shall be paid.[10]

In a case involving the Los Angeles City Junior College District a federal court of appeals held that under California law, where the dispute was between a materialman and the prime contractor, the materialman could resort to settlement of the dispute by arbitration, have the arbitration award confirmed in court, and recover from the prime contractor's surety even though the surety had not been notified of the arbitration prodecure.

It was not necessary for the materialman to sue the junior college district, said Judge Barnes, in an opinion in which Judges Hamley and Browning concurred, affirming the summary judgment of the federal district court below.[11]

---

[10] *Winchester* v. *Florida Electrical Supply Co., Inc.,* (Fla. App.), 161 So. 2d 668 (1964). Formerly before the court for adjudication of venue, (Fla. App.), 134 So. 2d 826 (1961).

[11] *Glens Falls Insurance Company* v. *Murray Plumbing and Heating Corporation,* (U.S.C.A., Cal.), 330 F. 2d 800 (1964).

Engineer-Builder Can Not Make Contract
for Architectural Services in Ohio

A private college in Ohio let a contract for the construction of several buildings, including "classroom buildings, library facilities, science facilities, administration facilities, student activity facilities, monastery and chapel." The contractor was a licensed engineer, and he agreed, among other obligations, to provide "necessary conferences, the preparation of preliminary studies, working drawings, specifications, large-scale and full-size detail drawings, for architectural, structural, plumbing, heating, electrical, and other mechanical work" in connection with the buildings.

When he sued to recover under this part of the contract, an Ohio court of common pleas sustained the college's demurrer and dismissed the petition, holding that the conferences, studies, and drawings mentioned were primarily architectural work, and that an engineer who is not an architect could not enter into a contract for such services and could not enforce such a contract. The Ohio supreme court dismissed an appeal, saying no constitutional question was involved.

Judge Griesinger of the court of common pleas had decided that in establishing the two professions of architecture and engineering, the legislature intended to protect each of the professions in its respective field of endeavor. It recognized that the two professions have some things in common; but the judge thought "Engineering practice is limited to such functions for which the educational qualifications are required to protect public health, safety, and property; and does not include services flowing primarily from the practice of architecture."[12]

---

[12] *Fanning* v. *College of Steubenville*, (Ohio Com. Pl.), 197 N.E. 2d 422 (1961). Appeal dismissed, 174 O. S. 343, 189 N.E. 2d 72 (1963).

CHAPTER 22

LIMITATIONS ON LAND-USE: ZONING; URBAN RENEWAL

"ZONING" of land-use in populous areas has been widely practiced for half a century. It is an exercise of the police power of the state, for the protection and advancement of the public health, safety, morals, and convenience. The states generally empower local units of government to enact zoning ordinances, and to provide for the granting of special exceptions or variances in hardship cases. Usually there must be a local zoning board of appeals to hear and determine remonstrances and other petitions; and there is an ultimate appeal to the courts, because there is some danger of an unjust deprivation of property without due process of law, in violation of the bills of rights embodied in the federal and state constitutions.

Generally the courts are rather lenient with colleges or universities, public or private, and tend to regard them as suitable for location in an area zoned even for high-class single-family residential use, if the local ordinance can be so construed. The courts also tend to deal liberally with them in the interpretation of local requirements as to vacant space, parking space, and the dimensions of buildings.

Tyler School of Fine Arts of Temple University
Permitted to Build Dormitory in Residential Section

The zoning ordinance in force in Cheltenham Township in Pennsylvania allowed buildings in residential districts "for educational, religious, or philanthropic use, *when authorized as a special exception*, but *excluding* hospital, sanitarium, rest home, or correctional institutions, and *including* dormitories of an educational institution." This seemed clearly to authorize, if not mandate, a special exception to allow the Tyler School of Fine Arts, a unit of Temple University in Philadelphia, to erect a dormitory for 50 men and 100 women in proximity to its campus located in the township.

The zoning board refused to grant the exception, however, and the appeal reached the supreme court of Pennsylvania. Local residents of the neighborhood, noisily remonstrating to the zoning board, had alleged that they anticipated parking difficulties, hamburger joints, evening disturbances, and various capers by young people "dressed like artists," whose conduct would be objectionable, "to wit, to woo in public and otherwise disrupt the tranquillity of the neighborhoood."

The court observed that the Tyler School had been in this location for 25 years, and over all those years students had come and gone, and only two minor untoward incidents were cited at the hearing which were said to involve people who "looked like artists" but were not proved to have been students at the school. Concluding that the local apprehensions seemed to be exaggerated, the court held that the zoning board had abused its discretion in denying the special exception which would permit the construction of the dormitory.[1]

Two Massachusetts Decisions Interpret Statute and Certain Local Ordinances in Boston Area

Recent cases reaching the Massachusetts supreme judicial court from the Town of Brookline and the City of Cambridge necessitated interpretations of *Massachusetts General Laws*, Chapter 40 A, Section 2, as *amended in 1959*: "No ordinance or by-law which prohibits or limits the use of land for . . . any educational purpose which is religious, sectarian, denominational or public shall be valid."

The Sisters of the Holy Cross of Massachusetts, operating Cardinal Cushing College on Fisher Hill in Brookline, intended to erect a

---

[1] *Temple University* v. *Zoning Board of Adjustment of Cheltenham Township*, 414 Pa. 191, 199 A. 2d 415 (1964).

general-purpose college building. The Town of Brookline held it strictly to the dimensional requirements applicable to that zone. The superior court granted declaratory relief on petition of the sisters, but the supreme judicial court reversed this decree and dismissed the sisters' petition, saying the court had no jurisdiction to make declaratory decrees as here; but this is not to be hastily taken as a decision adverse to the sisters, because Justice Spiegel, for the supreme judicial court, concluded: "Inasmuch as it is our view that the land owned by Holy Cross was *exempt* from the operation of the town's zoning bylaw, there is no need for us to comment on whether Holy Cross was entitled to a variance . . ."[2] (No need to sort out the details—the whole thing is simply inapplicable to Holy Cross under the terms of the statute!)

In this case the town asserted that the quoted part of the statute (exempting religious, sectarian, denominational educational institutions from the purview of local zoning ordinances) was in contravention of the establishment clause of the First Amendment to the United States Constitution: "Congress shall make no law respecting an establishment of religion, or prohibiting the free exercise thereof," made also applicable to the state legislatures by the Fourteenth Amendment. Not so, said the court, and cited *Lundberg* v. *County of Alameda*, 46 Cal. 2d 644, 298 P. 2d 1 (1956), in which the California supreme court held that the tax exemption of nonprofit denominational schools does not violate the establishment clause of the First Amendment; and pointed out that the United States Supreme Court dismissed an appeal from that decision, *for want of a substantial federal question* in *Heisey* v. *County of Alameda*, 352 U.S. 921, 77 S.Ct. 224, 1 L.Ed. 2d 157 (1956). From this disposition of the case Justices Black and Frankfurter dissented, and Mr. Chief Justice Earl Warren took no part.

The decision of the California court was by a vote of 4 to 3. The opinion of the majority was written by Chief Justice Gibson, with Justices Traynor, Spence, and McComb concurring without opinion. Justices Schauer, Shenk, and Carter joined in a dissenting opinion written by Schauer. The dissent, however, was based entirely on what the dissenting justices believed to be a contravention of the Cal-

---

[2] *Sisters of the Holy Cross of Massachusetts* v. *Town of Brookline*, 347 Mass. 486, 198 N.E. 2d 624 (1964).

ifornia constitution. The majority justices took an opposite view of this issue, and also maintained that there was no clash with the First Amendment to the United States Constitution, chiefly because tax exemption of religious and educational institutions began in Colonial days, and it is scarcely to be thought that the First Amendment was intended to put a stop to it. This leaves open, of course, the question of whether the First Amendment needs new interpretations to fit new conditions nearly two centuries later.

The issue before the California court was not tax exemption of universities or colleges, but of religious schools of less than collegiate grade, pursuant to an amendment added to Section 214 of the Revenue and Taxation Code in 1951, and approved in a popular referendum at the general election of 1952, authorizing such exemption.

Radcliffe College Is Declared Subject to Local
Regulations Regarding Ratio Between
Building Space and Parking Space

Two years later the same Massachusetts supreme judicial court, this time with Justice Whittemore writing the opinion, placed a different construction upon the same statute (Chapter 40 A, Section 2, *Massachusetts General Laws*, as quoted above).

Radcliffe College has a quadrangle of land containing dormitories for some 900 students. A new library building was being erected within the same quadrangle, and Radcliffe planned to provide only 36 new parking spaces (for library employees), although the Cambridge zoning ordinance stipulated that there must be one new parking space for each 1,000 square feet of floor space in each new building, and this would mean 90 additional car spaces for the new library.

Far from declaring Radcliffe exempt from the purview of the zoning ordinance, as had been done in the case of Cardinal Cushing College two years before, Justice Whittemore elaborated the following reasoning:

"Providing for the parking or housing of the automobiles of students, instructors, and employees of an educational institution is within the broad scope of the educational powers of the institution just as is providing for the feeding and housing of such personnel. These are secondary functions incidental to the main educational purpose. Hence, a regulation that requires that some of the college land be used for parking does not lessen the availability of all or any of the institution's land for some appropriate educational purpose. We think the statute does not bar such regulation."[3]

Two of the streets adjacent to the quadrangle in question are narrow, creating difficulty in the passage of fire vehicles and in snow clearance when automobiles are parked on them. Radcliffe had plans for additional dormitories within the same area. These might have to be modified or abandoned in the face of literal enforcement of the parking space requirements of the zoning ordinance. Justice Whittemore thought this hardship would not be ground for a variance under the present ordinance, but added that an amendment providing for an exception might perhaps be enacted.

Zoning Hurdles Surmounted for New York University's Elmer Holmes Bobst Library and Study Center

Designed by the architect Philip Johnson to house two million volumes and seat 4,800 readers, and to be named for a benefactor who has given $6 million toward its cost, a large new general library building at the Washington Square campus of New York University has been planned for several years, to be 15 stories high and cost $20 million.

The zoning regulations covering the site ordinarily require that any building more than 60 feet high must have a setback of 45 feet. The City Board of Estimate has approved an exception to permit the library building to rise 150 feet, flush with the sidewalk line and with no setbacks. The city has also transferred to the university a small "grassy plot" along West Broadway between Washington Square South and West Third Street, to constitute a part of the necessary site.

Representatives of certain neighborhood organizations sued the city and the board of estimate to invalidate these actions, but without avail. Late in 1966, Justice McGivern of the local supreme court dismissed the objections and held that "So long as the governmental

---

[3] *Radcliffe College* v. *City of Cambridge*, (Mass.), 215 N.E. 2d 892 (1966).

agencies have not been shown to have made their selection of public use in a corrupt manner or in bad faith, their choice is not subject to court review."

Universities and Urban Renewal: Some Birth-Pangs of Chicago Circle Campus of University of Illinois

A tract of 55 acres at Harrison and Halsted Streets in the near West Side of Chicago was designated as a blighted area in 1956. In 1958 a "Harrison-Halsted Redevelopment Plan" was adopted by the city, state, and federal housing authorities. By 1960 much of this tract had been cleared. It was to be developed as a residential area for moderate income families. Instead, as is now widely known, it became a part of the Chicago Circle campus of the University of Illinois, over the bitter protests of certain local interests, some of which were organized in "The Harrison-Halsted Community Group, Inc." They believed that in 1960 the city began to consider using the Harrison-Halsted tract as the nucleus of a new campus for the University of Illinois, but kept it secret and continued to promise residential development.

On February 10, 1961, the mayor announced an agreement with the trustees of the University of Illinois that the university would occupy this tract and two adjacent areas, about 105 acres. On April 13, 1961, the Planning and Housing Committee of the City Council held a hearing at which objectors were allowed to appear and make statements, but not to subpoena persons or papers or to cross-examine. On May 22 the City Council adopted ordinances approving the plan. The state Housing Board held hearings on it July 21-27, allegedly abruptly terminated before the objectors had time to bring in witnesses and cross-examine, and announced its approval of the plans and forwarded them to the federal Housing and Home Finance Agency. The objectors sent briefs to the HHFA, but no hearings were held, and on March 21, 1962, the HHFA Administrator announced approval of the plans and the inception of loan-and-grant contracts. On April 17, 1962, the city Land Clearance Commission filed its first condemnation suit against owners of Harrison-Halsted properties. Three days later they retaliated by instituting an action in federal court for a declaration of their rights.

They alleged various violations of provisions of the Federal Housing Act and regulations of the Housing and Home Finance Agency; that they were being deprived of property without due process of law and without just compensation; that the area was populated by Mexicans and Negroes, and that the loss of housing for these minority groups was not being replaced elsewhere in the community, thus bringing hardship upon them.

The court recognized that an abrupt change in the plans had indeed occurred. It was cognizant of the special hardship visited upon a Roman Catholic parish in the area, whose parochial school plant had been demolished a few years ago to make way for an arterial expressway. The parish had built a new school on a site selected after consultation with the public housing authorities, and completed it in 1959, only to learn less than three years later that the new school would now be razed.

But as to the main issue, the words of the United States court of appeals were simple and succinct:[4]

> Courts have consistently denied the standing of citizens to challenge the choice made by public authorities between different and competing public uses. The legislature, through its lawfully created agencies, rather than "interested" citizens, is the guardian of the public needs to be served by social legislation.

It was held that none of the plaintiffs had any private legal or vested interest in the type of public use redevelopment to be conducted. No substantial federal question was presented; and "Insofar as a legal controversy is presented, it belongs in the Illinois state courts."

On May 13, 1963, the United States Supreme Court denied a writ of *certiorari* in this case, but granted leave to file a supplement to the petition for *certiorari*.[5] Apparently nothing has come of this. The decision of the court of appeals has been cited in several subsequent urban renewal cases, and expressly followed in some of them. Its rationale is sound, on the principle of "the greatest good for the greatest number," even though it has meant temporary local hardship for some persons and institutions in some instances.

---

[4] *Harrison-Halsted Community Group, Inc.* v. *Housing and Home Finance Agency*, (U.S.C.A., Ill.), 310 F. 2d 99 (1962).
[5] 373 U.S. 914, 83 S.Ct. 1297, 10 L.Ed. 2d 414 (1963).

CHAPTER 23

THE TORT RESPONSIBILITY OF
PUBLIC INSTITUTIONS

The obstacles preventing an innocent injured party from recovering indemnity from a state or municipal college or university are being surmounted perhaps less rapidly than in the case of private institutions. New York permits the state to be sued in its court of claims, and damages have frequently been awarded for negligence in the state colleges. Somewhat similar judgments have also been had in California; but in other states it appears that governmental immunity is interposed in nearly all such cases, though occasionally a dissenting judge urges its abandonment.

Patient's Written Release Does Not Absolve University
Hospital for Negligence in California

At the medical center of the University of California at Los Angeles, a patient who received treatment in the research and teaching hospital alleged that he had been seriously injured on account of the negligence of certain physicians employed there, and sued the regents of the university for damages.

It was the custom at the hospital to have each incoming patient read and sign a written statement waiving any claims against the hospital for negligence. Such a paper was offered as a defense in this case; but the plaintiff testified he had never read it and did not recall having signed it; and it did in fact appear that at the time of his admission to the hospital he was in great pain, under heavy sedation, and probably unable to read. However, a jury in the superior court of Los Angeles returned a verdict that the release was valid, and the court, holding that such a release was not contrary to public policy in California, concluded that it was a good defense and rendered judgment in favor of the defendant university.

The judgment was affirmed in the court of appeal, but vacated by the California supreme court, pointing to Civil Code section 1668:

> All contracts which have for their object, directly or indirectly, to exempt anyone for responsibility for his own fraud, or willful injury to the person or property of another, or violation of law, whether willful or negligent, are against the policy of the law.

The opinion by Justice Tobriner, in which the six other justices concurred, emphasized that the operation of a hospital is an enterprise in which the public interest is very heavily involved. While statutes such as the one just quoted are not universally applied literally, the precedents in practically all states show that they are so applied when one of the parties is a concern deeply fraught with the public interest. Hence the conclusion was that the signed release was of no consequence.

In the final paragraph of his opinion, Justice Tobriner elaborated:[1]

> The integrated and specialized society of today, structured upon mutual dependency, cannot rigidly narrow the concept of the public interest. From the observance of simple standards of due care in the driving of a car to the performance of the high standards of hospital practice, the individual citizen must be completely dependent upon the responsibility of others.
> The fabric of this pattern is so closely woven that the snarling of a single thread affects the whole. We cannot lightly accept a sought immunity from careless failure to provide the hospital service upon which many must depend. Even if the hospital doors were open only to those in a specialized category, the hospital cannot claim isolated immunity in the interdependent community of our time. It, too, is part of the social

---

[1] *Tunkl* v. *Regents of University of California*, 60 Cal. 2d 92, 32 Cal. Rptr. 33, 383 P. 2d 441 (1963); vacating (Cal. App.), 23 Cal. Rptr. 328 (1962).

fabric, and prearranged exculpation from its negligence must
partly rend the pattern and necessarily affect the public interest.

There was no express mention of governmental immunity, though
the hospital operated by the state university is manifestly a state
agency. The pleadings of the hospital as defendant repetitiously described it as a "nonprofit, charitable institution," using the terminology
which is properly applicable to private colleges and private hospitals,
but hardly to state or municipal universities or hospitals. Even though
a public hospital receives nonpaying patients, often designated in the
vernacular as "charity patients," this does not change its legal character
as a public agency, and does not destroy the clear distinction between
it and private hospitals or private colleges or universities which are
chartered as private nonprofit charitable corporations.

It may be added that the California supreme court unequivocally
rejected any attempted distinction between paying and nonpaying
patients, as to their standing to sue the university for the torts of
its hospital employees. Thus the outworn doctrine that "beneficiaries
of the charity" can not recover indemnity for negligence was ruled
out in this case.

In this same year (1963) the legislature, after a two-year study,
eliminated the common-law defense of sovereign immunity ("the
King can do no wrong") in California, by enacting Division 3.6 of
the California Government Code. Sections 854 through 856.4 deal
specifically with medical, hospital, and public health activities.[2]

No Recovery Unless Negligence or Willful Intent to Injure Is Shown

A New York decision of 1965 was concerned with a claim for
damages against the state for alleged negligence of the State University College at Albany in allowing a male freshman student to participate in a "pushball" contest between freshmen and sophomores,
in which he received a serious injury. The contest was unsupervised
except by four upper-class students.

It seems that the "push-ball" game was one among many types of

---

[2] See anonymous note in *University of California at Los Angeles Law Review* 11: 639-645 ("Torts: Malpractice: Hospital's Exculpatory Release from
Liability for Future Negligence Held Invalid").

physical contests making up the activities of "Rivalry Week," a traditional period at the beginning of the academic year. All able freshmen and sophomores were not only permitted, but urged, to choose one or more of these activities and take part. It appeared that "pushball" contests had been one of these activities for 38 consecutive years, without any record of serious injury to any participant.

The plaintiff in this case, a 6-foot, 200-pound freshman aged 17 at the time, after observing the game and having opportunity to see that it was an activity involving rough physical contact and some hazard of injury, chose to participate in it. During the game he was "clipped" from behind (struck at or below the knees from behind) and fell forward violently, sustaining a severe injury to one arm, including bone dislocation and fracture.

New York has a court of claims in which suits of this kind may be brought against the state, and in many cases indemnity has been awarded to claimants alleging negligence against several of the state colleges. But of course damages will not be awarded if negligence is not proved.

In this case the court of claims held that the state should not be adjudged liable. The plaintiff assumed the risk of injury when he entered the game. There was no allegation that the playing field was in defective condition. There was no proof that the four student referees did not perform adequately, or that the injury would not have occurred if the college had provided professional referees.

Moreover, in view of the 38-year history of the activity, the college authorities were not upon notice that serious injury might result from the game, and hence had no duty to provide special supervision for it.

Judge Henry W. Lengel concluded that "We do not believe the State should be made the insurer of the safety of those who participate in this type of sport."[3]

---

[3] *Rubtchinsky* v. *State University College at Albany*, (N.Y. Ct. Cl.), 46 Misc. 2d 679, 260 N.Y.S. 2d 256 (1965). Compare this case with *Baum* v. *Reed College Student Body, Inc., and Reed Institute* (1965), and *Heimbuch* v. *President and Directors of Georgetown College* (1966), both cited and discussed in Chapter 24, *infra*. These cases arose from facts somewhat similar to the present one but were concerned with private colleges, not state institutions.

State Immunity in Louisiana; Access to
Court of Claims in Michigan

Two recent medical malpractice cases were both decided on what will probably seem to the layman to be "technicalities." In Louisiana a woman patient alleged that a transfusion of the wrong type of blood had caused a failure of her normal kidney function, after which she was moved to another hospital where Louisiana State University maintained an "experimental kidney station," and while being treated there by a physician in the employ of the university she was further seriously injured by an antibiotic drug negligently administered by him.

Her suit was brought in a federal district court and reached a United States court of appeals, in which Circuit Judges Brown and Gewin joined in an opinion by Moore. The suit was barred by the Eleventh Amendment to the United States Constitution, which provides that a state can not be sued in federal courts without its consent, by its own citizens or by citizens of other states. Moreover, in tort cases the federal courts interpret the law of the state concerned and apply it; and Louisiana law holds tightly to state immunity. Even if it did not, and would permit a suit in state courts, this would not confer a right to sue in federal court. The federal court of appeals decision decided only that the federal district court was not the tribunal in which to bring this suit and was expressly "without prejudice to appellants' right to pursue any remedies they may have in Louisiana state courts."[4]

In Michigan, a medical malpractice action against the regents of the University of Michigan in the Washtenaw County circuit court was met by a motion to dismiss. The court held that it did not have jurisdiction, but entered orders transferring the case to the state court of claims, saying that granting the motion to dismiss would result in serious injustice by reason of the running of the Statute of Limitations in a court of claims case. Against this decision the regents appealed, and the unanimous supreme court of Michigan, in an opinion written by Chief Justice Kavanagh, maintained that "When a court is without jurisdiction of the subject matter, any action with respect

---

[4] *Scott v. Board of Supervisors of Louisiana State University and Agricultural and Mechanical College*, (U.S.C.A., La.), 336 F. 2d 557 (1964).

to such a cause, other than to dismiss it, is absolutely void."[5] The justices cited their own recent decision in *Glass* v. *Dudley Paper Company*, 365 Mich. 227, 112 N.W. 2d 489 (1961), which involved a tort claim against the trustees of Michigan State University.[6]

A Crack in Rock of State Immunity in New Mexico

The state institutions of higher education have generally been held to be immune from responsibility for negligence in tort cases, on the familiar ground of "state immunity," which stems from the medieval doctrine that the King can do no wrong.

Consonant with the changes in this field of the law which are taking place slowly in many states, a 1965 New Mexico decision evidences a somewhat different spirit.

A female case worker for the State Welfare Department visited a blind student in his dormitory at New Mexico State University, to confer with him about his welfare assistance. While departing from the dormitory, she fell and was injured on a ramp-type walk at a point where it sloped downward.

There was conflicting testimony as to whether the walk was troweled glassy-smooth, or roughened on the surface to prevent slipping. The university director of physical plant testified that it was properly roughened, but a civil engineer as witness for the injured woman testified that it was smooth, slippery, and dangerous to pedestrian traffic.

The trial court rendered a summary judgment in favor of the university; but on appeal the New Mexico supreme court reversed this judgment and remanded the case with direction to proceed to trial of the disputed facts.

This plainly implies that if the university negligently maintained the walk in a slippery and dangerous conditon, then it might be responsible in damages to a person innocently injured thereon.

The decision was unanimous, with the opinion being written

---

[5] *Fox* v. *Board of Regents of University of Michigan*, 375 Mich. 238, 134 N.W. 2d 146 (1965).

[6] Digested at page 344 in *The Colleges and the Courts Since 1950*.

by Chief Justice Carmody and concurred in by Justices Chavez and Moise.[7]

---

[7] *Sandoval* v. *Board of Regents of New Mexico State University,* 75 N.M. 261, 403 P. 2d 699 (1965). Compare with *Livingston* v. *Regents of New Mexico College of Agriculture and Mechanic Arts,* 64 N.M. 306, 328 P. 2d 78 (1958), discussed at pages 341 and 342 in *The Colleges and the Courts Since 1950.*

CHAPTER 24

THE TORT RESPONSIBILITY
OF PRIVATE COLLEGES
AND UNIVERSITIES

A FEW OF THE RECENT CASES in this category seem to have arisen in states where the trend toward abolishing or modifying the doctrine of charitable immunity has as yet had little effect. The breakthrough of the period was the repudiation of the charitable immunity theory by the Pennsylvania supreme court in the *Flagiello* case, overruling the 1961 decision of the same court in the *Hahnemann Medical College* case.

There is also a Georgia decision which is a definite step toward establishing a simple and common-sense rule regarding the effect of liability insurance on the responsibility of a private college.

Efficacy of Liability Insurance Policy Held
by Nonprofit Educational Corporation

Confusion has existed in the recent past because some courts have held that as long as private colleges enjoy large immunity from tort liability by virtue of the judicial theory that all their assets are dedicated to charitable purposes and are not to be diverted to satisfy private grievances, it makes little or no difference whether they carry liability insurance or not, because their immunity can not be waived as long as that theory prevails. A closer view has now been taken in some jurisdictions, under which the maximum indemnity provided by a liability insurance policy is regarded as indeed an asset. It is one which is not and never has been intended to be a part of the charitable trust funds in any sense, but merely a piece of property which has been purchased for the express purpose of indemnifying innocent injured parties for possible negligence by the institution, and is therefore available for that purpose.

Morehouse College in Georgia has a large Olympic-size indoor swimming pool and undertakes to teach all freshmen to swim. On a recent occasion the professor of physical education in charge of swimming assembled a class of 15 freshmen at the pool and introduced to them two student-instructors, both of whom were upperclassmen and members of the college swimming team, and both of whom possessed the Red Cross senior life-saving certificate, but not the Red Cross instructor's certificate. The professor directed the freshmen who could swim to go to the deep end of the pool with one of these student-instructors, and those who could not swim to go to the shallow end with the other. He then departed, leaving no qualified instructor at the pool.

One freshman who could swim only a very short distance, awkwardly and with difficulty, nevertheless joined the deep-end group, jumped in with them and soon sank to the bottom at a depth of 12 feet. His body remained there five or six minutes before it was noticed by another student, whereupon the student-instructor immediately dived in, brought it to the surface, and began manual artificial respiration. Someone telephoned the Atlanta Fire Department for an artificial respirator squad, which arrived within five minutes after the call and worked on the body for 10 to 15 minutes, but to no avail. Soon a physician arrived and pronounced the boy dead from drowning. His mother sued the college for $100,000 indemnity, alleging negligence and alleging that the college was known to have a liability insurance policy thought to be large enough to cover that sum, and also averring that the college possessed other large sums from student fees as well as property not used for its charitable purposes.

These averments were met by one general demurrer and several special demurrers which were overruled by the trial court. A Georgia court of appeals affirmed this ruling in large part, but held that the special demurrer as to the property not used for charitable purposes should have been sustained, because there was no allegation that this was not a part of the college's endowment (perpetual charitable trust).

This decision was reached after the court of appeals had certified certain questions to the supreme court of Georgia and evoked a declaratory opinion by Presiding Justice Head, for all the justices. The law in Georgia, said the court, is that (1) funds in trust for charitable purposes are subject to a judgment against a charitable institution for negligence in the selection of competent servants, and (2) only noncharitable assets are subject to judgment for negligence of a servant under the doctrine of *respondeat superior*.

Translating this into a specific, the court added that a liability insurance policy is such a noncharitable asset as would support a cause of action for recovery under the doctrine of *respondeat superior* where the petition seeks to subject to the judgment only noncharitable assets of a charitable institution.[1]

With this encouragement, the opinion of the court of appeals went beyond the matter of liability insurance, and declared: "Funds derived from regular tuition paid by students do not constitute charitable funds and are not part of the charitable trust. They are not charitable donations but are payments for services rendered or to be rendered." [2]

One must hasten to remark that tuition fees constitute so large a part of the income of most private institutions (at least one-half of the average private college's annual operating income) that this holding could have the practical effect of virtually abolishing immunity for private colleges. Also, so great an extension of the concept of "noncharitable assets" tends to create confusion by seemingly running counter to the hard-won but now widely recognized principle that a private nonprofit charitable corporation holds all its assets impressed with a species of trust obligation.[3]

Insofar as the Georgia decisions establish the efficacy of a liability insurance policy in the hands of a charitable institution, they mark an important forward step; but it might have been better if, in-

---

[1] *Morehouse College* v. *Russell*, 219 Ga. 717, 135, S.E. 2d 432 (1964).
[2] *Morehouse College* v. *Russell*, 109 Ga. App. 301, 136 S.E. 2d 179 (1964).
[3] Discussed in Chapter 12, *supra*, in text appertaining to Footnotes 6, 7, and 8.

stead of the generalization of "noncharitable assets," the liability insurance policy had been designated as a *restricted charitable asset*
held exclusively for the purpose of indemnifying possible tort victims.

Responsibility for Safe Condition of Premises: Different Degrees of Care Required

If an alleged tort arises out of the unsafe condition of property, it is
necessary, of course, for the plaintiff to show that the defendant college
owned or was in control of the property in question. Thus a woman
employed in a nursing home in Prince Georges County, Maryland, habitually alighted from a bus at a certain stop and proceeded on foot
along La Salle Street past the grounds of De La Salle College toward
her place of employment, walking on a sidewalk about 24 inches from
the curb and outside a hedge on the grounds. On this route, on a
snowy day, when she crossed the apron of a driveway affording in-
gress and egress to and from the college grounds, she fell on the
ice and snow and was injured. When she sued the college for negligence, the trial court directed a verdict for the college, and this
was affirmed by the court of appeals of Maryland, because there was
no averment and no evidence that the college owned the ground on
which the plaintiff was injured.[4]

One in charge of property is not bound to the same degree of
care in keeping the premises safe for a trespasser as he is in keeping
them safe for other persons who are invitees on the premises. At Kentucky Christian College a new library building was being erected by
a contractor, when a wall of the uncompleted building callapsed because of an accident in the placing of steel A-beams for the roof.
An outsider came on the premises to employ a plumber who was at
work on the job, and while there for that purpose was injured by
the falling wall. When he sued the contractor, there was a directed
verdict for the defendant, and this was affirmed by the Kentucky
court of appeals, because the plaintiff was a trespasser, to whom the
defendant owed no duty except the exercise of ordinary care to avoid
injury to him after his position and peril were actually discovered.

---

[4] *Greene* v. *De La Salle College*, 237 Md. 615, 205 A. 2d 395 (1964).

What is required is abstention from "inflicting or exposing him to wanton or willful injury or from setting a trap for him."[5]

At Skidmore College an 80-year-old former music teacher was "taking a walk" in January 1960 and decided to visit his daughter who was at work in the college business office and have her drive him home. In negotiating a step upward to the slate-floored porch of the building in which she was at work, he fell and was injured. There were some irregularities in the concrete step and the slate floor, and some snow and ice were present. These conditions did not make the college liable for the injury, because the man's presence on the property was for purely personal reasons and had no connection with the business of the college, and was "at most, permissive." He was either a trespasser or at most a "bare licensee," and was thus classified as one who must take the premises as he finds them. "A landowner has no duty of ordinary care to a trespasser or licensee, but need only refrain from intentional, wanton injury or from setting a trap or the like." Thus there was summary judgment for the college.[6]

Standard of Care When Injured Person Is Employee of Institution

In the state of Washington, the Northwest Bible College built and maintained a chapel building, in the rear portion of which were separate restrooms for men and women. Large screens, weighing about 250 pounds each, were placed in the rear of the auditorium to block the view of the two restroom doors. These were not securely fastened to the ceiling, but had foam-rubber pads on their upper edges and were forced against the ceiling by screw jacks. The screens bore bulletin boards. The dean of women affixed a notice to one of these bulletin boards and stood inspecting other items on it, when the heavy screen fell on her, causing serious injuries.

She sued the college and the architect who had designed the building as joint defendants. The trial court directed a verdict for the plaintiff, and the jury awarded her damages of $45,000 against

---

[5] *Bradford* v. *Clifton and Sons*, (Ky.), 379 S.W. 2d 249 (1964).
[6] *Platt* v. *Skidmore College*, 36 Misc. 2d 631, 236 N.Y.S. 2d 186 (1962).

the college. On appeal the supreme court of Washington affirmed, and made the following statement in its opinion:[7]

> Even though we assume that the plans were defective, this would not relieve the college of its responsibility to provide a reasonably safe place to work. An employer has a positive, non-delegable duty to furnish his employees with a reasonably safe place to work. There is no distinction between responsibility for design and responsibility for maintenance, and the college cannot avoid liability by reason of allegedly defective plans of the architects it selected. The college, acting through its agents, built and maintained the screens. Construing all the evidence in favor of the college, we hold that the minds of reasonable men could not differ in concluding that the college was negligent in construction or maintenance.

Not impressed by the contention that the award of damages was excessive in amount, the court concluded: "After an examination of the record we find nothing to indicate that the verdict must have been the result of passion or prejudice. We are satisfied that the damages were within the range of the evidence."

Negligence Is Question of Fact for Jury

An architecture student severely injured his left hand while using a jointer (planer) in Yale University's woodworking shop. The man employed by the university to direct and supervise the shop was present and acting in that capacity at the time. The student used a "push stick" which is intended for use with a circular saw; and this required him to place his left hand on the wood he was planing. He should have been using a "push block"—a different tool intended for use with a jointer, which would have made it unnecessary for him to have his hand in contact with the wood. A directed verdict for the university was reversed and a new trial ordered, because a jury could have found on the evidence that Yale University was negligent in not providing a push block and instructing the student in how to use it.[8]

The problem of determining whether there actually was actionable negligence in a given case continues to appear, of course. This is a question of fact for a jury. Oregon furnishes a recent case of in-

---

[7] *Guy* v. *Northwest Bible College*, 64 Wash. 2d 116, 390 P. 2d 708 (1964).
[8] *Kirchner* v. *Yale University*, 150 Conn. 623, 192 A. 2d 641 (1963).

terest, involving Reed College, the well-known private institution at Portland.

A mother who resided in California visited her daughter, a student at Reed College living in a dormitory, during an Easter vacation. This was an ordinary unofficial visit, with no invitation from the college and no special arrangements.

Just prior to her departure for the return trip the mother and her daughter went to the Student Union Building to witness a folk-dancing session which was being conducted on a raised floor some three to four feet above the floor of the auditorium, and surrounded by benches of about the suitable height for seats, some of which were used for climbing on and off the dance-floor.

The daughter went up onto the floor to participate, while her mother sat on one of the benches nearby. A 200-pound male student stood very near to the edge of the platform, while the daughter and her partner conversed briefly with him. Suddenly the girl's partner poked the big boy in the stomach with his finger, causing him to fall off the platform and land with great force on the girl's mother seated on the bench below, injuring her severely.

When she sued the college for indemnity for negligent injury, the trial court jury awarded her a judgment for damages against the college; but this was reversed by the Oregon supreme court, holding that "An owner of premises is not an insurer of the safety of an invitee against injuries inflicted by other persons on the premises."

Deeming it unnecessary to decide whether the injured woman actually was an invitee, or merely in the lower category of "licensee" on the premises, the court said neither classification would entitle her to expect from the college the degree of care for her safety which would, if absent, support an allegation of negligence in this case.

The folk-dancing sessions were on a schedule, but they were no part of the curriculum of the college, and they were unsupervised. There was no evidence, thought the court, that the students attending these dances were ever rowdy or rough, either in the past or at the time of the injury; and there was nothing that "would put a reasonable person on notice that supervision was necessary." Hence the college was not negligent in failing to provide supervision.[9]

---

[9] *Baum* v. *Reed College Student Body, Inc., and Reed Institute*, 240 Ore. 338, 401 P. 2d 294 (1965).

Charitable Immunity Doctrine in Ohio
and North Carolina

In 1960 when two students at Wittenberg College sued the college for alleged negligence causing injuries to them, the Ohio court of appeals, closely following the state supreme court, was quick to assert the doctrine of charitable immunity. After noting that some courts have abandoned the doctrine in whole or in part, Judge Kerns went on to observe that although the Ohio supreme court had retreated from it in the case of *Avellone* v. *St. John's Hospital*, 165 Ohio St. 467, 135 N.E. 2d 410 (1965),[10] it had reasserted the doctrine (except as to hospitals) in its decision in *Gibbon, Admr.* v. *Y.W.C.A. of Hamilton, Ohio*, 170 Ohio St. 280, 164 N.E. 2d 563 (1960):

> A charitable or eleemosynary institution other than a hospital is, as a matter of public policy, not liable for tortious injury except (1) when the injured person is not a beneficiary of the institution, and (2) when a beneficiary suffers harm as a result of failure of the institution to exercise due care in the selection or retention of an employee.

"Any change in this rule must come from its source," said Judge Kerns, and the action of the lower court in sustaining Wittenberg College's demurrer (plea of no cause of action) was affirmed.[11]

North Carolina has made no move toward breaking down the wall of immunity protecting nonprofit charitable hospitals. A woman patient sued Duke University for the alleged negligence of a named intern in treating her while in the Duke University Hospital. The action was in the United States district court, but in such cases the federal courts interpret and apply the law of the state. Under North Carolina law, said Chief Judge Edwin M. Stanley, "Eleemosynary corporations are not liable for the negligence of their agents or servants, unless proved negligent in the selection of the employee responsible for the injury." Hence there was summary judgment in favor of the university.[12]

---

[10] Discussed at pages 355-356 in *The Colleges and the Courts Since 1950.*

[11] *Matthews* v. *Wittenberg College*, 113 Ohio App. 387, 178 N.E. 2d 526 (1960).

[12] *Berry* v. *Odom and Duke University*, (U.S.D.C., N.C.), 222 F. Supp. 467 (1963).

Pennsylvania Repudiates Charitable Immunity

In 1965 the Pennsylvania supreme court expressly overruled its 1961 decision which had sustained charitable immunity in the *Hahnemann Medical College* case.[13] The 1965 decision involved another private nonprofit hospital, and here the majority of the court declared that a charitable hospital's liability for negligence of its employees "must be governed by the same principles of law as apply to other employers."[14] The rationale of the opinions of the justices indicates that its effect is not intended to be restricted to cases involving hospitals, but to apply to other charitable institutions as well.

The long and scholarly opinion of the court was by Justice Musmanno, who had been the chief among three dissenters in the 1961 case. Justices Eagen and O'Brien concurred without drafting opinions. The former had been a dissenter in 1961, and the latter had become a member of the court more recently. Justice Cohen, who had also been a dissenter in 1961, concurred in the result only, not wishing to add anything to what the Michigan supreme court had said in *Parker* v. *Port Huron Hospital* (1960).[15] Justice Roberts, who had become a member of the court more recently, concurred in a brief opinion containing the following paragraph:

> I concur in what the Court does today for the fundamental reason that, no matter how viewed, the doctrine of charitable immunity cannot withstand unimpassioned analysis. Briefly put, there is really no supportable rationale upon which the judicially-created exception to the ordinary rules of liability can be predicated. The various theories advanced in favor of the doctrine seem to me, at root, as ethereal as the non-existent English precedent upon which the doctrine was first founded.

Chief Justice Bell dissented at great length, defending *stare decisis* and arguing for stability in the law. Justice B. R. Jones (to be distinguished from the former Chief Justice C. A. Jones, who had written the opinion of the majority of the court in 1961) dissented briefly,

---

[13] *Michael* v. *Hahnemann Medical College and Hospital of Philadelphia*, 404 Pa. 424, 172 A. 2d 769 (1961). Discussed at page 360 in *The Colleges and the Courts Since 1950*.

[14] *Flagiello* v. *Pennsylvania Hospital*, 417 Pa. 486, 208 A. 2d 193 (1965).

[15] *Parker* v. *Port Huron Hospital*, 361 Mich. 1, 105 N.W. 2d 1 (1960). Quoted by Justice Musmanno in his 1961 dissenting opinion. Cited and quoted at page 360 of *The Colleges and the Courts Since 1950*.

holding to the view that if change is necessary, it should be made by the legislature and not by the court.

Observe that the minority of three justices in 1961 led by Justice Musmanno became the majority of five in 1965. It seems that both of the recruits were new justices who had come to the court after 1961: Justices O'Brien and Roberts. Thus does the law progress.

District of Columbia Reaffirms Landmark Opinion of Justice Wiley Rutledge

At Georgetown University in Washington, D.C., a male freshman was compelled to participate in an "elephant walk," to be followed by a mud bath, under compulsion of the sophomores (including the "Sophomore Hazing Committee"). During the "elephant walk" he was violently tackled from the rear by a sophomore, and suffered a fracture of the femur and other injuries. When sued in the district court, the university defended on the ground that the student was a "beneficiary of its charity" and hence not entitled to sue. District Judge Matthews expressed his opinion that a student who was charged more than $1,800 a year for board, tuition, and incidentals, as was the case here, could hardly be called a "beneficiary of the charity"; he further pointed out that even if the student were so regarded, under District of Columbia law no doctrine of charitable immunity would prevent him from recovering suitable indemnity for his injuries. It also appeared the university was carrying liability insurance policies with annual premiums aggregating some $30,000 to $40,000. The court ordered that "The doctrine of charitable immunity from tort liability not being applicable in the District of Columbia, the action should be tried by a jury on the issue of negligence."[16]

The court added to its records another well-reasoned opinion on the decline and demise of charitable immunity, harking back to the convincing discourse of Justice Wiley Rutledge in the 1942 decision in the case of *Hughes* v. *President and Directors of Georgetown*

---

[16] *Heimbuch* v. *President and Directors of Georgetown College*, (U.S.D.C., D.C.), 251 F. Supp. 614 (1966).

College.[17] In that case the plaintiff was a private-duty nurse injured through the negligence of one of the hospital's own student nurses. The issue was whether recovery should be allowed because the injured nurse was a "stranger to the charity" and not a "beneficiary" thereof, or whether it should be allowed on a broader ground, without reference to that distinction. The district court had decided it on the narrow ground, but the court of appeals by a vote of three to three, affirmed the decision on the broader basis of total elimination of charitable immunity—with Justices Justin Miller and Edgerton joining in support of the memorable opinion by Rutledge.

In the 1966 case, the effect of Justice Rutledge's dissertation of a quarter of a century ago was highlighted by a quotation from Prosser's *Law of Torts,* 2d Ed., 1955, p. 787: "A devastating opinion of Judge Rutledge in the Court of Appeals of the District of Columbia reviewed all the arguments in favor of the immunity and demolished them so completely as to change the course of the law." And at a later point, "The immunity of charities is clearly in full retreat."

District Judge Matthews then went on to show (as has been done before) that the precedent in the United States which is at the root of the charitable immunity doctrine in this country (*McDonald* v. *Massachusetts General Hospital,* 120 Mass. 432, decided in 1876) relied solely on the English decision in *Holliday* v. *St. Leonard,* 11 C.B. (NS) 192 (1861), which "had already been judicially repudiated for some years in England," though the fact had not yet become known on this side of the Atlantic. This explains the acerb remark about the "non-existent English precedent" made by Justice Roberts of the Pennsylvania supreme court in the *Flagiello* decision of 1965.

The weight of judicial opinion against charitable immunity continues to accumulate and probably has already become somewhat heavier than a reading of the handful of decisions cited in this present chapter would alone indicate. This seems to be an instance in which *stare decisis* (especially when it stands on a very questionable base)

---

[17] *Hughes* v. *President and Directors of Georgetown College,* (U.S.C.A., D.C.), 130 F. 2d 820 (1942); affirming (U.S.D.C., D.C.), 33 F. Supp. 867 (1940). Discussed at pages 119-120 in *The Colleges and the Courts, 1941-45,* and page 93 in *The Colleges and the Courts, 1936-40.*

must yield to the logic and passion of justice for innocent injured parties who would otherwise be without a legal remedy.

Should Court Authorize Blood Transfusions To Save Life of Patient Who Objects on Religious Grounds?

Appended here is a case which involves no actual tort, but raises important questions regarding the protection of a private university hospital from possible actions for negligent or willful injury. It also raises grave questions concerning individual human rights and obligations.

The young mother of an infant aged seven months was in the Georgetown University Hospital, suffering from a hemorrhaging ulcer. The physicians decided that blood transfusions were necessary to save her life. She refused because this would be contrary to her religion (Jehovah's Witnesses), and was supported in this refusal by her husband, who was present.

The physicians were reluctant to violate religious scruples. However, if they knew the transfusions were necessary, but withheld them and the patient died as a consequence, would they and the hospital then be liable for negligence in failing to save her life? If they administered the transfusions against her will, would they be civilly and criminally liable for assault? Is the main question justiciable (suitable to be resolved by the courts) or is it wholly medical, to be decided by the physicians alone?

In this quandary two of the physicians sought the United States District Judge in his chambers and asked him for an order directing or permitting the transfusions, which he refused. They then hurried to Circuit Judge J. Skelly Wright of the United States court of appeals for the District of Columbia, who, after telephoning the hospital and going there in person to talk with the physicians and the patient and her husband, signed an order "that the applicant acting through its duly accredited and licensed physicians in attendance may administer such transfusions as are in the opinion of the physicians in attendance necessary to save her life."

The transfusions were administered, and the patient survived and was subsequently discharged from the hospital.

Circuit Judge Wright justified his order on the ground that the patient did not want to commit suicide, and both she and her husband said that if the transfusions were ordered, it would not then be their responsibility (meaning, apparently, that they would be freed from religious qualms). Further, he said, society would not allow her to abandon the care of her infant, even through suicide. And "If self-homicide is a crime, there is no exception to the law's command for those who believe the crime to be divinely ordained." "But whether attempted suicide is a crime is in doubt in some jurisdictions, including the District of Columbia." [18]

The conclusion was that the matter was properly justiciable, under the federal "all writs statute" (28 U.S.C.A. section 1651), and a rehearing before the United States court of appeals *en banc* was denied.

---

[18] *Application of President and Directors of Georgetown College, Inc.* (U.S.C.A., D.C.), 331 F. 2d 1000 (1964); rehearing *en banc* denied, 118 U.S. App. D.C., 90, 331 F. 2d 1010 (1964). *Certiorari* denied, 337 U.S. 978, 84 S.Ct. 1883, 12 L.Ed. 2d 746 (1964). Relevant is the comment by Kenny F. Hegland, "Unauthorized Rendition of Life-saving Medical Treatment," in *California Law Review* 53: 860-877 (August 1965).

CHAPTER 25

ACCESSORY EDUCATIONAL
CORPORATIONS AND
ASSOCIATIONS

In nearly all the cases included here from the period 1962-1966 it happens that the issue is that of exemption from property taxes. This is somewhat unusual, for the various types of "accessory" organizations always grouped about a university or college often become involved in other types of cases concerned with such matters as zoning ordinances, tort liability, or others.

It is well to observe here that Chapters 14 through 17 all deal exclusively with taxation: Chapter 14 with property tax exemption of colleges and universities; Chapter 15 with other types of charitable corporations having some educational functions but not in any way connected with a college or university; Chapter 16 with exemption from state taxes other than property taxes; and Chapter 17 with federal taxation.

This present chapter, as its title indicates, is distinguishable from all others because it is limited to the nonprofit organizations having some "accessory" relationship to a university or college—organizations which would not exist were it not for the presence of the college, and which have a mutual interdependence with it in one man-

289

ner or another. As is well known, a complete catalog of the subtypes would be lengthy. Those appearing in this chapter, however, are comparatively few: (1) corporations formed by two or more institutions, private or public, for purposes of cooperation; (2) a university press; (3) an industrial research institute in proximity to a university; (4) an organization of college administrative officers, faculty members, alumni, and students, operating a large food-service enterprise for the students and faculty, a bookstore, vending machines, and some faculty housing, and also owning and operating a lakeshore property used largely as a recreational center for the faculty and some students; and (5) a private university as owner of fraternity houses on or near its campus. (Actually in this last instance no "accessory corporation" is a party to the litigation; but college fraternities are "accessory organizations," and the cases relating to the taxation of fraternity houses are properly placed here.)

Nonprofit Development Corporation for Three Private Institutions in Physical Proximity

In the area in Cleveland wherein are located Western Reserve University, Case Institute of Technology, and the University Hospitals —all private charitable corporations—a nonprofit corporation styled the University Development Foundation was created to help plan, stimulate, and guide appropriate land use in the general area, for the mutual benefit of the institutions and all residents of the area, and of the city as a whole indirectly. The foundation bought two residence properties in the area, razed the houses, and landscaped the lots, "so as to provide open areas, pedestrian ways, and breathing-space for the institutions." After the Ohio Board of Tax Appeals had declared these lots taxable, all three judges of the court of appeals concurred in holding this determination was "unreasonable and unlawful," and reversed it.[1]

A larger enterprise of the same foundation was the acquisition, beginning in 1957, of 22 parcels of land, all to be used exclusively as vehicle parking areas for the three institutions named and for the

---

[1] *University Circle Development Foundation* v. *Auditor of Cuyahoga County*, (Ohio App.), 190 N.E. 2d 691 (1963).

Benjamin Rose Institute, which is also located in the vicinity. At the outset the foundation obtained loans of $100,000 from the three major institutions and a grant of $2 million from the Hanna Fund, a large philanthropic foundation. By late 1961 an additional $6 million had been raised by popular subscription, and the foundation undertook the operation of the joint parking facilities.

Students, faculty members, and employees of any of the institutions using the facilities were charged $11 a semester or $25 a calendar year, and there was a maximum daily charge of $1 to visitors. The areas were controlled by attendants and electronic gates, and there was free shuttle-bus service from Rapid Transit and from outlying parking lots. For the year 1962 expenditures were $387,000, income $276,000, leaving a deficit of $111,000. Over $1 million had been spent on acquiring and developing the facilities and on plans for additional facilities, either underground or multilevel.

The board of tax appeals declared these facilities taxable, saying "When such institutions charge for parking accommodations, where is the charity?" Again the court of appeals reversed this determination, pointing out that these facilities not only further the charitable purposes of the institutions, but are virtually indispensable to them; and their operation at an annual loss certainly would not militate against the idea that they are conducted on a charitable basis.[2]

Section 1958, New York Education Law, provided for the creation of a unique species of corporation in localities where it was desired to carry on specified educational services by means of joint action among local agencies, and to be styled "Board of Cooperative Educational Services." The board which had been brought into being in the Second Supervisory District of Westchester County had acquired ownership of certain facilities in the town of Rye, and sought to hold this property tax-exempt.

The trial court (Justice Frank S. McCullough) curtly held that the petition for exemption must be dismissed, because ownership of the property by the corporation was *ultra vires* (outside its powers). He believed the statute authorized corporations of this type to rent, but not to own, real property. Further, he said, an earlier opinion of the

---

[2] *University Development Foundation* v. *Perk*, 32 Ohio St., 213, 200 N.E. 2d 897 (1964).

state comptroller was correct, to the effect that such a board (Section 1958) is not a public corporation in the sense that that term is used in Section 405, Education Law, applicable to public school districts. This judgment was affirmed by the appellate division but *reversed* in 1965 by the New York Court of Appeals in a 40-word opinion: "Order reversed, without costs. The board possesses the power to own property (Education Law, Section 1958, Subdivision 6) which qualifies for an exemption under the Real Property Tax Law (Section 420). The mode of acquisition is deemed irrelevant for tax purposes. All concur."[3]

In New Jersey, Property of Princeton University Press Is Taxable

The *Princeton University Press*, a nonprofit corporation, owns its building and site under a deed which provides for reversion of the title to the university if and when the *Press* ceases to act in or serve the university's interests. The *Press* is managed by its own board of trustees of not more than 15 members, of whom 9 are alumni, faculty members, or trustees of Princeton University. Its fianance committee of 6 members has 4 affiliated with the university. Its editorial board consists of 5 faculty members, all appointed by the president of the university.

While its main business is publishing scholarly books, the *Press* also does printing work for educational and nonprofit organizations other than Princeton University. Its customers have included such institutions as Rutgers University, Stanford University, the Lawrenceville School, Sweet Briar College, and Mount Holyoke College. In the year 1957-58, 46 per cent of its work was its own scholarly publishing, 9 per cent was printing the Princeton *Alumni Weekly*, 21 per cent was printing bulletins of various kinds for Princeton University, and 24 per cent was "outside printing" for off-campus purchasers. Over a period of 11 recent years it earned a total surplus of $540,000, and during 3 recorded years in the late 1950's it made annual profits of more than $90,000.

---

[3] *Board of Cooperative Educational Services* v. *Buckley*, 42 Misc. 2d 450, 248 N.Y.S. 2d 270 (1964); affirmed in 21 A.D. 2d 784, 250 N.Y.S. 2d 528 (1964); but reversed in 15 N.Y. 2d 971, 259 N.Y.S. 2d 858, 207 N.E 2d 528 (1965).

The New Jersey supreme court concluded that the "outside" printing was a substantial part of the business, not negligible or minimal, and caused the *Press* "to take on the character of a commercial enterprise." Hence, said the court in its opinion by Justice Schettino: "There is no question but that (the *Press*) has been organized exclusively for the mental and moral improvement of men, women, and children (as required by the exemption statute), but "It cannot be said that the *Press* has satisfied, as it must, the statutory prerequisite that its property be 'actually and exclusively used' for the purposes stated in the statute." Thus the property was held taxable.[4]

Industrial Research Institute in Physical Proximity to University Is Taxable in New Jersey

The Textile Research Institute at Princeton is a nonprofit corporation consisting in part of "company members" (corporations engaged in the textile industry) which had power to elect its board of trustees and to place representatives on its various advisory committees, so as to control its policy and programming. In 1960 there were 90 such "company members," paying annual dues of from $200 to $2,250, depending on the size of their net textile shipments. From time to time some of these companies, or groups of them, sponsored research projects, in which they had the privilege of having publication of the results withheld for two years, and not made known during that time, even to other members of the institute. There were also 300 individual members who paid $20 annually but had no right to vote. Certain selected Princeton graduate students were appointed as Textile Research Institute Fellows, and did their thesis research at the institute; and some postdoctoral Fellows were supported by the member companies, but had no formal affiliation with Princeton University.

The institute sought tax exemption under the familiar New Jersey statute which exempts buildings and sites "actually used for colleges, schools, academies, or seminaries." "But the word 'college,' " said Justice Schettino for the unanimous supreme court of New Jersey, "does not embrace an organization which is controlled by a par-

---

[4] *Princeton University Press* v. *Borough of Princeton*, 35 N.J. 209, 172 A. 2d 420 (1961).

ticular profit-making segment of society and which is devoted principally and primarily to research for the benefit of that industry."[5]

Fifteen years earlier the same institute had been denied tax exemption for two reasons: (1) It was then incorporated in the state of
New York and was thus a "foreign corporation" not covered by the
New Jersey statute exempting "all buildings actually and exclusively
used for the moral and mental improvement of men, women, and
children," and (2) its purpose was primarily to benefit the textile
industry, and "Neither Princeton University nor any other college or
university has any jurisdiction over it."[6] Nearly contemporaneous
was an Ohio decision denying exemption to the Battelle Memorial Institute, a large organization for scientific research located near the
campus of the Ohio State University in Columbus, and bearing relationships to the university similar to those between Princeton
University and the Textile Research Institute.[7]

Property Used Primarily as Recreational Center for
Faculty Members and Owned by Nonprofit Accessory
Corporation Not Exempt from Taxation in New York State

The New York State University College at Plattsburgh has a
nonprofit accessory corporation consisting of 11 to 15 persons, of
whom 2 shall be administrative officers of the college, 2 members of
the faculty, 1 member of the alumni association, 1 member of the
board of visitors, and 3 student presidents of the house of delegates
(a student organization embracing the three upper classes). The president of the college is a member *ex officio*.

Among other activities, the corporation operates the food service
for about 2,000 students and some faculty members and campus
school children. Its operating surpluses for the fiscal year 1962-63 were:
food service, $54,000; bookstore, $10,000; vending machines, $2,000;
juke boxes, $500; and Court Street property for faculty housing, $250.

---

[5] *Textile Research Institute* v. *Township of Princeton*, 35 N.J. 218, 172 A. 2d
417 (1961).

[6] *Textile Research Institute* v. *Princeton Township*, (N.J. Dept. of Taxation
and Finance, Division of Tax Appeals), 50 A. 2d 829 (1946).

[7] *Battelle Memorial Institute* v. *Dunn*, 148 Ohio St. 53, 73 N.E. 2d 88 (1947).
Both this and the preceding case were digested at page 106 of *The Colleges and
the Courts, 1946-50*.

Its total cash balance at the end of the year was $85,000. In 1958 it was denied tax exemption of its faculty housing property.[8] In 1964 it was given the same treatment with respect to a parcel of property known as the "Valcour Educational Conference Center" on the shore of Lake Champlain about five miles from Plattsburgh. It had purchased this in 1963 for $98,000, out of its accumulated surplus. The property was used in part for meetings of teachers, students, and alumni; but much of its use was as a summer resort for faculty families and some students who used the beach and other recreational facilities for swimming and boating, and stored their boats in the boathouse. Use was only by special permit from the office of the president of the college.

The local supreme court was of the opinion that the Valcour property had been used primarily as a recreational area for "some selected faculty, students, and others," and that it was not in fact a regular adjunct to the college's program of physical education, and not used exclusively for educational purposes. Justice Soden spent some 3,500 words in reaching the astringent conclusion about accessory nonprofit corporations that is characteristic of New York courts: "The Court holds that a corporation which is not controlled by a *bona fide* educational institution but is autonomous and exists primarily to provide services, food and lodging for faculty and students is not organized exclusively for educational purposes because such services bear no primary or exclusive relationship to the educational process."[9]

Student House at Massachusetts Institute of Technology
Owned by Charitable Corporation Exempt from Taxation

At 111 Bay State Road in Boston is a house owned by a corporation styled M.I.T. Student House, Inc., and regularly used as a residence by students selected for that privilege upon nomination by

---

[8] *Plattsburg State Teachers College Benevolent and Educational Association* v. *Barnard*, 9 Misc. 2d 897, 170 N.Y.S. 2d 712 (1958). Digested at pages 370-371 in *The Colleges and the Courts Since 1950*. Briefly mentioned and criticized at page 1126 in Henry Sellin's "State and Local Taxation," *New York University Law Review* 33:1120-1132 (December 1958).

[9] *Plattsburg College Benevolent and Educational Association* v. *Board of Assessors of Town of Peru*, 43 Misc. 2d 741, 252 N.Y.S. 2d 229 (1964).

the dean of student aid at the Massachusetts Institute of Technology. The members of the corporation pay a $50 fee for membership, and its purpose is to aid needy students. Students residing in the house are not members of the corporation, but they have their own organization and pay for the operation of the house at rates which enable them to save about $200 a year each on their room and board bills.

Monthly room rentals are determined each year by the board of directors of the corporation. The student residents buy groceries, pay utility bills, and hire a cook. The students themselves perform the work of waiters, bus boys, assistant cook, dishwasher, and chambermaid.

On these facts the Massachusetts supreme judicial court, in an opinion by Justice Spiegel, readily held that the corporation is charitable within the meaning of the Massachusetts tax exemption statutes, and ordered abatement of the 1959 tax on the house in the amount of $1,771 with interest and costs, reversing an adverse ruling by the appellate tax board.[10]

University-Owned Fraternity Houses at Cornell University Not Exempt from Taxation

Cornell University has had for several years a "Group Housing Plan" under which the university constructs or rehabilitates a house on its own land and leases it to a fraternity chapter or other similar student organization.

Alumni members of the organization finance the construction, and the rent paid by the active chapter covers utilities, repairs and maintenance, insurance, and taxes.

The university, as owner, sought to have these premises held exempt from taxation, as "property held and used for educational purposes." The unanimous decision of the five-judge appellate division was adverse.

A New York statute exempts "real property of a corporation . . . organized exclusively for . . . education . . . purposes . . . and used exclusively for one or more of said purposes by the owning corporation or by another such corporation."

---

[10] *M.I.T. Student House, Inc.* v. *Board of Assessors of Boston*, (Mass.), 215 N.E. 2d 788 (1966).

The judgment holds that the university, as owner of the premises, qualifies for tax exemption; but the fraternity chapter, as occupant and user of the property, is not "another such corporation," and its use of the property is not exclusively for educational purposes, because fraternities are devoted in substantial part to social and other personal objectives of privately organized, self-perpetuating clubs controlled by graduate as well as student members.

"It is true, of course," said the court, "that the fraternities perform the essential function of housing and feeding students, but it is clear that in each case the use of the premises is also devoted in substantial part to social and other personal objectives."[11]

A different result prevails in Georgia regarding this issue, where a 1960 decision of the state supreme court held that fraternity houses at Emory University were tax-exempt, under a state of facts similar to the *Cornell* case, but under different exemption statutes.[12] The Georgia court viewed the fraternity as an integral educational unit of the college or university, with its living quarters forming a segment in the campus design, and serving much the same functions as college-owned residence halls for students not affiliated with fraternities. This is in harmony with current trends.

Charitable Corporation Formed by Alumni of Fraternity Chapter Primarily to Acquire and Maintain Chapter House Not Exempt from Federal Income Tax

The Texas Beta Student Aid Fund was incorporated in 1947, with its articles of incorporation declaring, "The specific educational purpose which this corporation is founded to achieve is that of aiding students of the University of Texas who are members of, or who are pledged to become members of, the Beta Omicron Chapter of Beta Theta Pi Fraternity."

A letter ruling dated December 1, 1949, recognized the purpose as educational and allowed gifts to the organization to be deducted in the federal tax returns of the donors. This was changed by a subsequent

---

[11] *Cornell University* v. *Board of Assessors*, 24 A.D. 2d 526, 250 N.Y.S. 2d 697 (1965).

[12] *Alford* v. *Emory University*, 216 Ga. 391, 116 S.E. 2d 596 (1960). Discussed at pages 377-378 in *The Colleges and the Courts Since 1950*.

letter ruling of March 26, 1957, which said: "The facts show that substantially all your funds have been used for the purpose of acquiring and maintaining a chapter house and leasing it to a local chapter of a fraternity . . . It has long been the position of the Service that college fraternities are not exempt educational organizations but are primarily social clubs." It went on to rule: "You are not entitled to exemption from federal income tax . . . , and after 1957 gifts to you are not deductible by the donors in computing income tax . . . nor gift tax . . ."

To test that ruling, a suit was brought for a refund of taxes paid under it by a donor, and the federal district court adjudged the refund to be proper; but this was reversed by the United States court of appeals in a penetrating opinion by Circuit Judge Rives:[13]

> The Fund, as incorporated, organized, and operated, has neither the educational activities of the University nor the social activities of the fraternity. Instead, its predominant activity is to provide and maintain the fraternity house. The fraternity house serves both the educational purposes of the University and the social purposes of the fraternity.

In order to be an exempt organization, "education must be its primary purpose or function, and such of its activities as do not serve to further education must be so minor in comparison as to be termed incidental. . . . In our opinion the Fund does not meet that test . . . Viewed realistically, it amounts to an elaborate scheme, skillfully devised for tax purposes, by which moneys primarily serving a fraternity can be earmarked for its more educational aspects. The purpose of serving the purely social purposes of the fraternity cannot be said to be minor and incidental to its broader educational purposes."

---

[13] *Phinney* v. *Dougherty*, (U.S.C.A., Tex.), 307 F. 2d 357 (1962).

BIBLIOGRAPHY

BOOKS

1. Chambers, M.M., *The Colleges and the Courts Since 1950.* Danville, Illinois: Interstate Printers & Publishers, Inc., 1964. 415 pp.
2. Desmond, Richard L., *Higher Education and Tax-Motivated Giving.* Washington, D.C.: American College Public Relations Association, 1967. 95 pp.

ARTICLES

Part One—Students

3. Hagie, Daryl G., "The Law and Student Dismissal Procedures." *Educational Record* 47: 518-524 (Fall, 1966).
4. Jacoby, John P., "Racial Discrimination in Fraternities and Sororities—State Action?" *University of Illinois Law Forum 631-645* (Fall, 1964).
5. Johnson, Michael T., Constitutional Rights of College Students." *Texas Law Review* 42: 344-363 (February, 1964).
6. McBurney, Floyd W., and Dale F. Fuller, "Restricted Scholarships: Problems in Standing to Challenge Constitutionality. Cy pres, and Legislative Policy." *Wisconsin Law Review* 254-320 (1963).
7. Silard, John., "A Constitutional Forecast: Demise of the 'State Action' Limit on the Equal Protection Guarantee." *Columbia Law Review 66:* 855-872 (May, 1964).

8. Wrightsel, R. Douglas, "College Education as a Legal Necessary." *Vanderbilt Law Review* 18: 1400-1428 (June, 1965).

Part Two—Members of the Faculty and Other Employees

9. Bishop, Arthur N., Jr., "Fair Use of Copyrighted Books." *Houston Law Review* 2: 206-221 (Fall, 1964).
10. Black, Hugo L., "The Bill of Rights." *New York University Law Review* 35: 865 (1960).
11. Heilprin, Laurence B., "Technology and the Future of the Copyright Principle." *Phi Delta Kappan* 48: 220-225 (January, 1967).
12. "Joint and Several Liability for Copyright Infringement: A New Look at Section 101 (b) of the Copyright Act." *University of Chicago Law Review* 32: 98-123 (Autumn, 1964).
13. Joughin, Louis, "Academic Due Process." *AAUP Bulletin* 50: 19-35 (March, 1964).
14. "Judicial Review of the Tenure Contract of a Professor in a Private College." *Ohio State Law Journal* 25: 289-298 (Spring, 1964).
15. Kaplan, Benjamin, "An Unhurried View of Copyright: Proposals and Prospects." *Columbia Law Review* 66: 831-854 (May, 1966).
16. Morris, Arval A., "The University of Washington Loyalty Oath Case." *AAUP Bulletin* 50:221-231 (September, 1964).
17. Munster J. H., Jr., and Justin C. Smith. "The Care and Feeding of Intellectual Property." *Science* 148: 739-743 (May 7, 1965).
18. Nelson, Greg J., "The Copyrightability of Computer Programs." *Arizona Law Review* 7: 204-218 (Spring, 1966).
19. Palmer, Archie M., *University Research and Patent Policies, Practices, and Procedures.* Washington: National Academy of Sciences, 1962. 291 pp.
20. "Protection of Inventive Ideas Through Post-Employment Assignment Covenants." *Washington University Law Quarterly* 335-361 (June, 1965).
21. Throckmorton, Rex D., "Copyright Revision: Preemption as a Panacea." *Ohio State Law Journal* 27: 176-192 (Winter, 1966).
22. Treece, James M., "Patent Policy and Preemption: The Stiffel and Compco Cases." *University of Chicago Law Review* 32: 80-96 (Autumn, 1964).

Part Three—Government and Charity

23. Casad, R. C., "On Teaching Religion at the State University." Kansas Law Review 12: 405 (March, 1964).
24. Chidlaw, B. E., "Nonprofit and Charitable Corporations in Colorado." University of Colorado Law Review 36: 9 (Fall, 1963).
25. "The Charitable Corporation." Harvard Law Review 64: 1168-1181 (May, 1951).
26. Finkelstein, Maurice, "Tax-Exempt Charitable Corporations: Revenue Act of 1950." Michigan Law Review 50: 427-434 (1952).
27. Fisch, Edith L., "Restrictions on Charitable Giving." New York Law Forum 10: 307-332 (September, 1964).
28. Glander, C. Emory, and Earl E. Mayer, Jr., "Tax Saving Through Gifts to Education." Ohio State Law Journal 25: 222-233 (Spring, 1964).
29. Gross, Kenneth L., "Federal Income Tax—Summer Resort Not Operated for Social Welfare Does Not Qualify for Exemption." Villanova Law Review 10: 385-390 (Winter, 1965).
30. Heckerling, Philip E., "The Federal Taxation of Legal Education." Ohio State Law Journal 27: 117-142 (Winter, 1966).
31. Karst, Kenneth L., "The Tax Exemption of Donor-Controlled Foundations." Ohio State Law Journal 25: 183-221 (Spring, 1964).
32. Oliver, William W., "The Deductibility of Expenses: A Professors' Research and a Study in his Home." AAUP Bulletin 50: 14-18 (March, 1964).
33. Raskind, Leo J., "Changes in the Tax Treatment of Employee Moving Expenses." AAUP Bulletin 51: 38-41 (March, 1965).
34. Schoenfeld, Marcus, "Federal Tax Aspects of Non-Profit Organizations." Villanova Law Review 10: 487-502 (Spring, 1965).
35. Schwartz, Richard W., "The Ohio Mortmain Statute—As Amended." Western Reserve Law Review 17: 83-101 (October, 1965).
36. Sederstrom, Charles V., "The Exemption of Educational, Charitable, and Religious Institutions in South Dakota." South Dakota Law Review 11: 132-143 (Winter, 1966).
37. Sugarman, and Pomeroy, "Business Income of Exempt Organizations." Virginia Law Review 46: 424 (1960).

38. Wittenberg, Susan, "A Charitable Armageddon: Commissioner v. Clay B. Brown." *UCLA Law Review* 13: 167-177 (November, 1965).

Part Four—Institutional Property and Other Matters

39. Cooper, James Truman, "Torts—The Fall of the Charitable Immunity Doctrine." *West Virginia Law Review* 68: 99-103 (December, 1965).
40. Fisch, Edith L., "Charitable Liability for Tort." *Villanova Law Review* 10: 71-91 (Fall, 1964).
41. Harris, Judah J., and Nick M. Nibi, "College Housing Loan Program." *New York Law Forum* 10: 555-572 (December, 1964).
42. Peck, Cornelius J., "The Role of the Courts and the Legislatures in the Reform of Tort Law." *Minnesota Law Review* 48: 265-312 (1963).

TABLE OF CASES

FEDERAL

United States Supreme Court

303

Page

1964   Application of President and Directors of
       Georgetown College, Inc...................... 287
1963   Due v. Florida Agricultural and Mechanical
       University 22
1963   Gantt v. Clemson Agricultural College of
       South Carolina 43
1963   United States v. Wallace...................... 45
1963   NAACP v. Flowers.............................. 49
1963   Baggett v. Bullitt............................ 92
1963   United States v. Michaelson (and Commissioner of
       Internal Revenue v. Johnson).................. 111
1963   Cleveland Chiropractic College v. Commissioner of
       Internal Revenue 212
1963   Commissioner of Internal Revenue v. Brown.......... 219
1963   City National Bank and Trust Company of Columbus
       v. United States.............................. 222
1963   State Street Bank and Trust Company v.
       United States 223
1963   Berry v. Odom and Duke University............. 282
1962   Fireman's Fund Insurance Company v. Brandt........ 65
1962   Wihtol v. Crow............................... 105
1962   Dennehy v. Commissioner of Internal Revenue........ 110
1962   Davis v. Commissioner of Internal Revenue........... 113
1962   Wallingford v. Zenith Radio Corporation.......... 121
1962   Hall v. United States......................... 209
1962   Hulman Foundation, Inc. v. United States........... 216
1962   Harrison-Halsted Community Group, Inc. v. Housing
       and Home Finance Agency...................... 265
1962   Phinney v. Dougherty......................... 298
1961   Dixon v. Alabama State Board of Education........23, 37
1961   NAACP v. Gallion............................. 48
1959   Mercantile—Safe Deposit and Trust Company v.
       United States 224
1958   Marlor v. Commissioner of Internal Revenue.......... 113
1958   John Roberts Manufacturing Company v. University
       of Notre Dame du Lac......................... 165
1956   Samuel Friedland Foundation v. United States........ 216

STATE

Alabama

Arizona

Arkansas

California

North Carolina

North Dakota

Ohio

INDEX

A

Academic freedom, 29-30, 91-102
Academy of Medicine of New Jersey, 190
Accumulation, "unreasonable," by charitable trust, 213-216
Achor, Judge (Ind.), 27
Activists, student, accused of violating criminal statutes, 26-29
Alabama State College, 43, 49-50
Alabama, University of, 44-45, 47, 48, 114
Alcoholic beverages, prohibiting sale of near colleges, 57-60
Alcoholics Anonymous, 232
American Association of University Professors, 30, 96
American Cancer Society, 232
American Institute of Architects, 71
American University, 25
Aptheker, Herbert, 29
Architecture and engineering, differentiated, 257
Arizona loyalty oath case, 97-98
Arnold Arboretum, 236-237
Arterburn, Chief Justice (Ind.), 27
Ashland Community College (Ky.), 151-152
Association of American Medical Colleges, 156
Athletics, cases arising out of, 60-62, 114-115, 117-119, 204
Auburn University (Ala.), 43
Automobile accident cases, 57, 64-65
Autonomy of state universities and colleges, 137-138, 140-142

B

Bache, Kaye, 33
Bar mitzvah ceremonial, 8
Barnes, U.S. Circuit Judge, 256
Battelle Memorial Institute (Ohio), 294
Bell, Chief Justice (Pa.), 283
Bell, Griffin B., U.S. Circuit Judge, 52, 96
Beloit College, 69
Benjamin Rose Institute (Ohio), 291
Bergan, Judge (N. Y.), 80, 163
Bernstein, Justice (Ariz.), 97
Beta Theta Pi Fraternity, 297
"Bible as literature" can be taught at state university, 143
Bishop, Arthur N., Jr., 300
Black, Mr. Justice Hugo L., 27, 50, 99, 100, 220, 261, 300
Blackwell, Thomas E., 145, 159
Bluefield State College (W. Va.), 145
Blue Shield contract, 84
Bobbitt, Judge (Ind.), 6
Bond issues for capital improvements, 241-248
Bookstein, Isadore, Justice (N. Y.), 250
Bookstores, college, 203-204
Boston University, 190
Botein, Presiding Justice (N. Y.), 161
Bowling Green State University (Ohio), 57
Breitel, Presiding Justice (N. Y.), 80-82
Breitenstein, Jean S., U.S. Circuit Judge, 33
Brennan, Mr. Justice William J., 27, 50, 99-100

319